Repossessing Ernestine

Novels by Marsha Hunt

Joy
Free

Repossessing Ernestine

A GRANDDAUGHTER UNCOVERS THE SECRET HISTORY OF HER AMERICAN FAMILY

—☙ MARSHA HUNT

HarperCollins*Publishers*

Photo credits:
Karis Hunt Jagger, by Stefan Ruiz
The Hooks, Ernestine and Marsha, by Archie Lachlan
Marsha hugging Ernestine, by Ros Orpin
Ernestine embracing Marsha, by Alan Gilsenan
Portrait of Marsha and Ernestine, by Ros Orpin
Ernestine with the Bible, by Ros Orpin
All other photographs are from the collection of the author.

HarperCollins books may be purchased for educational, business, or sales promotional use. For information please write: Special Markets Department, HarperCollins Publishers, Inc., 10 East 53rd Street, New York, NY 10022.

FIRST EDITION

Designed by Caitlin Daniels

Library of Congress Cataloging-in-Publication Data

Hunt, Marsha, 1946–
   Repossessing Ernestine: a granddaughter uncovers the secret history of her American family / Marsha Hunt.—1st ed.
      p.   cm.
   ISBN 0-06-017443-9
   1. Hunt, Marsha, 1946–   —Family. 2. Afro-American women novelists—20th century—Family relationships. 3. Psychiatric hospital patients—United States—Biography. 4. Grandmothers—United States—Biography. 5. Aged women—United States—Biography. 6. Afro-American families. I. Title.
PS3558.U4678Z475   1996
813' .54—dc20   95-48436

96 97 98 99 00 ❖/RRD 10 9 8 7 6 5 4 3 2 1

This book is dedicated to carers everywhere

CONTENTS

Photographs follow pages 120, 152, and 216.

1

France

⁓⟋ A PHONE CALL

THE BABY PICTURE OF MY DEAD FATHER had been mysteriously fading for three days when the phone rang that Saturday. I'm still not sure if this story starts with the phone call or the spooky way Blair's baby image was disappearing.

In any case, I was in the sunroom hunched over my typewriter and pages of my manuscript were strewn about the stone floor. It was the nearest thing I could get to organization. Writing was still a little new to me and I was pursuing it with a vengeance. The bell on the phone was so loud that the first ring made me jump. But I didn't reach to answer it because there was nobody I needed to talk to. What I needed to do was finish the novel I was working on, which was why I had buried myself away in that craggy French village ninety miles north of Paris. The isolation helped me avoid friends and eliminated temptation.

I use the sunroom as my study because it gets good light and lets me see for miles across the farmlands; so to help me resist answering the phone I stared at my neighbor's cows grazing in the distance. It being late spring, the sky was blue, the meadows green, and the roses abundant. The setting was totally different from the inner city ghetto where I'd started out in Philadelphia or the streets of Berkeley where I'd been as a student before I headed for England and made it my base.

Though I shot an evil glance at the phone, it wouldn't stop ringing so I gritted my teeth and answered it. Few people have my number and the rare calls I get are long distance. Nobody French ever rings, and I said hello in English. The hiss on the line meant that it was a call from abroad. The man's accent was American.

"Hey, this is Alan," he said, as if he expected me to know him.

I was guarded because journalists still manage to find me, interrupting my life when I least expect it to ask some ridiculous question about Mick Jagger, the father of my child who is no longer a child and is away studying at Yale.

The man said, "This is your cousin, Alan Hunt."

There was no reason why I should have recognized his voice because we'd only met a few times and he never phoned. I was pleasantly surprised to hear from him until I remembered what was happening to my father's baby picture.

I checked my watch: being noon in France meant it was dawn in Boston, assuming he was calling me from home. He was a mature student, a single parent with a ten-year-old son, and knowing how strapped he was for cash I guessed he wasn't ringing for an idle chat.

Alan's father, Wilson, and my own had been brothers. Wilson was the last of my father's small clan. When I'd first met him, I was in my late twenties and based in London, where I'd been for eight years, singing and acting. Wilson had come to town for a psychologists' convention. That he looked so much like Blair made me take to Wilson immediately—he even sounded like Blair, tentative, Bostonian, and soft-spoken.

My typewriter was humming. I switched it off and sat upright. I hadn't had much contact with Wilson since that first meeting in the 1970s but he was my last direct link with my father and I tried to see him whenever I was on the East Coast.

"Wilson's okay?" I asked Alan anxiously. My uncle was probably seventy, yet even with his thick white hair he looked ten years younger. But he'd recently retired as far as I'd heard and sometimes that's a killer.

Alan said, "Everybody's fine, but I stumbled upon something which I thought you ought to know." His speech was sprinkled with long pauses like his father's, but otherwise they couldn't have been more different. Wilson was the sort of man who paid his taxes on time, hung up his coat as soon as he came home, and sat down to a sensible breakfast early each morning. Alan, on the other hand, was a college dropout like me and over the years his various trades had ranged from driving a taxi to pottery, although now he was back to studying. Whenever I saw him he was in overalls and sandals. He was training for the Unitarian Universalist ministry and worked part-time as a substance abuse counselor. Though he lived in a Boston ghetto, his background was middle-class, because Wilson had been a psychologist and university lecturer while Alan was growing up. I could imagine my cousin being mistaken for an outsider in the ghetto, because he looked white and with his heavy beard and thick wavy black hair he resembled a Greek Orthodox priest.

Our small family had had more than its share of tragedies and I hoped he wasn't phoning to report another one.

Alan asked, "Do you remember what you said when we were all having dessert?"

I guessed he was referring to my last visit to his parents, which had taken place three months earlier on St. Valentine's Day 1991. I had been in the States for a book tour with a stop in Boston and Alan's mother, Dorothea, had invited me for dinner. American troops were fighting in the Middle East and yellow ribbons were pinned to doorways. Hard rain had knocked the edge off the cold winds. The house and family were a welcoming sight. It was a three-bedroom semi-detached on two floors, and Dorothea kept it cleaner than it would have been had they had a full-time house-keeper. The paintings on the walls were in quiet good taste and the cane furniture was handsome and sober in a long room which served as the sitting room at one end and the dining room at the other. Nine of us gathered around the table, including Alan; his elder brother, Wilson Jr., and his wife; and their children.

The scent of the blueberry pie which Dorothea baked had seeped from the kitchen to the dining room, and while I can recall that I ate too much of it, I had no recollection that I said anything worth remembering. But as I opened my sunroom door in France, admitting more heat and flies, Alan's voice taunted me. "Remember? You asked what happened to Ernestine."

I blushed. Ernestine was Wilson's mother and our grandmother, but though no spoken rule stopped us from discussing her, no one ever mentioned her. Somehow she'd become the skeleton in the family cupboard. I knew that she'd spent her life in a mental institution in Tennessee and I presumed that she'd died there. But I could have spoiled our pleasant dinner by bringing her up and don't know what made me do it, especially with Wilson's three grandchildren there.

Inasmuch as Ernestine was Uncle Wilson's mother, and I had had so little contact with my father's family, I thought I had no right to pry, but I was curious to know when she had died and where she was buried.

I sat at my uncle's table as an outsider, because the others sitting there fell somewhat under his control, especially since he and Dorothea were so involved in the raising of their sons' children. A pall fell over the table, and my uncle, his gentle voice with each word measured, said his mother was still alive, still in the mental hospital. He obviously didn't like to talk about her.

Alan must have wondered why I was being so defensive on the phone. I said, "I thought your father didn't want to admit that she was dead because the children were at the table."

My father's mother had been put away when my father and his two brothers were hardly out of diapers. I hadn't asked why but accepted that she was beyond hope or help. It was said she had been no more than a vegetable since the Depression, and who was I to question that or to question Wilson? Wasn't the loss his, and didn't he have a right to deal with it however he saw fit?

That Alan had even mentioned Ernestine's name seemed lawless, and I felt like a juvenile delinquent abetting a crime. My uncle was late to welcome my daughter Karis and me into his realm and, in deference to him, I was prepared to let Ernestine remain taboo. The few times that I had dared ask Wilson about his mother, he was gently dismissive; it was at such times that I remembered that he was a psychologist and had made a career of handling people, but I respected his right to avoid talking about her. As he had survived her loss, my father's suicide in 1956, and their youngest brother Ernest's murder in 1970, it was a miracle that Uncle Wilson was a good father, a faithful husband, and a doting granddad.

Above a crackle on the phone Alan said, "Come on, you said if Ernestine was alive you wanted to see her, and I said I did too. And I met a man through the Unitarian Universalists who claims Ernestine's living in a nursing home in Memphis."

The possibility seemed so preposterous that I laughed. Ernestine had been locked away in the 1920s when the "lost generation" was burning itself out on bootleg and the Charleston, when Al Capone ruled the underworld, and "colored boys" could be hanged down south for sport. She'd been erased for so long she wasn't even a memory and the idea that she was in a nursing home was absurd.

"Grandfather was ninety when he died in 1978," I said. "She'd have to be older than Methuselah." I didn't even feel comfortable mentioning her name. But I was thinking about my father's fading baby picture. Maybe it was an omen. "Who did you say saw her?"

"A man from Memphis named O'Ferrell V. Nelson who was up here campaigning for a national Unitarian office. His publicity handout said that he was a retired Memphis school principal who graduated from Booker T. Washington High School when Grandaddy was still principal."

Booker T. Washington was the oldest black high school in Memphis, and our grandfather, Blair T. Hunt, had run it for nearly four decades before he retired in the late 1950s; he had also been the minister of the Mississippi Boulevard Christian Church, one of the most prestigious in the black community. He had remained married to Ernestine, shut behind the walls of a Tennessee asylum. That she was catatonic, suffering bouts of violence, and unable to recognize anybody was what I'd heard. When I was tricycle age I was able to say, "My grandmother's in a mental institution." As a child it had seemed brave to admit it, and my mental picture of a dribbling she-monster crouched in the shadows, smelling of decay, made me eager to forget her, relieved me of any sense of responsibility, and made me happy that she was in a mental hospital receiving care and help.

I felt uneasy discussing her with Alan, although he was obviously excited about his find. To think that she was alive and possibly living outside of an asylum: I felt as though we'd stumbled upon a secret and it made me uncomfortable. Assuming what Alan had been told was true, why had he discovered it by accident and how could someone who had been so mentally disturbed since 1929 get well?

Alan had an answer. "Maybe she was never crazy. They used to lock women up just to stop them talking. Keep 'em quiet and shut 'em up." His laughter on the telephone was mocking, and I grimaced as if I'd been asked to inspect a mutilated body.

Was it possible that my father's mother hadn't needed to spend her life in an asylum? For his sake, I hated to think about it, especially as his suicide may have been related to what had happened during a childhood in which he'd been deprived of her love.

I asked Alan, "Have you told your father any of this?"

"No."

"Have you told your brother or your mother?"

"Nope." Alan sighed.

His brother, Wilson Jr., was eight years older than Alan. Will was a career planning counselor at Harvard, where he'd also been a student in the 1960s. He was nearly fifty and was happily married with two young children. He wore sober cardigans and ties and was as sensible as his father. He and his Jewish wife seemed to have a stronger relationship with Wilson and Dorothea than Alan, and I assumed this might explain why Will hadn't been told.

I stood up and stared out to the front lawn, where the hot red roses grew in thick clumps under the catalpa tree. The birdsong was dense: cuckoos and rooks, blackbirds, and tits, thrushes and finches forming a blanket of sound which made me more conscious of my idyllic surroundings. Birds, flowers, and calm country. The spring light made me feel suddenly guilty. How could I have a right to my sweet life if my father's mother had endured a life-time of suffering which may have been unnecessary?

Alan repeated, "They used to do all kinds of things to women."

His words stabbed me like a pickaxe in the back. Had my asking no questions been party to a crime against my grandmother?

I asked, "*If* it's Ernestine. How do we find out if it's Ernestine?"

"I've got the Nelson man's address."

"Can you get to Memphis?"

"I'm pretty broke. But maybe I can hitch down. Once I've set my mind to something there's no stopping me."

Like most people, he probably thought that I was supported by Mick Jagger. But the $6000 a year Mick contributed to Karis's upbringing between 1979 and 1988 hadn't made me rich, and I'd eked a living from my acting and books. I had a shopping bag full of bills and no way of getting to Memphis.

"Get some sleep," I told him, "and I'll write to the Nelson man."

—◦ THE SIGN

WHEN I HUNG UP THE PHONE AFTER SPEAKING TO ALAN, I heard myself saying "Ernestine," but I was actually thinking about my father and replaying those events which had occurred three days earlier when I'd first seen what was happening to his baby picture. . . . A scene that I'd been trying to write hadn't been working, so I'd stomped off upstairs to dust my bedroom, since housework helps, like gardening, to whip up my imagination.

The furniture polish was by the foot of the bed where I'd left it the day before. I threw open the French doors and stepped onto the flat roof which serves as a terrace. I'd had the place for a couple of years but couldn't think of the two rolling acres as mine. The pines and fruit trees, the well and sloping lawns remind me that I started out on Philly's mean streets.

I don't know how long I stood there staring, but after three gongs from the village church bell, I slipped back inside and grabbed my duster. Swinging it at a fly, I overturned the two framed pictures sitting on the bedside table, and when I lifted the one of my father, what I saw made me want to drop it.

His eye was dripping onto his cheek, his mouth was distorted and fading down the right side, his sepia image looked freakish. I called out, "Blair?", as if he might answer, because I come from a long line of women on my mother's side who believe in the spirit world. But therefore I was also hesitant to beckon a dead spirit in that house which had been there before the French Revolution. It was no place to call up the dead, because it stood on high ground overlooking the village in a region which had been part of the killing fields called the Western Front during the First World War, where a million and a half soldiers had been slaughtered. Still, I dared to call Blair's name a second time to indicate that I'd seen the photograph. There was no explanation for it disappearing. I took it to be a sign.

Blair had been dead for thirty-five years and my having his baby picture in my bedroom could lead anybody to think that we'd been close, but in fact I'd hardly known him, because he and my mother separated and divorced before I can remember.

Obviously they remained on friendly terms, because he made a few visits and once even brought his young brother, Ernest, with him. We were living in a small house in Germantown by then and even had a backyard, but crapshooters occupied the corner opposite the bar at the end of the street and my father looked as if he needed protection against those types my mother called hoodlums and gangsters. He wore glasses and spoke with a soft Bostonian accent. I couldn't have imagined him raising his voice or his hand to anyone, even in self-defense.

I must have been seven then, and it impressed me that my father and his brother had such pale skin and straight hair that they looked like the Italian family that lived in the middle of the block. Skin color and hair texture established class among blacks back then, and I wondered if I was an embarrassment with my dark skin and kinky braids.

It was important to me that he was a psychiatrist, that he lived in Boston and had gone to Harvard. His profession felt like my achievement and his Boston address told me that there was life for me beyond my ghetto, where most people had never heard of psychiatry.

I was ten when he died in 1956, aged thirty-seven. My mother didn't say that it was suicide. She said, "Blair died in a car accident," and I gulped the news without tears, pleased that nobody could see the lump in my throat when I went off to play at a friend's. Maybe his death even brought an odd relief, because I sensed he needed protection.

At that age I couldn't have said whether he snored or took cream in his coffee, whether he liked baseball or believed in God. But what made me sure that the ghetto wasn't all life would offer me was that Blair was my father, my get-out clause.

I felt I owed him a lot, though he'd done little for me.

 THE BLANKS

AFTER ALAN'S PHONE CALL ENDED, I reached to the bookshelf for the first book I'd been commissioned to write. It chronicled my adventurous and unexpected life. There was a picture of Ernestine, wearing a cap and gown, next to one of my maternal grandmother. I'd been given the photograph by my grandfather, Blair Hunt Sr., when I'd taken Karis to meet him in Memphis in 1977. She was six and he was eighty-nine. Seeing Ernestine's graduation picture brought back memories of the visit.

I had never been to see him and can't say that I'd ever been invited. Night had fallen by the time our plane landed, so I couldn't see much of the city as we drove to the north of it. Memphis had been Elvis Presley's base; Graceland was there, and because he had just died there were posters of him on some of the buildings we passed. But my mind was on my daughter, and my grandfather whom I didn't know. It was Karis's third visit to the States. She'd only ever lived in London and Grandfather's southern accent was strange to her. He had an articulate southern drawl and sat in front of us talking to his companion, Harry Mae Simons, who had driven him to the airport to meet us. Although he'd introduced her jokingly as his landlady, she made it clear that their forty-seven years living under the same roof had been satisfying and intimate. My father had always referred to Miss Simons as grandfather's girlfriend so I wasn't surprised that she had driven him to the airport to meet us.

Miss Simons was charm itself. She was a lot younger than he was. Her honey complexion might have been what most people thought was her best feature; she had a prominent nose and wore glasses that shielded her large eyes. Grandfather, wearing a hat, sat beside her in his light blue summer suit. I couldn't get over how thin he was. I'd last seen him in Philadelphia when I was twelve and then he'd been portly, his long face had been full. He didn't look like the same man—his cheekbones were as bony as his nose and his pale skin was dull. After the three operations he'd undergone, it was a miracle he was still alive. That's why I'd brought Karis to see him. She was his only great-grandchild.

He'd been important in Memphis and had been the third black there to get a college degree. He'd been head of La Rose

Elementary School for six years from 1926 before he went to head Booker T. Washington High which had an enrollment of 2500. It was one of only two black high schools in Memphis and had been the first. That grandfather headed it until 1959 meant that he had been a major influence on students and teachers. Since the 1920s he had also headed one of the most prestigious black churches and his sermons were printed weekly in the *Memphis World*. But it was his long-term association with Mayor Crump, a white supremacist who ran Memphis, which established Grandfather as the political spokesman for the black community. He could get school supplies for his students when other black schools couldn't. Being what he called a "gradualist" meant that he wasn't a forerunner of the civil rights movement. But I figured that he'd officiated over enough births, deaths, marriages, and graduations to have affected the lives of many people. He didn't slow down even after retirement when he became the first black to serve on the Shelby County School Board. But I'd always wondered why he had lived in Memphis while his sons were raised by Ernestine's mother in Boston.

His work should have given him a good income, so I was surprised when we pulled into his neighborhood and passed ramshackle wooden houses. What made them look poorer still was to see people fanning themselves on their rickety porches, some of them in chairs but most sitting on the top step, dressed in old work clothes.

Karis had always lived with me in London in a two-story St. John's Wood apartment near Regent's Park. Tall trees and graceful Victorian houses lined the streets, which were swept daily. The Royal Cavalry, based nearby, rode immaculate chestnut horses down our road every morning and children in uniforms were escorted by nannies to neighborhood prep schools. I was glad that now she was seeing a segregated district, but I couldn't understand why my grandfather was living on the side of town that other black professionals would have avoided.

I didn't pretend to know him and couldn't have related any stories about his family or childhood. It was only during that visit that

I discovered he had a sister in Chicago and a brother in Los Angeles. My parents' divorce and my father's suicide were always the reasons I gave for losing touch with my father's family.

Having grown up in Philadelphia and moved to Oakland when I was fourteen, I'd been to schools where there were only small numbers of black students, and to imagine the large segregated high school my grandfather ran was difficult. But he was nearly ninety and had experienced being the first generation in his family to be born free.

I had always been proud of him and loved getting his occasional letters scrawled in his large uneven handwriting on the stationery of the Mississippi Boulevard Christian Church, yet I realized I didn't know what denomination it was as we pulled into the driveway of where he had lived for decades, a single-story bungalow no larger than my London apartment. We entered through the back door which opened into a den lined with plaques commemorating his work. Several people, teachers that he'd worked with, had been invited to meet us. Considering his health, it was a miracle that he'd been to the airport and could still sit among his gathering of friends drinking Coca-Cola.

The morning following our arrival was dense, humid, and sitting in my grandfather's bedroom with the shades drawn, I had no sense of time or place. The room was at the front of the house but, despite being close to the street, I could hear no cars passing, no children playing, no sounds of nature. If death hovered over him, he was making admirable efforts not to show it. His mood was cheerful, though the room suffered from a dismal heaviness.

Blair Sr. was propped up in bed sharing a batch of family photographs while Karis was on my lap. My thighs were stuck together with perspiration but I held on to her, conscious of how different the setting was to places she'd been before. Occasionally I'd have to translate one of his sentences for her which I sensed that she hadn't understood because of his accent.

Karis was holding a picture of him in his First World War uniform. As I reached to accept another, his slow, measured drawl said, "This is your grandmother, Ernestine."

Until then, I'd never heard that name or seen images of her. His having referred to her as "your grandmother" shocked me as much as realizing that this pretty, healthy-looking teenager was the pitiable she-monster of my childhood imagination.

My grandfather continued. "My poor, dear sick wife is still at the hospital, incurably insane. . . . Of course, divorce is not permitted in the state of Tennessee."

I wasn't sure why he mentioned this and was only half-listening because the picture had my attention. I was smiling at it. Blair's mother—a whole person. My father's mother in a cap and gown, her expression pensive.

"Look," I told Karis, "this is your *great*-grandmother—my daddy's mummy—who I told you lives in a hospital because she's not well."

Blair Sr.'s tone was despairing when he went on to say that his wife's condition was hereditary.

While he spoke, Harry Mae had joined us. She was plumping his pillows. She was twenty-two years his junior and he had been living there throughout most of the time that Ernestine was in the hospital and his sons were growing up in Boston. She was obviously very proud of his achievements. On the wall of her den, lined with his awards and citations, there was a photograph showing him being sworn in to the Shelby County School Board.

Ernestine's graduation photograph hadn't reproduced well in my autobiography. Her pale face lacked definition and her black cap and gown were swallowed up by the dark background. While I sat at my desk staring at it, my cousin's voice replayed in my ears. "They used to put women away . . . they used to put . . . "

The sound of the geese calling from the neighbors' farm was topped by two dogs barking and the rattle of a tractor rolling down the main street. Despite these sounds, I was aware of a dense silence filling the sunroom. Memphis was thousands of miles away and again my thoughts slipped back to that visit to my grandfather. I recalled his pale, bony fingers passing me my father's baby picture, the original of the one which was now looking ominous upstairs on my bedside table. I wondered how it had been possible for him to have allowed his three sons to have grown up so far away from him. To give them the chance to grow up in the integrated North was the accepted family explanation, but nonetheless it seemed odd that he hadn't had more to do with their upbringing while they were deprived of their mother.

Flicking my typewriter on, I reached over to place the pages I'd gathered up back onto the flagstone floor and thought, Mustn't let Alan's call disrupt my whole day. But he'd raised some disturbing questions and had drawn me into a family matter which, as a woman and as Blair's daughter, made me anxious. I decided to ring Karis, who was twenty and wise and in her third year at Yale.

She was as excited as I wanted to be. "Mum, if she's alive you've got to go see her, and I want to go too."

"You do?" Her reactions often surprised me. She'd never known my father, and although she enjoyed the few trips we had made to visit Wilson and his family, I thought she'd turned down her acceptance from Harvard because they lived nearby and my cousin Will worked there.

Karis's tone implied that my sounding surprised was irritating. "Of course I want to go. It's too exciting, isn't it? Ol' Ernestine alive. We've gotta go." Her enthusiasm made me laugh, and so did her American accent—after three years studying in the States she was sounding like her roommates. She had moved off campus and was sharing an apartment in a neighborhood which was no better than the last one my family had lived in before moving from Philadelphia to the West Coast in 1960, but her ghetto experience would never be like mine. She was as calm as the little river which runs through our village, and however hard she may try to bury her English reserve, it's as natural as my American aggression is to me. She was my daughter but she was also Mick Jagger's daughter and the combination gave her an unusual scope. And to compli-

cate things further she was smart and pretty with her slim hips, her
father's infamous lips, and tight chestnut curls that hung like thick
rope to her waist. She was used to my swearing and probably
enjoyed hearing me say, "Shit, Miss Karis, I can hardly afford gas to
drive to the next village. How am I supposed to get to Memphis?"

"Mum, if you can get to New York, I'll drive you down when
I've taken my finals." After what had seemed a lifetime of chauf-
feuring her to schools, lessons, and airports, now I was being
offered the passenger seat of the car her father had bought her the
previous year; that stung and felt sweet at the same time.

My autobiography was still lying open on my desk and
Ernestine's picture seemed to be staring up at me. All that connected us was blood, and just how important is the bloodline? I
was tempted to tell Karis about Blair's baby picture, but held my
tongue in case omens aren't supposed to be discussed.

THE LETTER

WEEKS OF WAITING FOLLOWED ALAN'S CALL and I'd given up rushing to meet the postwoman, expecting a reply from my letter to
O'Ferrell V. Nelson, so the day it arrived I was out back hanging
up a wash.

Having invested so much time in the hope of resurrecting my
father's mother, my heart was shaking as I handled Mr. Nelson's
small blue airmail envelope. It was 10:30 A.M. and I'd been up
hours trying to understand the labors of one of my characters, a
raped slave turned washerwoman. I'd been handwashing thick cot-

ton sheets and heavy bath towels in a tub. The smell of detergent on my hands was overwhelming and I wanted to put off opening the letter. What was I afraid of? I started getting edgy, and every second increased my dread as I tracked into the kitchen to boost myself with coffee.

But while the kettle boiled, I erratically ran outside, envelope in hand, and tore into it. Mr. Nelson's elaborate handwriting didn't obscure his message: In a Memphis boarding home where his father had spent a few weeks, Nelson had seen an elderly woman with long white hair who was said to be Blair Hunt's widow.

I let out a whoop, leaping like a cheerleader with one of Nelson's two squares of stationery in each hand. I started singing "Zip-A-Dee-Doo-Dah" but suddenly stopped. Was there cause for celebration? The whereabouts of the widow of the renowned Memphis principal, the Rev. Blair T. Hunt, was a secret? Why had she been released from a mental hospital after fifty years of segregated asylum wards without her family being informed? I sat down on the drive and knew that things weren't right. How the family figured in my grandmother's life was still a big question, and I didn't know who to trust to help me answer it. I needed more information but knew that I'd have to wait hours before Memphis would be waking up.

Mr. Nelson had included his phone number and said that he'd seen my grandmother alive earlier in the year. But I knew nothing about him and tried to pose my questions carefully when he answered his phone hours later. His voice took me off guard. It rumbled, dark and deep, it was educated and southern and had the lilt of a Tennessee Williams as well as the soul of Muddy Waters. He sounded old and proper, like a man who always thought before he spoke.

When his wife joined us on the line, it seemed premature that she was offering to let me stay with them. After all, I was a stranger. But perhaps my relationship to the man who had been Mr. Nelson's high school principal, my being Blair T. Hunt's granddaughter, suggested that I was all right. Had they seen me as I was in a weather-beaten tracksuit they might have been less welcoming.

The Nelsons let me know that they were well-traveled and socialized both north and south, but I was the wrong person to talk to about clubs and fraternities. Berkeley in the sixties made me avoid those sorts of associations.

Mr. Nelson said, "Don't come in July or August, whatever you do. Definitely avoid August; the heat and humidity are unbearable. It's too hot to breathe."

I took the number of the nursing home. Thinking about my Uncle Wilson, I said, "You really think it was Blair T. Hunt's wife you saw?"

Although I wanted Mr. Nelson to be right, I was also hoping he wasn't. I didn't want to rock the family boat but I sensed that something was wrong and knew I had to find out what it was.

"It was Blair T. Hunt's wife all right. Not that we've spoken—I don't think she talks."

I was in a no-win situation. My conscience told me that I had to inquire about my grandmother, but I felt guilty doing so. What might be right for Ernestine could upset some people and expose something that was meant to remain hidden. I thought about Ernestine, my uncle, and my grandfather, not knowing which I was meant to serve, but I think it was for my father's sake that I inched forward. His disappearing baby picture might have been trying to tell me something.

WOMAN TO WOMAN

I WAS ALMOST RELIEVED WHEN WEEKS WENT BY with no reply from the nursing home. That Mr. Nelson may have been wrong about seeing Ernestine was easier to accept than the possibility that my father's mother might have been purposely hidden away. But that midnight when Mr. Nelson gave me the nursing home number, I took a breath and called it.

The rough, confrontational hello that greeted me triggered memories of the TV news from my fifties childhood. I'd sat in front of the black-and-white set watching militant maids march to work rather than ride at the backs of buses, or saw respectable-looking black men in suits being mauled at lunch counters by jeering gangs of whites. My view of the South was based on stories of rampant racism and memories of the civil rights struggle depicted on TV. It was as foreign to me as Russia, but I'd grown up reading about it.

The woman on the line waited for me to speak. "I'm sorry to trouble you," I said nervously, "but I'm ringing from France." It was a bum start. My transatlantic accent was all wrong to engage the woman I was talking to.

She boomed, "I'm the onliest one here." Her voice was husky but brisk. She sounded like she wasn't planning to talk long.

To let her know I wasn't white, I switched to ghetto dialect to explain. "I'm Reverend Blair T. Hunt's granddaughter, and I'm trying to find his widow. Her name's Ernestine Hunt." My mouth suddenly went dry. I swallowed. "She's my . . . I'm her granddaughter."

It was after midnight, so every light in the village was out except mine. Moonlight eased the darkness and toned down the stars. I could hear an owl in one ear, while the other connected to Memphis heard a voice that conjured up Hattie McDaniel playing the maid in *Gone With the Wind.*

The voice from Memphis said, "Lord ha' mercy! I been prayin' some of Miss Hunt's people would come for her. Yes I have, been prayin' and prayin'. 'Cause she ain't had nobody all these years. No. Not nobody."

Though I had no picture of Ernestine in my mind I was appalled to hear that she needed her family and had no one. It seemed inexcusable, and I listened as the voice rolled on.

"You don't know how good this feels. Couldn't nobody know. It sure feels good!" The woman's laughter made her lungs rattle like a heavy smoker's. When she said, "Miss Hunt's my baby!" a picture of a soft, huggable old woman began to take shape. I could see the old women in my village who weeded their gardens in housedresses and woolen slippers. But my lifelong impression of my father's mother as a haunting shadow made me blurt out, "Can she do anything?"

A long pause was followed by, "Miss Hunt can do anything anybody else can."

I was sitting on my bed in the open loft. Below in the living room only the loud ticks of the clock broke the silence. The phone made me feel that the phantom I'd always thought of as Blair's mother was within arm's reach. But I couldn't see her, couldn't even begin to imagine her apart from the long white hair which Mr. Nelson had mentioned. I pressed the phone to my ear and asked, "She walks?"

"Don't talk to me about walkin'," said the woman, who sounded middle-aged and robust. "She's up and down these halls 'til it about wears me out just watching her. Miss Hunt can outwalk me. We go out and I'm the one ready to head back first."

"Is my grandmother violent?"

"*Vi-o-lent?*" the woman repeated as if it was too incredible to mouth. "Miss Hunt? Miss Hunt ain't violent! She a sweet ol' lady. Couldn't nobody ask her to be no sweeter."

Who was I to believe? Mr. Nelson who had insinuated that Ernestine couldn't talk or this strange woman who denied it?

"Miss Hunt can talk. 'Fact, sometimes she gets back there in her room and gets to cussin' that dead husband of hers. Callin' him you so-and-so . . . you this-and-that!"

I recalled my grandfather's face during my visit in 1977 and could hear his voice saying, "My poor, dear sick wife." I thought about what Ernestine might have been doing that morning while we had been in his bedroom looking at her graduation picture.

Sitting there in France in bed in a big tee-shirt, I was facing the open doors leading to my terrace. Moonlight threw shadows around my room while the voice on the telephone did nothing to help me picture the nursing home. But the word "nursing" made me think of bright light and airy windows and I wanted to see my father's mother walking the halls.

When the woman's voice snapped me back to the moment, I heard, "Miss Hunt don't mess with nobody. But she don't let 'em mess with her neither. And she just loves playin' in water! Plays in that sink"—the woman laughed—"plays in that sink every chance and will set in that tub hours if you let her. So happy to be . . . "

The pause gave me a chance to try to take on board the picture that was being painted of a tough but sweet little old lady who had won the affection and admiration of the no-nonsense woman who had answered the phone and who sounded like one of the domestic staff rather than a nursing aide.

She said, "Wait now, see. There she go . . . just a-walkin'. Hey, Miss Hunt!"

"Where?" I yelled, trying to grapple with the moment, with the fact that with every tick of the clock my grandmother was becoming more real. It was as frustrating as trying to shape and order a dream. But all I could imagine were the cloth slippers worn by Madame de Jardin, the old widow who lived across the street. "Where? Where is she?" I begged, as if my grandmother would walk out of the frame and never walk into it again.

"She right in the hall," the woman said before calling out louder, "Miss Hunt! This somebody callin' for you." Then her voice fell as the person she called drew near. "This is your granddaughter on the phone. Go on and say hello to her."

The receiver changed hands and I could hear coaxing in the background before a loud, flat "Hi" resounded in my ear. I was so startled I forgot to reply and sat there grinning with my hand over my mouth. My grandmother had a voice that was strong, black, and steeped in the South. That "Hi" was Ernestine.

"Miss Hunt, go on and say something else. That's your granddaughter callin' for you . . . "

I said, "Hi, Grandma," like a bashful six-year-old.

There was some fumbling with the phone. "Miss Hunt's gone. Headin' back to her room, I expect."

I imagined her heading for a single bedroom with a large window that let the light pour in. I asked, "How long have you known her? How long has she been there?"

"She been here years. Way 'fore I started workin' here."

I took a deep breath. I was scared. As the family outsider, had I uncovered something that was meant to remain hidden? I had liked the feeling that I'd been accepted by my father's brother Wilson. But was this discovery going to alienate me again? Despite my dread I still knew that I had a responsibility to my father to let her see she wasn't alone. With trepidation, I said, "I can't get there right away." The disappearing baby picture was within sight on my bedside table.

"You come whenever you want. We'll be here waitin' on you. But it's Miss Cummings that runs the place that can tell you all about Miss Hunt. She been knowing her way longer than I have. And her number's right here. She might be home by now."

"And your name?"

"Miss Dukes, Essie Mae Dukes. And I'm so glad you called, 'cause all these years Miss Hunt ain't had nobody. And that ain't right. We all need *some*body."

⟋⟍ ELEVEN YEARS

MRS. CUMMINGS SAID, "I hate to tell you what your grandmother's feet looked like when I got her. I'll never forget it. Just terrible—

her toenails practically curling under. And they had her on about ten pills twice a day—"

"They?" I interrupted.

"Western State. The hospital she came from. Anyway, when I took her to our doctor, he said leave her off the pills to see how she'd do, and sure enough, she seemed better right away. She got calmer."

I was sitting up in bed grateful for my chronic insomnia because it had been three in the morning French time before Mrs. Cummings had answered her phone. She admitted receiving my letters but said she hadn't got around to answering them.

"How long has she been with you?"

"Eleven years."

As I clutched the phone, my joy at finding Ernestine became a flood of rage. "Do you know how many letters and gifts and cards I've sent to people all over the world in the past eleven years and my *grandmother's* never had a Christmas card from me? Can you understand how that makes me feel?"

My heart was pounding. I didn't know what to do and got out of bed. Memphis was a whole culture away, maybe two if you count America's as one and the South's as another. The woman on the phone was a stranger but my two letters had told her a good deal about me, about Karis. I'd even sent our photographs. So why hadn't she been in touch if, as Essie Mae Dukes said, Ernestine had no one?

Mounting suspicion should have made me ask Mrs. Cummings what was the real reason Ernestine had suffered a half-century lockup. But I was afraid of the answer. I wanted to scream or break something. Had Ernestine been deliberately abandoned?

Mrs. Cummings asked, "Are there nursing homes like mine over there where you are?"

"Sure," I answered sullenly, hoping that Ernestine was merely a victim of Reagan's mental health policy which turfed long-term inmates from mental wards. But I couldn't get a picture of Mrs.

Cummings's care facility and assumed it was part of some government plan.

She laughed. "The government? Both my places are private."

"Then how is my grandmother with you?"

"Her guardian takes care of things."

"She has a guardian?"

"Miss Simons."

"As in Harry Mae Simons?" I asked, hardly able to move my lips. That Ernestine was the charge of the woman who had replaced her was the last thing I expected, but I sensed that there was no need to tell my uncle. I assumed he knew.

"Mrs. Cummings, you've been very good to talk to me. I can't thank you enough for looking after my grandmother and hopefully we can have lunch when I'm in Memphis."

"You're coming?"

I didn't think I was left much choice.

⎯⎯⏤ QUESTION TIME

I WAS STUNNED AFTER THE CUMMINGS CONVERSATION, staring into the night. My heart drummed in my ears, my jaws were rigid. I was scared that I had found something which I wasn't supposed to turn my back on but hadn't the resources to tackle, because my grandmother was four thousand miles away. My cousin Alan was her only hope. Putting my head in my hands, I prayed, "Please God, don't let this be what I think it is."

With my father's disfigured baby picture lying face down on

the bedside table, I thought about his life. Perhaps his suicide was related to what had happened to his mother; it seemed possible that he'd become a psychiatrist because of her.

Having isolated myself so that I could write, I was a long way from family. The price for my writing and independence was that I was too broke to fly to Memphis in the morning. But I knew I had a duty to see my grandmother, so that she wouldn't end her days abandoned because nobody cared. I sat on the edge of my bed, hardly breathing. The owl's cry was mixed with a few barks from the Alsatian that guarded the farm next door. I ran my hand over the duvet and was sorry that I had nobody to talk to about right and wrong and duty.

Mrs. Cummings had said Ernestine was ninety-three. It was too late to do anything about the decades she had spent in an asylum, but there was still time to love her.

I hadn't spoken to Harry Mae Simons since 1985 when I'd phoned her to ask for pictures of Grandfather for the book I was putting together about my life. Her number was still in my phone book and she answered on the fourth ring.

I didn't know where to begin and wasn't sure I knew exactly what I was meant to say. I didn't expect her to be happy that I was ringing other people in Memphis and realized that she had chosen not to tell me that Ernestine was no longer in an asylum. But why the big secret?

Miss Simons sounded jaunty. I could imagine her looking just as she had back in 1977 when she wore her silver-gray hair in a neat chignon on the crown of her head and covered her high forehead with bangs. Her eyes looked large in her glasses and she was quick to flash her slightly lopsided grin.

On the phone, her voice had the lift of a woman half her age. Forcing a smile, I remembered that she must be at least eighty and addressed her with due respect. But all the time we talked, I was angry and wanted to say, Why didn't you tell me about Ernestine, and how could you let her wither away without knowing that she's got a family?

But all I said was that I was coming to Memphis and Harry Mae didn't give me a chance to say more. She sounded happy. "Sugar, you can ring me from the airport. I'll come get you. I don't need but a moment's notice."

"That's kind of you, Harry Mae, but I don't know when I'm coming and I'll probably stay in a motel."

She laughed. "A motel! Darlin', your grandaddy would turn over in his grave if you were in Memphis and weren't in this house ... now we can't have him turning over in his grave."

She had the command and charm she'd once needed as the first black female principal of La Rose School. She'd replaced Grandfather, although she hadn't been teaching long. He was already boarding in her house at that time, but I didn't know exactly what the arrangements were or how long Ernestine had been committed. I wanted to see Harry Mae's expression. I felt that she was being as cagey as I was. I knew she'd heard from O'Ferrell V. Nelson that I'd written to him about Ernestine.

Harry Mae and I exchanged small talk before we got around to discussing Ernestine who, she said, got out of control and had to be sedated. She also said that when my father and his brothers were teenagers they had asked Harry Mae to tell their father that they didn't want to see Ernestine any more and thought that their father should also stop seeing her.

"But I think my father would want me to see her," I said, "and my daughter Karis wants to come too."

Harry Mae's tone was a warning. "Sugar, you can't let her see your grandmother. It's hereditary and will only worry her if she sees it."

"I don't agree," I said, out of breath with anger, wondering where the notion about hereditary insanity came from. My mind was fatigued and stumbling over questions I dared not ask. Why was my grandmother hidden? Why had Alan found where she was by accident? What I did say was, "For you to have to pay for my grandmother's upkeep is unfair."

But Harry Mae explained that my grandfather had made financial provisions. "He always took care of her," she said.

The next day I rang Alan to say that I'd talked to Harry Mae. I vowed it would be my last call to him. "I'm chalking up a bill I can't pay. We've got to start writing."

His letter of 30 July said that he'd told his parents and his brother that we'd found Ernestine. Wilson's reaction mattered most, because I was sure that my uncle would feel that Ernestine was not my business. Alan wrote, "He said he had no objections to anyone going to see Ernestine, but had no urgency himself about going. He said he was glad to hear that she was doing well and that he didn't know if she would want to deal with family after all this time."

Alan had found a place to stay in Memphis if he could get there by 19 August. He was sure he could make it.

⟋⟍ THE BREAKTHROUGH

THE ROUND-TRIP TICKET TO MEMPHIS was more than I could afford until an unexpected acting offer came from London. That changed everything—with rehearsals beginning in early September, I booked a flight and notified the nursing home to expect me after lunch on 27 August.

Whether I had some ulterior motive behind my growing determination to get to Ernestine was a question several people asked, but none as directly as my mother, who wondered how Wilson and Dorothea felt about my imminent plan.

"He's given the go-ahead," I said, "but he's probably not ecstatic. I can sympathize with why he may not want to see her, but it doesn't eliminate my responsibility."

My mother knew how absent the Hunts had been in my life and snapped, "That's not your family! It's not your business to get involved in that."

"Well, whose family is it, if it's not mine? She's my grandmother, and nothing will change that . . . and she's got nobody. For all I know, Inez, she shouldn't have spent her life in that asylum!"

The prospect of leaving France and being London-based for possibly a year made me edgy and I was happier than usual to have phone interruptions, hoping each time there was a ring that it was Alan calling from Memphis, because I had an eerie suspicion that Ernestine would die before we could get to her.

Walks along the country lanes among the lime trees and red poppies calmed my anxiety but nothing erased the fear that my grandmother would be dead before 27 August.

Two weeks before I was scheduled to leave, the phone rang while I was up in my bedroom. It was a warm night, but the trees rustled as if we were in for a storm and the rooks were making a racket. Writing had gone well that day and I grabbed the receiver with fingers crossed, hoping that it was Alan. My hello was a plea, and I was surprised that it was Karis.

"Mum?" she said, seeming to have heard the disappointment in my voice when I realized it was her.

"Hey, what's up?" She'd been working in San Francisco that summer and had taken an apartment there with Alisa, one of her roommates from Yale. They had driven from Connecticut to California and were less excited about driving back.

Karis was old enough not to keep me posted on her where-abouts from day to day, and I always felt I was lucky when I knew where she was. But I knew exactly who she was refer-ring to when she said, "I've just seen her. I'm in Memphis, but I can't talk long. We've been driving for two days and we're wrecked."

She had said that she might head for Memphis on her way to the East Coast, but I thought she'd change her mind when she got

on the road. I didn't muffle my scream. The whole village must
have heard me.

"I don't believe it!" I yelled, not sure what to do with myself. I
didn't know whether to stand or sit, so I stood on the bed. "Trust
you! You made it!" I kept saying, but I finally stopped because I
knew she was getting bored.

She was nonchalant. "I said I was coming . . . you're not going
to believe how tiny she is."

"Hoooo-ray!" I started yelling, rocking the bed. Understatement
is Karis. Some of it has to do with her being English, but shyness
accounts for the rest. I tried to picture her with Ernestine, but
while I could see Karis with her waist-length hair, olive skin, and
high cheekbones, and imagined that she'd gone to see Ernestine in
a pair of jeans and a tee-shirt, picturing Ernestine was still impossible. So I said, "What does she look like?"

"Short hair. Really tiny. Alisa took pictures," Karis said, yawn-
ing.

Alisa was white. At least I thought she was and wondered if it
was a good idea for the two of them to be traveling down south
together.

Karis asked, "Are you sure everybody in the home is black?"

"Why?"

"There's one woman with red hair. Alisa and I thought she
wasn't."

Having parents of different races, nationalities, and incomes
broadens my daughter's view, and we see things differently.
Although she calls herself an African American when she's in the
States, she doesn't carry the baggage that comes with growing up
in race-conscious America, and southern racism would have been
something she had yet to experience. The open way she carries
herself would have told people that she was foreign, though she
didn't like me to tell her this.

My daughter had been with Ernestine. I drank that thought like
mellow wine.

Karis has a thin frame which I thought came from her father, but I'd always told people that she looked like my father's family, and if Ernestine was petite, maybe that was a feature which Karis inherited from her.

Had the telephone cord reached the balcony, I would have gone to stand outside, because the night air blowing into the bedroom was sweet, and I wanted to finish the call under the stars. I couldn't see them, but I knew they were out.

Karis said, "I wanted to take her some flowers, but we couldn't find anything nice, so I took her a couple of plants."

"You did good. I'm proud of you. Are you driving out of there today?"

"We're spending the night in Memphis. At a motel."

"Be careful and keep your doors locked," I said, though locks kept nobody out who really wanted in. I wasn't comfortable about her being in Memphis.

"Mum, I've got to sleep."

"When will you be leaving?" I asked.

"Tomorrow," she said, to my relief.

2

Memphis

27 AUGUST 1991

WHEN MR. NELSON ANSWERED THE PHONE I said, "I'm here."

"Where's here?" He laughed.

"Memphis. In an Econo Lodge not far from the airport."

"I know exactly where you are . . . I guess it's all right." The way he stressed "guess" said it wasn't. "You're right there next to the Rebel Inn where James Earl Ray spent the night 'fore he murdered Martin Luther King."

"Are you sure?" I asked, rushing over to the window to draw back a curtain. I saw a six-lane highway, some tractor trailers and telephone poles, and a gas station. All that was left of nature within view was a patch of lawn. Beyond was the rooftop of the next motel. It was as unremarkable as the freeway I'd taken from the car rental office at the airport. Billboards and fast-food concessions lined the route.

Mr. Nelson said, "To get to Anne and me, turn right into Airways Boulevard at the Burger King."

But my mind was still on the Rebel Inn, which was a reminder that however innocuous the area looked, I had to remember that average-looking citizens might be armed and dangerous.

"Mr. Nelson, I'm sorry but I'm going to have to cancel our appointment. It's nearly three and I've just arrived. My Nashville to Memphis connection was two hours late and I was due at the nursing home an hour ago. Jet lag's already got me, because I've been traveling for twenty-two hours."

"It doesn't take twenty-two hours to get from London," he said, with the certainty of somebody who has made the journey more than once.

"I started from my place in Folkestone down on the south coast . . . I went there to pick up some pictures for my grandmother. Anyway, since the trains are unreliable, I left at dawn for London. And in truth I've been traveling for two days, because I left France the day before yesterday; closing the house was a nightmare." My nerves were frayed and my hands shook. I wound a clump of hair around the curling iron while gripping the phone between my ear and shoulder. "I'm used to the steering wheel on the left and get lost with street maps. Goodness knows how I'm going to drive to the nursing home."

"Want me to drive you?"

"What I really want is bed," I said, eyeing the double where I'd tossed Ernestine's gifts. But I knew that if I closed my eyes for a nap, I'd sleep through to the next day.

"I'll come right over."

As I hung up, I was overcome by a sense of dread. Had I the good grace at that moment to deal with a retired principal and keen church deacon? I expected Mr. Nelson to be stodgy. Staring from my window, I eyed the roof of the Rebel Inn, mostly concealed by a wooden fence. The highway could have been in California or Connecticut, New Mexico or New Jersey, and knowing that Burger King and McDonald's, Taco Bell and Kentucky Fried were half a mile down the road only enhanced that feeling. As I wrapped another clump of hair around the curling iron, a thought which had kept me awake throughout the transatlantic flight still worried me: Would Ernestine take her last breath before I could reach her? I had visions of arriving at the nursing home just as an ambulance pulled away with my grandmother's body.

Within minutes Mr. Nelson was tapping at my motel room door. Glimpsing him from the window, I was relieved to see him puffing a cigarette. His hair, thinning on top, was snow-white; his

broad face was as smooth as polished walnut. Nothing had prepared me for his impish grin, and his trousers told me more about
him than his new Lincoln Continental. He wore black baggy
painter's pants, gathered at the ankle and hand-painted in bright
swirls. To call him Mr. Nelson seemed inappropriate so I opened
the door to say, "Okay, O'Ferrell, I can see you're really working
those pants."

Suddenly I wondered why I was making such a fuss wearing a
dress and heels, bothering with makeup and curled hair. But
Ernestine's parcels on the bed told me to look my best. I wanted
to make a good impression at the nursing home. I suddenly knew
that walking in with Mr. Nelson would be the wrong thing to do,
but there wasn't time for a protracted excuse.

"I hope you'll forgive me for letting you come over," I said, "but
I think I should visit my grandmother alone this first time."

He didn't flinch. "Anne and I are five minutes from here. Come
when you're ready." He gave me directions to Elvis Presley
Boulevard, the main street to the nursing home.

I said, "My manners are usually better. I haven't even thanked
you properly for helping me find my grandmother. But like I said
in my second letter, if it weren't for you—"

He laughed. "I expect you'll act better when you've had some
sleep."

I caught my reflection in the mirror as we stood at the open
door. "With all the makeup and curls, you'd think I was getting
ready for a night out."

"Don't leave any valuables in this room," Mr. Nelson said as he
looked out over the parking lot. A semi was parked ten yards away
and blocked some of the torrid sun.

"Is this district dangerous?" I asked. I had been living away from
the States for so long, it was possible that I'd lost my instincts for
that kind of judgment. The highway didn't look like a mean
street, but that didn't say it wasn't. During my childhood the
South had been lethal for anyone my color. The Ku Klux Klan
had power and used it, so images of lynched men were branded

into my consciousness. I had left the States in the sixties, so the atrocities that occurred during the civil rights movement remained my lasting impression of the South. With the Rebel Inn next door I felt as expendable in Memphis as vapor in the noonday sun.

Pointing to the roof next door, I said, "The Rebel Inn?"

"Yep." Mr. Nelson grunted. That sole utterance summarized all he had seen and survived in his sixty-odd years.

When I climbed into the rental car, my father was as much on my mind as his mother. I was thinking of something Alan had said about Blair having gone to Memphis after he'd become a psychiatrist in the hope of helping Ernestine. But his entertaining such a hope in the 1950s was either brave or naïve, since contempt for him as a Northerner and as a Negro—an educated northern Negro—could have been lethal.

But the Memphis I was about to experience was officially integrated, though driving along Elvis Presley Boulevard there were no European faces to be seen, and the only black people walking looked too poor even to catch a bus.

It had a strangeness—the broad streets and single-story buildings plastered with billboards and advertisements accommodated cars and commerce, but there was nothing beautiful. Not much for the people apart from one open park I passed during the twenty-minute drive to the nursing home.

Signs for Graceland, Presley's home, suggested it was the main tourist attraction, and I wondered why Presley made this town his base. But maybe I was judging too quickly. I'd hardly been in Memphis for an hour as I pulled in to the curb outside the nursing home. Perspiration trailed my back and temples, as I sat in the car staring at the house on a street that had once been for whites only. Now it was an all-black neighborhood. To discover that Ernestine had been living for eleven years in a house with no bars on the windows, no guard at the door, numbed me. Since childhood I'd been repeating, "My grandmother's in a mental institution," and it had never crossed my mind to challenge that.

Suddenly I knew I had to question everything I had ever been told about Ernestine. What was she doing here?

The street was deserted. A couple of cars were parked on the opposite side, and in the distance I heard children playing.

Braced for a cool reception, I paused.

Maybe my grandmother wouldn't accept that her fair-skinned son had fathered somebody with dark skin and kinky hair. Since slavery our class structure has always been defined by skin color and hair texture. So has beauty. Janet and Michael Jackson are testimony to the fact that smooth hair and pale skin still count. But I had come too far to worry about it. Even if the skeleton in the family closet was best left alone, it was too late to turn back.

 ERNESTINE

OUTSIDE THE PEELING FRONT DOOR my eyes couldn't avoid the filthy gray sofa to my right or the rusty porch chair to my left. No sign indicated that the house was a nursing home.

It was 27 August 1991; only three months had passed since my cousin Alan's call. The series of shocks which had driven me to find my grandmother and get to her hadn't prepared me for this moment. The grimy sofa took me off guard, as did the dirty white paintwork on the house. I couldn't relate to this place. In my mind I could see my uncle's pretty living room in Brookline with the tall white azalea peeking in. I could also visualize the dark brown shutters on my house in France, flanked by pink and yellow rosebushes.

Clutching Ernestine's gifts, I tapped lightly on the door pane, reminding myself that, whatever I found, I had seven dollars in my purse and was powerless to change anything.

Several voices called out, "It's open!"

Stepping directly into the medium-sized front room of a single-family dwelling, I saw a morbid collection of silent old women of varying shades of brown, except for one huddled in a big plastic chair that was patched with wide strips of silver tape. I was frozen in the moment, and the rest of the gloomy gathering faded away. I could see only Blair's mother. She was the size that Karis had been at ten—so small and frail, so bony and pale. I wanted to drop the packages I was holding, sweep her up, and run out of there. I wanted to be in a tracksuit instead of high heels and a designer dress so that I could run my fastest with this woman who hadn't yet looked at me. Like the others she was staring at the black-and-white TV, which was blaring.

I was too conscious of how white she looked. I hated myself for it and for noticing how straight her hair was. I couldn't shake my lifetime of training to see color as relevant, to see her straight hair as a status symbol. Since slavery these factors had come to mean something that registered with me no matter how much I knew they shouldn't.

Hovering in the doorway while heat and light tried to squeeze in behind me, I resisted shouting Ernestine! above the din of the television. It felt as if I'd entered a waiting room for dying patients who'd given up expecting to be called. One heavyset woman with her stockings knotted at the calves was so bent over in her chair I couldn't see her face.

Nobody moved.

What makes people avoid death after they cease to be interested in life?

I stood within feet of my father's mother and tried not to notice the depressing room where she sat. The sickly pale-green walls cried out for fresh paint and the linoleum on the floor needed replacing. No chair looked clean enough to sit on and I wondered what state the sofa cover was in. It had a stained sleeping bag slung over it. Pity crowded my joy. I didn't know whether to laugh or cry. But a voice in my head said, At least you got here. You can only do what you can do. Now make the best of it.

For Ernestine's sake I knew that I had to fit in to this strange environment in which I was obviously an outsider. My refusal to straighten or oil my hair set me apart as much as my expensive Milanese outfit and my air of confidence, which comes from twenty-five years of a public profile in Britain and Europe. In my flowery dress with my lips painted red, I guessed I provoked suspicion. Even my accent would have been out of place, so I needed to change how I spoke. Although I love the English that I learned in the ghetto, it was no longer natural to me. Nevertheless I had leaned toward it when speaking to O'Ferrell Nelson, despite his being so educated, and I knew it was appropriate to lean toward it again.

I reminded myself that this gloomy gathering of old women could probably have been a think tank of mother wit in their younger days. Surely these were some of the militants that I'd seen on the TV news as a child, those women who had marched into the face of the racism that clouded their youth and mine. It felt like they could read my thoughts. Maybe there was even a seer among them who could have predicted, This gal that come through that door will pry in all that done happen to Ernestine.

The electric glow from the TV cast highlights across a room starved of natural light to fend off the heat. Having come in from the glaring afternoon sunlight, I squinted to see who called from across the room. The female voice was dark and bluesy and belonged to Essie Mae Dukes, whom I had spoken to the first time I rang the home. "Miss Hunt, Miss Hunt!" she called to Ernestine. "Look, sugar! That's somebody here for you."

As Miss Dukes rose to greet me, the voice in my head said, Don't give your grandmother the impression that you're here to see somebody else.

But I welcomed Miss Dukes's smile. She was slimmer and prettier than I expected. Her square unlined face could have belonged to a woman thirty-five or fifty-five, and her dark hair glistening with oil framed her round cheeks. Wearing black trousers and a white tunic, she was in socks without shoes. Working their long shifts alone, she and Lula Mae ran the home: made the beds, cooked the meals, did the laundry and cleaning and cared for the twelve adults living in the house.

When Miss Dukes was near enough to hear me whisper, I said, "Let's don't tell my grandmother who I am. It might upset her." I guessed that I would have to choose my moment to explain that I was Blair's daughter. Ernestine's blank expression told me that although she was looking at the television she was unable to take it in.

I apologized for being late and hoped that I hadn't arrived at teatime or naptime, assuming that the home ran by a fixed schedule. Ernestine's eyes never turned from the television and, with her hands clasped tightly on her lap, she hadn't reacted to Miss Dukes's call. It was hot in that room and I was surprised that the seven women sitting there weren't sweating like I was. With my arms laden with handbag and packages, I couldn't mop my brow and felt the beads turn to trickles on my forehead.

When I asked Miss Dukes if there was someplace private to sit, she offered the kitchen and pointed toward a short passage. "Miss Hunt! Miss Hunt! Come on, baby," she commanded, and without asking why or looking our way, Ernestine lifted herself from the seat. It was like seeing a corpse rise from a coffin. She came alive— until then she had been as still as a wax model.

Ernestine had thick gray hair. Cropped short, it was cut in bangs at the front and looked oddly young compared to her pale, lined face, which was as stoic as an old Apache chief's. Her blue eyes gave away nothing. Her body was straight for a woman of ninety-three and there was no sign of rheumatism or arthritis, but she shuffled along with the dullness of a long-term prisoner in a concentration camp. Her blue and gray plaid dress hung on her as it would on a hanger and exposed her calves, which were thinner than my forearms and didn't look strong enough to support her, but only her feet looked misshapen. The tops of her white wedgies had been cut away to make room for hammertoes and bunions hidden by white ankle socks.

This stranger was my grandmother. This sleepwalker had been holding on, for what and for whom? Was I missing my moment? Was I meant to grab her, to yell, It's okay now, you're not alone? But I didn't dare touch her, remembering some autistic children that I'd once worked with as a volunteer. How one entered their space was crucial, but nonetheless I wanted to put my arms around her to comfort her. I recalled my uncle telling me that when he'd last visited his mother in his late teens, he'd arrived at the mental institution to discover that they had pulled out all her teeth. He had no explanation as to why, but said, "She didn't look like my beautiful mother any more." Ernestine would have been in her late thirties. It's possible that having her teeth removed was a punishment, not an uncommon practice in asylums then.

But still, as Miss Dukes led us to the kitchen, I wanted to scoop my grandmother into my arms and rush with her into the streets, where there was at least some air and light. I couldn't imagine how Miss Dukes cooked for so many people in that small kitchen; it was clean, but no more could be said for it. The leaden smell of over-cooked greens clung to the dismal paintwork. Yet this would be the place where I would speak to Ernestine for the first time, touch her for the first time.

Miss Dukes offered me a bench in the breakfast nook adjoining the kitchen. Placing my gifts on the table, I said, "How would you like to sit on my lap? I've got a nice soft lap." Though I coaxed her as I would a child, I thought she'd scream Noooo! or hide behind Miss Dukes's shoulders. But instead, Ernestine positioned herself to be drawn onto my lap, although she sat as rigid as a plank with her legs thrust out in front of her. It hadn't dawned on me yet that during her long life she might have been forced to sit on many strange laps.

I looked at her veiny arms, their thick dark ridges, the white skin. . . . Again I could hear my grandfather referring to her as "my poor, dear sick wife." She had outlived him by thirteen years, and though I assumed her mind was gone, she was still standing, and her dementia (if that was what she was suffering from) was probably no worse than the senility of many people her age.

The TV blared on in the other room. Sitting at a Formica table where the residents ate, I held my arms around Ernestine's waist while sun streamed in through the window on our left. Miss Dukes sat opposite us. She didn't ask why I was running the silky edge of my dress along my grandmother's forearm or letting her sniff my perfumed wrists. But I was remembering how the autistic children I'd worked with responded to sweet scents and silky things to touch. When Ernestine chuckled I kissed the backs of her hands and Miss Dukes's eyes welled with tears. She said, "Miss Hunt loves gettin' babied, don't you, Miss Hunt?"

Despite the three planes, including one across the Atlantic, which I had taken to get here, I was decades late. Realizing that no amount of babying would change that, a silence crept over us like a deadly spider, until Miss Dukes tossed her glory among us to say, "Miss Hunt, ain't you gon' give her a kiss?"

That's when it dawned on me that Ernestine might have sat on my lap because she had had to put up with sexual advances during a lifetime of "care." I said, "You don't have to kiss me. In fact you don't have to do anything you don't want to while I'm here. Understand?"

Ernestine didn't answer. Nor did she kiss me, and I winked at Miss Dukes. As pure as her intentions seemed, I was scared to trust even her. I felt foreign, as if I couldn't read all the underlying signs, and I had nobody to ask, Does this all seem suspicious to you? Why has she been *here* for eleven years? My mind was telling me that if the woman on my lap had been abused, it was because I hadn't prevented it. I thought about the seventy-two people in my village in France, most of them poor and struggling to make a living off the land. They had air and sun and light in their lives. But this woman didn't.

I felt so sorry for her. She smelled decayed. I tried to convince myself that old people always did. Because what if they didn't? Something in me kept saying, This is your grandmother and you've got to get her out of here. But I refused to listen to that voice and concentrated on Miss Dukes, who was saying, "This here's Marsha. Can you say that? Say Marsha . . . go 'head. Say it, Miss Hunt: Marsha . . . Mar . . . sha."

The refrigerator hummed and I rubbed Ernestine's back. Spine and ribs were prominent. She released a couple of sighs from somewhere deep, sounding like she was suffering from molecular fatigue. After a minute she suddenly said, "Mar . . . sha."

Miss Dukes's laugh reminded me of women I'd heard laughing while I was growing up. Her joy was contagious and I laughed with her.

Ernestine didn't know who I was and didn't have the ability to ask. But I wanted to believe that with my arms around her waist she felt safe while I stroked and rocked her.

Miss Dukes offered me a cup of coffee and though I declined, she rose to make herself one, trailing cigarette smoke into the kitchen and saying, "I told you she could talk. And takes herself to the bathroom good as anybody, can't ch'you, Miss Hunt? Can't ch'you, sugar?"

"Yeah, hon," said Ernestine.

Her voice. She had a voice. And I longed to hear what she could tell me about the past. Maybe her silence was a ploy or a defense, but whatever had driven her into silence had left her trapped there. Had she always had that heavy voice? Her sticklike frame said that she had once spoken with the high, feminine lilt of a genteel southern girl.

Miss Dukes sat back down, taking sips from a Styrofoam cup, as I reached to grab a small box wrapped in shiny blue paper which I'd brought for Ernestine. "It's not much, but maybe you'll like it," I told my grandmother. I was losing control over my jet lag. My eyes were burning and I was getting edgy. The heat didn't help and, with Ernestine on my lap, my thighs were sweating

more than my back and forehead. I wondered how much longer
I could stay awake as my grandmother fiddled with the wrapping
paper.

"Miss Hunt," said Miss Dukes, "you gon' be spoiled rotten by
the time she leaves. . . . She brung you all them presents."

The gift that Ernestine was trying to open was only a box of
heart-shaped soaps and I was relieved when Miss Dukes yanked
the paper off for her. Ernestine sniffed the see-through box on
command but she wasn't interested and I derided myself for coming to Memphis. What had I hoped to achieve? Having treated my
credit card like a magic wand to pay for the journey, the gifts, and
the motel, the trip to see Ernestine suddenly seemed pointless. The
soaps lay in their box on the scratched Formica and Ernestine
watched Miss Dukes smoothing out the torn bits of paper. Were all
my instincts wrong? I wondered, as I shifted my grandmother from
my lap.

She stared at the top of the refrigerator and Miss Dukes laughed.
"Miss Hunt got her eye on that bowl where I keep the bananas,
ain't ch'you, baby? I told you she love bananas. If you don't watch
her, she come in here and steal 'em. One time she ate 'bout seven
of 'em."

"You told me to bring bananas, but I forgot. Me and my big
ideas."

Fatigue had me confused but, with Ernestine now seated on
my left, my tired eyes had the first chance to study her profile.
Without teeth her jaw seemed too small and her ears too large. A
strange peace surrounded her, although her clasped hands had
begun to jerk involuntarily. Despite unsmiling lips, her blue eyes
were soft and she had a certain grace. With a chest as flat as an
adolescent's and her spindly arms, she could have been a wrinkled
child.

I wanted to tell her that I was Blair's daughter, to explain that I
was family, but I'd hardly been there for ten minutes and knew it
wasn't the right time.

Among my gifts was a copy of Blair's baby picture which I'd

traveled via Folkestone to collect. I'd bought a Victorian frame for it and was relieved that the pane was plastic instead of glass, because I still half believed that my grandmother was violent. Myths take a long time to die.

Blair, born in 1919, had probably been no more than a year old when the photograph was taken. He looks knowing, posed on a carved chair, wearing a handsome white coat with a cape collar and cuffs and high buttoned shoes. Maybe it had been Ernestine who had brushed his hair for the professional sitting at the Hooks Brothers studio whose name is stamped on the back of the picture.

I didn't expect her to notice that the Victorian frame suited the sepia print and even wondered if she'd be able to see it, because it was only three inches by five and she needed glasses.

As laughter pealed from the TV in the other room, I used the photograph as a fan before handing it to her. Ernestine accepted it in both hands. Her expression didn't change, but she stared at it momentarily before bringing it to her lips. "Bee Tee," she said quietly after she had kissed it. B.T. were the initials of my father's first and middle names. The sound of her voice clung to the heavy heat of the afternoon as she raised her hand to her brow.

"Lord ha' mercy," whispered Miss Dukes.

Seventy years of isolation and confusion might have clouded her memory and relegated her to a dusty tomb, but she remembered her baby. I wanted to hang on to that moment but the seconds pressed on as I waited, hoping that Miss Dukes would say nothing, in case Ernestine was about to speak. But the three of us sat motionless, until Ernestine turned toward the window.

Miss Dukes took a drag from her cigarette and looked down at her hands to avoid my eyes. It's likely that she had questions she wasn't sure she should ask. I suspected that she wanted to know why Ernestine had been disowned, which is what I sat there asking myself.

—ଙ RECALL

I ROSE MOMENTARILY FROM THE WOODEN BENCH in the breakfast nook because my dress was sticking to my thighs. It gave me a second to think. My heart pumped at such a rate after seeing Ernestine kiss that picture that I was gritting my teeth to stay calm. Why had I been told that Ernestine could recognize no one, and what else had been said about her that wasn't true?

My grandfather had said that Ernestine's condition was hereditary. So had her guardian, Harry Mae Simons, who'd also told me that my grandmother could be violent. But Essie Mae Dukes had denied this, and she had known Ernestine for years.

I was in Memphis for Ernestine's benefit, because hearing that she'd had no one hit me as hard as discovering that she had been able enough to live outside of the asylum. The visit was more than I could afford in time or money, and although I didn't know what it would accomplish, the least I had hoped for was to let my father's mother see that she was remembered and wasn't a disease to be avoided.

A few weeks after my cousin Alan had phoned me in France to say Ernestine was possibly in Memphis, he'd sent me a ten-page autobiographical piece which he'd written for his Unitarian Universalist ministry studies. His church was liberal and early members had included some of the American transcendentalists like Ralph Waldo Emerson and Henry David Thoreau, who wrote *Walden* and *Civil Disobedience.* So I was ready for Alan's piece to be as open as it was. He'd mentioned things about our family which I didn't know, but sitting there on that bench in the breakfast nook with my backside aching from having had Ernestine on my lap, I tried to recall what Alan had said about her and Grandfather.

He'd written that Ernestine had been one of Grandfather's students, and although Grandfather had told me this himself, I hadn't thought about the teacher-student relationship or wondered whether theirs had been a healthy one. When I was in high school, an affair with a teacher would have been more than a scandal; the teacher would have been written off the books. But when Ernestine and Grandfather married this must not have been the case.

He had died in 1978 aged ninety and she was said to be ninety-three now. So there was ten or more years' difference in their ages. Assuming that she graduated when she was eighteen, Grandfather would then have been about thirty. He too had pale skin, smooth hair, and European features and therefore would have been considered handsome, so her classmates may have envied her.

Alan's piece described Grandfather as a Disciples of Christ minister and the name alone sounded odd to me. I assumed that it was a Baptist denomination but knew nothing about my grandfather's religion. He wrote to me on church stationery and I knew that his church being in Memphis meant that his congregation was all black. But he struck me as a conservative man and I doubted if he had been a Bible-thumping minister whose church members got happy and had to be carried out. The Mississippi Boulevard Church included some of the most prosperous members of the community.

Alan wrote that his father, Wilson, and the other two boys, Blair and Ernest, had been raised by their maternal grandmother in Boston so that the brothers could avoid the Jim Crow laws in the South, but I didn't know if that had been said to eliminate questions about why Grandfather didn't raise his sons at home. As a high school principal, he had had a reputation for strict discipline, which must have been necessary to run an inner-city school at that time.

With Ernestine sitting beside me, my father's baby picture still in her hand, I reached out to stroke her forearm. What was she thinking, sitting there with the sun plaiting silver streaks in her hair? Did that photograph remind her of a happy period in her life when she became a mother? Or was it motherhood which had brought her down? Ernestine, hardly more than a teenager, had

had her three sons in quick succession. Her first was born in 1919, so she would have been pregnant, giving birth, or recovering from delivery for thirty-five consecutive months. When my father, Blair, was two, Wilson would have been one while Ernest was a newborn. So she would have had three babies in diapers at the same time and who knows what other pressures to cope with. Although this wasn't unusual for women of her generation, I assume they were as susceptible to post-partum depression as women are today. Was a condition as simple as this responsible for her spending over half a century in an asylum? That possibility was as hard to face as her dispossession.

——&ep; FAMILY ALBUM

MISS DUKES LIT UP A KOOL. She enjoyed her first draw so much, it made me wish I still smoked. It was four o'clock and I expected one of the other residents to interrupt us at any moment. I said, "Do you mind if I call you Essie Mae? "Miss Dukes" sounds so formal."

"Call me whatever you like. I'm so glad you're here, I don't know what to do." The sadness of her black eyes didn't match her sparky voice.

"Are we keeping you from getting on with your work?"

"Don't worry 'bout me, don't worry one bit. I'm just so glad you're here," she repeated, staring over at Ernestine as if seeing her for the first time. Maybe she had thought that memory, spontaneity, and feelings were more than Ernestine was capable of. Picking up her Styrofoam cup, she shook it slightly and said, "Here Miss Hunt . . . let me see that picture you got."

Despite Ernestine's fingers flicking involuntarily, she managed to hold the cup.

Essie Mae said, "She ain't s'posed to have coffee, but if she find my cup on the table, she'll drink from it."

The frame of the picture was fabric, maroon with tiny flowers. Some of Essie Mae's smoke circled it and she hooted. "Miss Hunt! This here's your baby and Bee Tee is what you call your husband!"

How often had Ernestine had the privilege of being right since she was certified insane? I sprang to her defense. "Her son and her husband had the same initials. Bee Tee is obviously what she called her baby."

Essie Mae disagreed. "That's what she calls her husband. I hear her back in that room just a-fussin' at him. Callin' him you this-and-that, you so-and-so!"

Ernestine was the only one who could resolve the question but she was still staring at the banana bowl, which made me suspect she wasn't getting enough to eat.

Essie Mae laughed. "She always in here trying to steal bananas. But she had her a good lunch, didn't you, Miss Hunt?"

The table we were sitting at couldn't have seated all thirteen residents and I wondered if they ate in shifts as I passed Ernestine her third gift, her graduation picture in a frame. She didn't react. Her blue eyes, so much paler in real life than they looked in the photograph, were focused upon it, but her sigh seemed unrelated.

Graduation is usually a proud moment and would have been the more so for Ernestine and her classmates, whose parents or grandparents might have been slaves forbidden to learn reading and writing. Throughout her high school years, the First World War was decimating her generation in Europe. It brought to mind my village in France with its geraniums growing outside on window ledges, and I imagined Ernestine watching my neighbor's cows being herded up our road.

Essie Mae studied Ernestine's graduation picture and shook her head. "Pitiful . . . just pitiful, ain't it . . . a pretty girl like that."

With Ernestine beside me I noticed that her nose was almost flat and the bridge was bent, though it had been straight when she was young and her nose pointed. It hurt to think that it might have been broken. Being small, she must have attracted bullies in the asylum from time to time. Between the Depression and 1981 when she was released, her pale skin, straight hair, and blue eyes could have singled her out for favors and abuse in the racially seg-regated wards.

The breakfast nook was about eight feet long. On my right was a door leading to a passage and opposite it was a bathroom with the door open. It was hard to imagine where all the residents slept and I wanted to see Ernestine's bedroom. "Would you like to rest?" I asked, although there were two gifts unopened on the table.

Essie Mae said, "Miss Hunt's having a good time."

My grandmother stared up at the banana bowl and said noth-ing.

"You ain't ready for her to go, is you?" Essie Mae asked.

"Shall I get you some bananas?" I said. It was a faint offer, because I was exhausted. My eyes burned, my head throbbed, and it was unlikely that I could drive back to the motel.

Essie Mae yelled, "Hold it!" and rushed to the kitchen, return-ing with one black-speckled banana. Ernestine gobbled chunks, mashing them between her gums—but the dull expression in her blue-gray eyes didn't change. She was a deserted house.

After she had swallowed her last piece of banana, I handed her a 10-by-12-inch ribboned parcel. Knowing what was inside, I was excited, but Ernestine's expression was blank. In the half hour that I'd been there, she hadn't yet looked at me, so I leaned forward, hair brushing the table, face upturned.

Her pale eyes met mine. She blinked and blinked again. It was as if she'd touched me. I laughed. "Who's got beautiful eyes!" And they were. Speckly blue with the surrounding whites clear and bright. For a moment they were knowing eyes and I was suddenly uncertain about the present I'd just given her.

It was a family album, a dozen pictures which included grand-children and great-grandchildren that I was sure she didn't know she had. Essie Mae smoked, the refrigerator hummed, and I yanked the ribbon and paisley paper from the album and opened it to the first page.

The portrait of Grandfather was slightly sinister because of deep circles around his eyes. His dark hair was already receding, and his white shirt, black jacket, and tie bled into a dark background. It had been taken at the Hooks Brothers studio like my father's baby picture. Grandfather might have been in his forties and already living with Harry Mae.

I asked Ernestine, "Know who this is?"

"Mistah Hunt," she said. Immediate and certain.

"Mister Hunt" . . . was that how she had addressed him? Wives often did in the old days.

In France my grandfather could have been mistaken for an Algerian, but both his parents were American slaves. His mother, Emma Shouse, was born in Danville, Kentucky. Her mother, Annie, was owned by a Jewish immigrant from Germany who was also Emma's father. After Abolition, he carted them down the Mississippi River and abandoned them on the Memphis shore when Emma was five.

Grandfather's father was owned by a Memphis family, the Hunts. Also called Blair, he was about six in 1862 when the Civil War forced the Hunts to vacate their Beale Street plantation and it was captured by Union soldiers. The Hunts returned when the war ended, and still being a child, Blair remained with them and eventually became their carpenter. Their wedding gift to him when he married Emma Shouse was a house at 693 Linden Avenue where my grandfather was born, the second of four children.

Although Ernestine called him "Mister Hunt" when she identified his picture, did she also call him "Bee Tee" as Essie Mae claimed? Stubbing out her cigarette, Essie Mae dismissed his image with a glare and a "hmmph." But it wasn't the time to ask why.

My grandmother didn't kiss her husband's picture. Nor did she kiss the one I turned to of her mother, Mattie, seated in front of three of her sisters outside a hotel where they had worked in Hyannis Port, Massachusetts, on Cape Cod, which Americans now associate with the Kennedy family, who have a home there.

Mattie looks older than her three fair-skinned sisters standing behind her. When Wilson had given me the photograph, he'd explained that one of the three was the grandmother of Benjamin Hooks, chief executive of the National Association for the Advancement of Colored People, referred to as the NAACP, which was the largest black political coalition in the United States. Mattie was already middle-aged and overweight in the picture. My Uncle Wilson had explained that his gran's maiden name had been Mattie Lewis. I had asked if she had had the same parents as the others, because she was so much darker than they were. He said yes, so I assumed Mattie was a genetic throwback and had the coloring of an African ancestor, unlike the rest of her family, who were fair. Not only did this set her apart in the picture, it would have set her apart in life.

She had been one of fourteen children born to emancipated slaves in Huntsville, Alabama, a decade after the Civil War. That her father, Wilson Lewis (after whom my uncle was named), had looked German may have increased his market value during slavery. It also raised his status in the Huntsville community after emancipation, because ex-slave masters with their pre-Abolition value judgments about Negroes continued to control things.

Mattie's dark skin would have singled her out from birth for teasing and whispers about why she wasn't as pale as her parents and siblings. Looking more "white" or European improved work opportunities and social standing, so compared to her family she was disadvantaged.

Although I had asked my uncle why Mattie was darker than the others, I didn't ask why Wilson Lewis looked German. I didn't expect to know why some members of the family looked white. Slaves couldn't make claims upon their white fathers—or white mothers—and it was unusual that Emma Shouse, my grandfather's mother, could identify her father as German-Jewish.

Europeans are sensitive about their cultures and heritage: a Scotsman would laugh at being mistaken for German and no Englishman would expect to be mistaken for French. But in America as immigrants they shed their national identities and became "white."

I knew who Ernestine's mother was, although Mattie's heritage became impossible to pinpoint beyond her parents. But who was Ernestine's father? He might have been Polish for all I knew, or Russian, or perhaps he was a genetic throwback like Mattie and together they had produced a fair child who resembled the fairer members of their families.

The pictures of Mattie had probably been taken after Ernestine had entered the asylum. The style of the cotton dresses Mattie and her sisters are wearing suggests the late thirties. Ernestine still hadn't reacted to her mother's picture. So I said, "Isn't that your mama with your aunts Cora and Mildred and Bessie?"

I wondered if having a pale, blue-eyed child had caused Mattie problems. Having had a pale child myself, I know that people asked why Karis looked like she did. I could say her father was English. Essie Mae was curious about the picture of the four Lewis sisters and was surprised that Ernestine's mother was the dark one seated.

Ernestine was born in Roanoke, Virginia. Mattie's mother had been from that area, and mining there offered work and attracted laborers. But I didn't know whether Mattie had arrived pregnant from Huntsville. Immigration and migration cloud the picture.

Why had Ernestine's maiden name been Martin, and if she suffered from a hereditary problem, could it have come from her father's family?

Sitting there in the kitchen nook, I decided not to torment myself with questions. Ernestine was alive and I had managed to get to her. That was my miracle for the day.

‿ℭ꒰ THE DILEMMA

THE RED CHEVY HAD BEEN SITTING IN THE SUN. It was an oven. Sliding into the driver's seat, I planned to park a few streets away and collapse in the back, but as the air-conditioning blew in my face, all I could think about was Ernestine. Having spent that hour with her, I was more riddled with questions than I'd been on the planes flying to Memphis. She was no drooling vegetable, nor was she violent, and I had a gut feeling that she hadn't spent over half a century in an asylum because of inherited insanity.

To find out who she had been before they locked her away meant asking questions, but with only two days in town would I get any answers?

My grandfather's myth or my grandmother—which needed protection? Suspicion can be as harmful as accusation, and if asking what happened to her would damage his reputation, did I have a right to ask?

Turning right into McLemore Street I passed a red brick church, small with no frills. It looked like the houses that little children draw, square with an A-line roof. The cross over the front door was wooden and painted white. The streets were empty and I hadn't yet passed a tree to park under before I saw a sign for Elvis Presley Boulevard, an ugly street lined with chain stores. What would Elvis have thought of the street which bore his name?

O'FERRELL AND ANNE

THE ECONO LODGE MOTEL ON LAMAR is set back from the road. I hadn't given it a good look when I checked in from the airport, so returning to it that evening I noticed for the first time that the façade was meant to resemble a southern plantation house. Tall white columns standing either side of the entrance made it look stately and out of place on the six-lane thoroughfare. Traffic was slack. I'd slept in the car through rush hour but I was still breathing gas fumes as I pulled into the parking space outside my room. I was glad I didn't have to see anybody but was already thinking about whom I should phone.

Collapsing on the low double bed, I listened to the air conditioner. I was sorry that I wasn't at home, because my house helped me think, and the smell of honeysuckle eased my mind. Feeding the finches that gathered outside the sunroom between six and seven each night cleared my head faster than a sniff of eucalyptus oil. I could talk to my house, but I couldn't talk to that motel room. The white walls were as soulless as the laminated round table with two chairs and the mock-brass standing lamp. A 24-inch TV sat on a long, low wooden chest of drawers, and from the bed I could see the mirrored dressing alcove next to the little bathroom. The telephone was on a built-in shelf next to the bed, so I hardly had to move to dial O'Ferrell. His wife, Anne, answered and I apologized for having missed my appointment earlier.

Anne's low, smooth voice was soothing, her southern accent contagious. I sounded more like her than myself when I told her that I'd just come from seeing my grandmother. Maybe I'd been wrong to refuse Anne's original phone invitation to stay with them during my visit. Without the long-distance connection getting in the way, she sounded less formal.

"We've got some friends here from Atlanta," she said. "Why don't you come by?"

I took a deep breath. I wanted to talk but hadn't the strength to clean myself up and be social—but I accepted her invitation anyway.

The Nelsons' place was easy to find. Before I knocked on the back door, I reminded myself to be careful about what I said. Grandfather had been O'Ferrell's high school principal and Anne was in a social club with Harry Mae Simons. The city of Memphis wasn't large and was predominantly black, though it hadn't always been. My grandfather had taught at least three generations of Memphians. Over the years many teachers had taught under him. He had been a prominent minister and had presided over the births, marriages, and deaths of who knows how many people. I wasn't sure if he had enemies, but I figured he had a lot of friends. Despite being his granddaughter, I was not an insider.

The Nelsons' back door overlooked their driveway, where three cars were parked. A white one was next to O'Ferrell's Continental. Their house was a two-story in a nice setting of individual houses separated by driveways and well-tended front lawns. Trees and flowers grew and the Nelsons' roses were bigger than a heavy-weight's fist.

The gentle clinking I heard before O'Ferrell answered the door was the ice cubes in the glass of bourbon he was carrying when he came to open it. He had changed from the afternoon: white trousers, white sandals, and crisp striped shirt. Obviously clothes mattered to him. Seeing his smile reminded me how much I miss my people. My people, Americans with slavery in their family history.

Magazines on a glass coffee table in a bright carpeted family room surrounded by windows caught my eye as he walked me through to an attractive room which was both a kitchen and lounge. Color, light, comfort, and design also mattered to him—to them. Anne was standing at the sink and their two guests were sitting on stools at the red counter.

Anne was a nurse and had a very sympathetic face. She looked soft and round without being fat, her honest eyes were dark and almond-shaped, and the few freckles on her soft cheeks didn't flaw her complexion. She was the color of acacia honey and there were only a few strands of gray in her smooth black hair. She looked fifty at most but I figured she was at least ten years older.

Somehow it felt like I'd known her and O'Ferrell all my life, though we'd hardly spoken. She introduced her friends before offering me a peach chiller from the fridge.

The four of them wanted to hear about me finding Ernestine and I leaned heavily on the fading of Blair's baby picture being the start of events that had me standing in their stylish kitchen that evening. I didn't say that I couldn't understand why Ernestine had been in Memphis for eleven years without Alan or me knowing about it. Nor could I tell them that I thought the conditions that she was living in were unacceptable, because O'Ferrell's father had also been there. (Had I mentioned this, they might have made it clear that he'd only stayed there for a short time and that Anne had visited the old man every day.)

Anne wanted to know about my family.

"I grew up in Philadelphia." I rambled on. "My mother, her sister, and their mother raised my brother, my sister, and me. But Dennis and Pam weren't Blair's children, so the whole thing of me finding Ernestine doesn't really concern any of them. My mother's worried that I'm sticking my nose in something that isn't my business. I sort of see her point, because she and my aunt and my grandmother did everything for me. But the thought of Ernestine having nobody cut deep."

O'Ferrell asked, "Where's your mother?"

"California. Berkeley. My sister lives next door. My brother's in LA. He's a music critic on the *LA Times.* My mother remarried, but she and her husband are just splitting up after twenty-five years. She's a tough customer and we argue at the drop of a hat. I was almost tempted not to tell her that I was coming to Memphis—don't get the wrong idea . . . you'd adore my mother, everybody does—but I want to keep her out of my business."

Anne laughed and said, "Did Ernestine know who you were?"

"No, and I didn't tell her." I had slipped into my black accent. "For one thing I don't know if she realizes that my father's dead, and for another I don't know if she has a color problem. She may not want a little, dark, nappy-headed granddaughter. . . . Did I tell you that she's related to the Hookses?"

O'Ferrell said, "I went to school with Ben Hooks. I used to be in his mother's house all the time."

"Well, his maternal grandmother and Ernestine's mother, Mattie, were sisters."

Apart from knowing that Benjamin Hooks headed the NAACP, I knew nothing about him or his family. O'Ferrell said that Ben's three sisters were living nearby, so I asked, "Can you help me get in touch with them?"

"I doubt that Ben and Frances are around. Now that he heads the NAACP he's in Washington most of the time. Benny knew your grandfather. He and his sisters graduated from Booker T. Washington just like I did."

I didn't know whether that was lucky or unlucky. The Hookses as distant cousins may have been the nearest thing to family that Ernestine had in Memphis. Maybe they knew something about her, but wouldn't their allegiance be to my grandfather, who had been their high school principal? "Ben gave the eulogy at your grandfather's funeral," O'Ferrell said.

THE HOOKS CONNECTION

HUNTSVILLE, ALABAMA, IS ABOUT TWO HUNDRED MILES due east of Memphis and not far south of the Tennessee-Alabama state line.

Job opportunities may have attracted Mattie and some of her sisters to move to Memphis because, despite being born in Huntsville, at least three of them were in the Memphis area in the early 1900s. Mattie had become a seamstress, her younger sister Cora worked in a coffee shop, and their sister Bessie married.

Four of Bessie's grandchildren, Julia, Mildred, Bessie, and Benjamin Hooks, were living in Memphis that August of 1991 when Anne and O'Ferrell took me to meet them on my last night in town. The three sisters were living together within two miles of the nursing home.

Julia answered the door. She was a small woman who walked with a cane, because she'd been in a car accident when she was young. Although she was in her seventies, her pale face had no wrinkles. She wore a short wig which was as beige as her skin. In dark blue trousers and a sweater, she hobbled across to her special chair in the den as the three of us followed her in. She was polite, as she might have been to an insurance salesman. I wondered if her family's name and her brother Ben's position had attracted other strangers who claimed to be related.

O'Ferrell had introduced me as Blair Hunt's granddaughter, which had been my calling card, but maybe she wasn't convinced that I was Blair Jr.'s daughter. Anne and O'Ferrell looked embarrassed by her reception of me. In the time I'd seen them over my sixty-hour stay, they'd been quick to laugh and smile—but now they were quiet. I mentioned that I lived in England and France and had a daughter at Yale.

The den was large and dimly lit. At the far end from the door was a fifties-style bar and a huge television set. The far wall was lined with books. I was perched on the edge of the sofa and Julia sat in an upright chair with a pillow to give her hip extra support. Her mood brightened so sharply after I dropped some trivia about Karis going into her senior year that it seemed as if she'd switched the overhead lights on.

Anne and O'Ferrell relaxed. He even lit a cigarette when I produced the picture of Mattie with her three sisters in Hyannis Port.

Crossing the room to give it to Julia, I said, "My great-grand-mother and your grandmother were working in a hotel or restau-rant in Massachusetts."

Julia held the picture under the lamplight. Her nails were man-icured and polished. She pointed to the sister who stood behind Mattie looking bashful. "That's Aunt Cora—no, wait. Maybe that's Mildred. But that one," said Julia, pointing to the middle sister who had her graying hair pulled back from her face, "that one's Aunt Florence, I think. We didn't really know my grandmother. But I remember Aunt Mattie."

Finally. I rushed back to my perch anticipating the stories I thought she might tell. Anne winked at me, and O'Ferrell confi-dently blew a puff of smoke over the moment.

Julia Hooks would have hardly been more than school age when Ernestine was put away. She was fifteen years younger than my grandmother. About Mattie she said, "She used to live in a great big house on that hill on Mississippi Boulevard. And one time we went to visit and she gave us some ice cream. We licked the bowls, and boy, did we get it when we got home!" Julia's south-ern accent was refined. "Mama and Daddy used to give us ice cream every Sunday, and Mama said she didn't know why we had to act like we'd never seen ice cream before."

"Do you remember Ernestine?" I said.

"No. But her sister Roberta was a friend of mine. We used to write to each other; she wrote me just before she died. She was a beautiful girl."

Ernestine had a half-sister, Roberta Jacobs, who looked like Mattie, dark brown with smooth dark hair. She was nine years younger than Ernestine and I'd included a picture of her in the photo album which I'd given my grandmother.

Sitting in Julia's den, I thought about the front room of the nurs-ing home. I could picture Ernestine slumped on the sofa as I'd found her when I'd arrived unexpectedly. The soiled sleeping bag was still covering it. For an instant, I'd thought she was dead, but she was napping. I knew that Julia would never have been left in such a place but entertained the hope that she might visit, because it wasn't far.

Julia said, "I remember Mama saying that Ernestine had told her she could smell green snakes in the grass. . . . Mama said she had those children too close together, one after another."

"Wouldn't you have heard Mattie talking about her?"

"I was just a little girl. Ernestine wasn't my generation."

"Didn't her sister Roberta talk about her?"

"No," said Julia.

"Did you know my father?"

"I met him once or twice, but it's Ernest I remember. He was so good-looking and had a wonderful sense of humor. But they didn't really come down here much."

Julia was proud of her family and gave me a biography about her grandmother called *The Angel of Beale Street.* Julia's father and her Uncle Charles had owned one of the first black photographic studios in Memphis. Suddenly the penny dropped and I realized that the studio she was talking about was the Hooks Brothers studio, responsible for so many of my family pictures, including my father's baby picture. I got excited and when I showed it to her she shifted herself from her chair and winced.

"Oh, this hip. It gets worse and worse. I can't tell you the pain." She sighed, making her way to the door which led to the rest of the house, which was actually two semi-detached homes combined. "Come, let me show you something."

Leaving Anne and O'Ferrell I followed her down a narrow hallway. I could hear a small dog sniffing behind one of the three closed doors we passed.

In her sitting room a fully decorated Christmas tree occupied one corner. I didn't ask why, because that wasn't what she'd brought me in to see. Pointing to a carved mahogany chair near the dining-room archway, Julia said, "That's the chair your father was standing on."

I ran my hand over the smooth, polished wood. In my father's baby picture the chair looked imposing, but among Julia's furniture it was hardly noticeable. Though it was exciting to see it, I resisted sitting on it. I was never sure what was bad manners while I was in Memphis, in part because I was dealing with people of an older generation who had old-fashioned ways.

Julia's sisters, Mildred and Bessie, were both in bed ill, but she said that her brother, whom she referred to as Ben, was in town and insisted on ringing. I didn't want him disturbed and knew I couldn't ask him about Ernestine. But when his wife, Frances, answered the phone she gave me their numbers in Baltimore and Washington. She sounded enthusiastic and used to making small talk with strangers. She was her husband's diplomat.

I had seen newspaper pictures of Ben Hooks, and there were photographs of him and his sisters on the den wall. One studio portrait of the three sisters looked like a promo picture for a fifties singing trio, smiling, confident, and used to cameras.

When I was young, their pale skin and smooth hair would have secured their social status and it would have mattered to me that I was related to them—but times had changed. Nonetheless, we had blood ties. That may have been why Mildred and Bessie popped down in their dressing-gowns to say goodbye.

THE ROCKER

I WANTED TO TALK TO ANYBODY who had information about Ernestine. I wanted to raise my grandfather from the dead and ask him to explain exactly what behavior and what incidents led up to her being committed to an asylum, because each time I saw her she did a little more to suggest that with greater care and attention she would break her silence.

As kind as Essie Mae may have wanted to be, her duties didn't allow her time to talk to Ernestine. The residents in the home suffered from a lack of activities. No one took the mobile ones out for walks; had Essie Mae tried to, she would have been leaving others unattended.

To complain would have been fruitless, even had there been anyone to complain to. For conditions at the home to be as they were implied that the owner and the licensing board didn't feel that the environment, the care, or the facilities needed improvement.

Ernestine was eager to get outside. For her, a stroll along the street to Walgreen's Drugstore around the corner was an adventure. She was agile and moved at a moderate pace, holding on to my arm. Twice I'd arrived and found her sitting alone, head bent, in the small bedroom she shared with two others, sitting on the edge of an unwelcoming single bed with a grubby mustard coverlet. Hardly any light came into the room, and there was nothing for her eyes to be stimulated by or her ears to hear.

My last morning in town, I had invited Mrs. Cummings, the owner of the nursing home, for breakfast, hoping I could talk about my grandmother's history and future. As old as Ernestine was, she still had a future and needed some joy.

The recommendation for the restaurant that I chose was that it accepted my credit card. The grits and gravy, hickory ham, and applesauce on the menu were as southern as the big rocking chairs set up to the checkerboard opposite the open fireplace. I had studied the menu the day before when I'd arrived with Harry Mae Simons, whom I had grilled over a bowl of grits, knowing beforehand that as guardian she must have thought Ernestine's circumstances were suitable. Grandfather's pensions continued to pay for Ernestine's care, but I doubted that he would have chosen that place for his wife.

At breakfast with the nursing home owner we talked about her divorce mostly and she explained that Ernestine was her longest-stay resident. She wasn't in any way apologetic about the conditions at the home, so I made no mention of them but said, "Did you notice the rocking chairs they have out front? I'd love for my grandmother to have something nice to sit on. If you'd let me, I'd love to buy one of those rockers for her."

Mrs. Cummings approved and the wooden rocker with its rattan seat just fitted into the open trunk of my rental car. Essie Mae was on duty when I delivered it and Ernestine was sitting alone on the edge of her bed in the back. I called out, "Grandma!" when I saw her and she actually rushed to the door, clapped her hands together, and smiled at me. She was wearing an old red plaid dress. Her hair wasn't properly combed and was flattened against her scalp at the top.

The rocking chair was still in the living room, so I went to bring it through. It looked large in that bedroom and her feet hardly touched the floor when she sat down in it. Expressionless—the joy had passed. For her it was fleeting, but on me she had bestowed some everlasting memories, like the day before when we were heading for Walgreen's and I asked, "What do you want me to call you: Ernestine, Grandma, or Miss Hunt?"

She was holding on to my forearm, her feet stepping lightly along the pavement.

Her strong voice cut through the afternoon's heat. "Grandma," she said.

⟶℘ GRANDMA AT THE ECONO LODGE

WITH THE CURTAINS OPEN, anybody passing my motel room could have seen Ernestine seated at the round table, but they wouldn't have heard her silence. It had density, like the constant hum of a furnace, and settled on everything like a layer of dust. I pretended not to notice it. Competing for space in the room, I babbled, because she'd forgotten that talking was part of being.

"Well, here we are," I said. "I know this room is hot, but at least it's not as bad as the car. What d'you say, Grandma? But if you're really hot, we can switch on the air conditioner. That's a new-fangled thing that they don't have where you live. See it? . . . It's over there under the window. What you do is just press the button . . . but it turns the place into an icebox, and with you in those short socks, your little legs would freeze. . . ."

Ernestine's head was bowed. She controlled her jerking hands by clasping them together and drawing them close to her side. She was wearing her blue-gray plaid dress and her legs were crossed, because she always crossed her legs when she sat and smoothed her dress over her knees. It was her only habit and a most beguiling one.

At the nursing home, where the old residents sat around the television silently, Ernestine's emptiness blended with the rest. But on my own with her, it was noticeable that she was unable to communicate. She'd lost the skill—or the will—to express herself. Something had virtually silenced her, and I became more satisfied to hear her say "Yeah, hon" or "No, hon," not that she offered these often.

I tried to picture her asylum life. Silence may have been her only defense, shutting her mouth as close as she could get to controlling her rage and frustration. But I wanted to remind her of the art of conversation, touching another person with voice and images. So my nonsense spewed forth. "I bet you want to go to the toilet, don't you? I forgot that you may not tell me when you have to go. It's over there, near where the mirror is . . . see?"

Ernestine looked at me. The muscles of her face were relaxed, but I wasn't sure that she was listening. Yet I waited for a break-through and knew that I mustn't give in to her silence. To let her remain vacant would have been too easy.

I jumped off the bed, saying, "The bathroom's clean and if you want a bath or shower . . . we could even wash your hair. How 'bout it?"

At that moment I felt an affinity with caregivers everywhere. I thought of middle-aged women shut up with senile mothers, parents with retarded children, nurses in wards with patients in comas, and of my friend who was caring for her lover with motor neuron disease. I thought of a musician I knew with an autistic daughter. Their prisons became mine that afternoon.

The motel bathroom was stark: white curtain and tiles, white floor and tub and toilet, white soap and towels. Assuming that she had never seen such cleanliness, and thinking about the dirty bathroom at the nursing home, I wondered if a bath might excite her interest. Ernestine rubbed a hand over her bangs.

She didn't smell good. Was I prepared to see her emaciated body? If I took her clothes off would she think she was about to be molested? I laughed. I knew who she was, but she didn't know who I was. She wasn't an old granny who could indulge a granddaughter's whims. She was alone, lost in her isolation.

"I know you love water, and I've been saving all my shampoos and bath gels for you. They're not first-class in this joint, but they smell fine."

Anybody listening would have taken *me* for the ex-mental patient.

In the motel breakfast room was a side table with four kinds of doughnuts, coffee, and orange juice. I reminded myself that everywhere I took her was a new experience. Her world was so small that merely watching the candy machine operate in the breakfast room might occupy her mind.

Twenty minutes—that's all the time it took to get the breakfast rations. Back in my room I had nothing that could occupy her, no storybooks or crayons. Television was the easy option, but snatching the remote control I knew was a defeat. I said, "I hate to do this but maybe you'll enjoy the big color screen."

Ernestine had been silently gobbling the bits of doughnut

which I'd broken for her on a napkin at the round table. Suddenly she looked at me with knowingness. I thought she was going to speak, but she said nothing, so I flicked on the TV and grabbed the brush to restyle her hair. She continued to eat, pinching chunks of doughnut between her tiny thumb and forefinger. Her silence crawled in and around me and settled into the corners of the room like the humidity. When she rested her sticky fingers upon her lap, it was pointless to reprimand her. I dampened a washcloth and cleaned her hands.

There had been movies about people running away with children, but had anybody run off with their grandmother?

I had been in Memphis for three days and it was hard to recall when Ernestine hadn't been part of me. Without words, she had consumed my thoughts. But I couldn't defend her against the dismal life she was leading.

After an hour or so, I had to take her back to it.

3

France

—ᨠ Middle Passage

I WORKED THE FOLLOWING WINTER in a West End London theater and returned to France when the play's run had ended.

Ernestine was out of the closet.

Every day I thought about her and spoke her name. It was difficult to remember that she had not existed for me for forty-five of my forty-six years. I sent her occasional gifts via Anne Nelson and hoped the phone calls and cards registered with this grandmother, but I suspected they didn't.

I'd taken a picture of her in my motel room. She was seated at the table with her legs crossed, her hair recombed, a hint of makeup on her face and a shawl of mine thrown over her shoulders to brighten her drab dress. I sent a copy to Wilson hoping it would show him and his family that Ernestine wasn't a monster, that she wasn't as he had last seen her in his teens. Then I lived on the edge of expectation for that day when the phone would ring and it would be him or one of his sons to say that they'd been to see her or were on their way. It was important that she be accepted.

Nine months after my trip to Memphis, Karis graduated from Yale, so I went to Connecticut for her May 1992 graduation but couldn't afford another flight to see Ernestine.

Karis drove to see her in January of 1993 and sent me a picture of the two of them which I pinned on the kitchen wall in France. Ernestine's hair had been cut so short she looked like a little old man: she was as vulnerable and unprotected as a two-year-old. There had been no improvement in her living conditions and antagonizing those in charge of her with complaints wouldn't change anything. Could I tell the nursing home owner anything she didn't know? Harry Mae Simons never visited her and it was unrealistic to think that she would take an interest in Ernestine, who had prevented her from marrying my grandfather.

From the moment that I'd seen Ernestine kiss my father's baby picture, I'd had a feeling that she'd suffered some grave injustice. But assuming that was true, it was too late to rectify it. At that point it seemed the only thing I could give her was her story. She had been erased; whether by accident or design remained the question. When I promised my grandmother that I would write about her, I wasn't sure she understood what this meant. In a way nor did I, but a promise is a promise.

4

Memphis

— RETURN

BY MAY 1993 I HAD RAISED ENOUGH MONEY to spend three weeks in Memphis and one week in Boston to uncover what had happened to Ernestine.

Nearly two years had passed since I'd visited Ernestine in 1991. Having flown in from London, I was eager to see her again. I'd refused to accept that hereditary insanity had been the reason she was put away, but had only twenty-eight days to rake through her past. I suspected that my Uncle Wilson both liked and hated the idea of my snooping into his mother's life. He had assured me that everyone who had known her would be dead. But I think he was himself curious about what had happened to her.

Brochures for the Memphis-in-May 1993 Festival were on the counter of the Alamo Car Rental office serving Memphis airport. I picked one up and stuck it in my handbag as a plane took off. The blonde with the Dolly Parton hairdo who was sorting out my rental agreement kept her eyes on a computer screen when I asked about motels.

"We offer a pretty good reduction at the Econo Lodge on Lamar."

It was a good omen. "Next to the Rebel Inn?" I knew the sheets and towels were changed regularly and asked her to book it.

Being May, it was cooler than it had been when I'd landed in August, but the air was warm and I was glad to be there. I'd rung Ernestine regularly from France. I knew phone calls didn't register with her, but they were a reminder to other people that she wasn't alone. Having kept in touch with the Nelsons, who had visited her occasionally, I returned feeling that I had friends in town.

My rented car was a garish royal blue. When I climbed in, I was less weighed down with gifts than I'd been on my first trip to see Ernestine.

She and Essie Mae sat with me in the breakfast nook and neither of them had aged. Essie Mae said, "After you left here the last time, Miss Hunt used to stand at that front door just looking and looking. And I'd say, 'She looking for her granddaughter. Lookin' for that little ol' red car.'"

I didn't expect Ernestine to remember me, but a look in her eye when I slipped her arms into a sweater I'd bought her said that maybe she hadn't forgotten.

My second day in town, I arrived to take her out for lunch. All we needed was a snack bar, but I gave up looking for one—fast-food chains seemed to dominate every corner. As we drove into the McDonald's on Elvis Presley Boulevard, Ernestine looked happy to be in the passenger seat. Her hands were shaking and one eye was bloodshot, but otherwise she seemed fine.

"Chicken, hamburger, or fish, Grandma?"

She blurted, "Fish, hon," and I hoped that she wasn't expecting catfish straight from a hot skillet.

It was humid. She had on the same blue-and-gray plaid dress that she'd worn two years earlier; it had been machine-washed until it was paper-thin and hemmed so that all the stitches showed, and seeing her like that made me angry.

We ate in the car overlooking a busy corner where trucks bounced over the four-lane roads. She crammed handfuls of fries into her mouth and I was happy to see her eating. The fish she'd asked for came as a sandwich, thick with mayonnaise which spilled on her dress. She was oblivious, but it was the first time I'd taken her out to eat and I didn't care if she made a mess.

With the radio on, we sat watching the traffic. She didn't speak or look at me, but it felt like we were having a wild adventure as I sat trying to think of the best way to pursue her past.

 BOLIVAR

WHEN THE MANAGER OF THE ECONO LODGE told me she was writing a book, I wanted to talk. When she heard that I wrote too and might stay there three weeks, she lowered my room rate and said, "You ought to come to my writers' group. We're meeting next Monday." She had a fifty-inch waist, wore glasses, and had short, frizzy hair. Her smile was infectious.

"Thanks for the offer, but I have to leave my schedule open. I may need to spend some time in Bolivar."

"Bolivar! My husband and I just bought us a trailer home there . . . closed the deal yesterday. 'Course, we live upstairs here but we wanted to be able to get away weekends."

We were in the reception room, which had been redecorated since I'd last been there. The furniture was in better taste than I'd expect in a motel lobby, and the big plants beside the new sofas were thriving in all that light. She was behind the long counter where the receptionist also sat, and reaching to shake my hand she said, "My name's Annabelle. What have you got to do in Bolivar? There ain't much out there."

"My grandmother spent fifty-two years at Western State."

"Holy shit!"

"I don't know much about it, but I thought it might be useful to check it out. You're not interested in renting your trailer, are you?"

"Could be. But it's pretty basic and it's got no phone. I could take you out there tomorrow afternoon, as long as you drive, 'cause Bob, my husband, is gonna have the truck."

I was excited. "You know where the mental institution is?"

"It can't be far from my place. We can find it."

The two-piece dress Annabelle wore for our journey was the same royal blue as my car. It started drizzling when we fastened our seatbelts, and within minutes there was so much rain I could hardly see the road that took us north out of Memphis.

Annabelle was speaking from experience when she said, "The trouble with being in a mental institution is that if you laugh, they say you're crazy, and if you don't they say you're crazy. Talk, they say you're crazy. Don't talk, they say you're crazy. You can't win, see."

There was nothing unnatural about us being in the car together, but I didn't think it was the norm for a black woman and a white woman to be driving out to the country. I was stuck in the sixties, thinking that rednecks were still rife and that every old pickup we passed with red-faced men in straw hats meant trouble.

Occasionally we'd pass a Civil War plaque which mentioned some battle lost or won, or Annabelle would point out a plantation house back from the main road.

But mostly she talked about her life, her seven grown-up children and the time *she'd* been placed in a mental institution. She said, "I was twelve." Nobody had believed that her father was sexually abusing her. "Everybody liked my dad so my family didn't want to hear that he was messing with me. But he finally admitted it."

It was a sixty-mile journey and the weather switched back and forth from brilliant sun to teeming rain which slowed my driving. It was nearly 4:00 P.M. when we got to Bolivar. "Maybe we ought to head straight for the hospital," Annabelle suggested. "You can check out my trailer later."

As we turned off the highway, she started talking about how

informative her medical records from the mental institution had been to her and said, "You oughta get your grandmother's."

"She hasn't been there for years. They probably got rid of them."

"Well, I got hold of mine recently," said Annabelle, "and I was twelve when they put me in there."

We were on a two-lane back road driving past few houses and no people. The open country either side looked like undeveloped farmland. The windshield wipers slopped the rain back and forth; it was heavy until we descended a hill, then it stopped as I looked to my right and saw the sign for Western State.

Annabelle shook her head and said, "'Bolivar'—that's how it was known."

I had imagined Ernestine being shut behind forbidding stone walls, so I was surprised to see none. A long, neat drive led to what could have been a deserted campus of a few buildings surrounded by tended lawns and tall trees. The administration building stood alone; it was of brick and looked Victorian. I hadn't seen anything so imposing since I'd arrived in Memphis. The general atmosphere reminded me of an English boarding school during half-term, as if it had been set up for a lot of people but they'd disappeared.

I parked in front of a three-story building. Annabelle adjusted her glasses nervously; she'd been talking boldly but suddenly sounded meek when she asked, "What are you gonna do?"

"Go in," I told her, grabbing my briefcase off the back seat. In it it I had the family album I'd given Ernestine in 1991. If I needed to tell her story, I thought pictures would help.

But the door I tried was locked, so I rushed back to the car to head in the direction of some women who were gathering outside the glass door of a more modern building. A tall black attendant was herding them in. Her long mahogany arm reached for a young patient with short hair who was passing the door and I managed to walk in behind her. The room I'd entered looked like a reception area. There was a vending machine which sold snacks, and just beyond it were some leather sofas arranged in a square. The atten-

dant seemed too preoccupied with the patients to worry about
me, though I had expected her to ask what I was doing there. In a
pale summer suit and heels, I was obviously an outsider.

Her voice was sharp and demanding. "This way, this way!" she
ordered the women. She could have been a handsome Masai from
Kenya. Her dark face was beautiful, her neck long, and she seemed
to stand head and shoulders above me as I approached her, smiling
and clutching that family album. It was one of those moments
when I knew I had ten seconds to state my case. She could have
been a bouncer and I could have been somebody trying to talk my
way into a private club.

"Hi," I began. "Wonder if you can help. My grandmother spent
most of her life here, and I'm trying to find out anything I can
about her past. I was hoping there might still be somebody working here who might remember her." The attendant's black eyes
looked me over. "She left here twelve years ago."

The attendant didn't smile back at me. "I've been working here
way longer than that," she said. "What was her name?"

Just as I said, "Ernestine Hunt," the door that she had ushered
the patients through and then closed was opened and a heavy,
dark-skinned woman with gray hair and glasses emerged. Tight
trousers covered her big thighs; she was wearing a white smock
and obviously worked there too. She said, "Hey, what time you
takin' your break?"

I don't think she noticed me until the tall attendant said, "This
here's Ernestine Hunt's granddaughter." She mentioned Ernestine's
name with a hint of contempt as well as familiarity. Her co-worker
came out into the reception area, and the heavy door clicked shut
again.

It seemed impossible that the first person that I'd spoken to had
remembered my grandmother. Twelve years was a long time. The
woman with the glasses was older, friendlier, and curious. She
asked, "Where you from?"

I eased into a slightly black accent and told them about how I'd
found Ernestine. But before I could open the family album, the tall

attendant said huffily, "Ernestine . . . she looked white. Looked like a white woman. And she didn't let you forget she was Blair T. Hunt's wife."

Having never heard Ernestine refer to her husband, I couldn't imagine her bragging about their relationship. But maybe the attendant had known another Ernestine, unravaged by age.

But I didn't like the way she referred to Ernestine's appearance. It sounded too much like angst from the ghetto when people with dark complexions ganged up on the pale ones for looking too white. In my school days, it would have been something that I needed to be ready to fight about, but I was middle-aged and standing in the reception room of an asylum and wasn't ready for a full-out confrontation over my grandmother's color.

I wanted to know what these two women knew about her. But I was forgetting that I'd already learned two things: how she looked and that her relationship to Grandfather seemed to have bred resentment among the staff.

The heavy one with glasses reached to touch my hair, which made me step back slightly. Her eyes were intense but warm.

"You kind of favor her," she said. "She had long hair too. Long, long hair. But straighter."

A barrier was up between them and me. I didn't know why. Maybe it was clothes; I was sorry that I'd come in a city suit and that my briefcase suggested that I was on business. I said, "Ernestine was here for over fifty years; can't you remember anything specific about her? Did she have friends?"

The one with glasses touched my hair again admiringly. "I'll tell you one thing about your grandmother. Ernestine was always a lady. Always. . . . She was a *real* lady. She always remembered her manners."

O'Ferrell had said that the hospital had a bad reputation and had been written up in the papers more than once because of it. For all I knew, I was talking to two attendants who abused patients.

"Have you worked here long?" I asked.

The tall one said, "Thirty-five years," as I passed her the photo album. I assumed that they were both still on duty and would suddenly feel I was wasting their time.

Nearby was a glass-partitioned office with a woman seated behind a desk. It seemed too quiet to be an asylum. Nobody came or went. The cold atmosphere made me think about my grandmother's fifty-two years there. I couldn't understand how she'd survived it.

Two more women appeared behind the partitioned glass. They weren't wearing uniforms and moved about that small space, from desk to filing cabinet, with a smile passing between them from time to time.

I thought about Ernestine moving along these corridors. Did she have friends here or had she been isolated for half a century? She would have seemed so small and inconsequential in that reception room where we stood. But at least it was clean—cleaner than the nursing home.

A vending machine stood by the doorway. Had she ever had change to buy something? I could imagine her alone, incapable of blending in, especially when the asylum had been racially segregated. Favor and disfavor must have found her because of her appearance and because of her husband's position in the Memphis community sixty miles away.

But I didn't dare ask how much abuse her looks had caused her to suffer, because I had more basic things to find out about her, so I asked the women if they knew any other employees who had worked there as long as thirty-five years.

"Jackie over at Dunn. She must have worked with your grandmother. We all did," said the one with glasses, before they both excused themselves. "We better get back to work," they said, but only the tall dark one slipped behind the door. The other headed outside with me and said if I returned the following day she'd tell me more.

The rain was coming down hard and Annabelle was eager to hear what had taken me so long when I climbed into the car. I hoped that the woman in glasses hadn't seen that I had a white pas-

MEMPHIS   85

senger, because it might have mattered to her. I couldn't forget that I was in the South and there was an uneasy peace between black and white—a truce without trust.

What I had noticed in the hospital reception room I expressed in the car. "Those two women were too nice, and they avoided looking at each other, avoided each other's eyes."

Being questioned about the past would surely make some hospital staff guarded, in case I had a concealed motive for asking.

The windshield wipers flapped back and forth, but they couldn't fend off the sheets of blowing rain. I pulled into a Kentucky Fried Chicken concession, because I couldn't see where I was going, and a cream Buick pulled in behind me flashing its lights.

It was the older worker from the hospital. Seeing her roll down her window, I rolled down mine. Rain splashed her glasses and she held her hand above them like a visor and yelled, "If you're going to Memphis you're headed in the wrong direction."

"I hope I didn't ruin your break," I called to her.

"I didn't have nothing to do in this rain and I'm glad I got to meet you. Glad for your grandmother too."

I felt guilty for suspecting her of withholding information.

"We'll talk again tomorrow?"

"Yeah, but you got to be here early. That other girl and me will be waiting for you at twelve. We're on late tomorrow."

This was a working woman, probably in her late fifties, who spent her days dealing with mental patients who were probably difficult, abusive, or so withdrawn they made her want to scream. But she had a quick smile and an air of helpfulness that warmed me to her as she sat there with the rain blowing into her face while we spoke.

"This must be your break. You shouldn't waste it," I said.

"There wasn't much I could've done in this rain," she repeated. "I'm glad for your grandmother that you're bothering."

Annabelle and I were back on the highway headed for Memphis when she said, "That woman's got something to tell you. I could just feel it from her eyes."

OBITUARY

As O'Ferrell poured himself a bourbon, I could smell it from the other side of his kitchen. The book he was lending me about prominent black families in Memphis was lying on the sofa next to me. I had scanned the page about my grandfather and said, "Most of the families in here couldn't be any paler. The ones on the cover look Portuguese."

Anne was wiping the sink. She laughed.

O'Ferrell said, "Haven't you noticed that the race is getting darker?"

"Not really."

"Well, it is. The further we get from slavery, the darker we're getting, because all that mixing that used to go on has stopped."

I picked up the book and turned to the page with a picture of my grandfather. It must have been a shot taken after he retired.

O'Ferrell perched on a stool at the counter and took a sip of his drink. His wide suspenders had multicolored stripes, the yellow jumping out from the rest. "You can borrow that but I want it back."

"There's not much about my grandfather in here that I didn't already know. But maybe there will be something about somebody else that will relate to Ernestine."

"Our main library has an excellent genealogy section," he suggested.

Since I felt like I was searching for a needle in the dark, I was prepared to try anything. But I didn't expect the library to be much help, so I put off going until my first Saturday in town, arriving early so I could be gone before the crowds came. Located in midtown, it was surrounded by tree-lined streets with large houses, so I imagined it was a white district. I didn't see a sign telling when it was built but I was sure that it had been there before integration.

My uncle had once said that Ernestine used to pass for white to get books out of the library for herself and others back in the days when blacks weren't allowed in.

I had arrived early enough to talk to the head of the history department. His badge read JIM JOHNSON. The sleeves of his white shirt were already rolled up. His straight, sandy hair was receding, his gold-rimmed glasses were old-fashioned, but he had a kind face though it could have used some sun. When I was in Europe, I was usually unconscious about what race people were, but Memphis was different and the first thing I noticed about Jim Johnson was that he was white.

When I told him that I needed some information about my family he said, "Blair T. Hunt was one of our leading citizens. We've got a lot about him. Just a minute." He rushed off to a room behind the checkout desk.

The history department had high ceilings and large windows; sun splashed the long wooden tables situated between aisles of book stacks, and a small room that looked private had a sign saying MEMPHIS ROOM tacked above the door. It resembled a library in someone's home and had a fireplace with expensively upholstered wing chairs on either side of it. The lights were on and Jim Johnson suggested that I sit in there to look at the stapled pamphlet he handed me. BLAIR THEODORE HUNT was printed in bold black letters across the top. The dates 1888 and 1978 were on the bottom. There was a Hooks Brothers photograph of Grandfather on the cover and Jim said, "This lists what we hold in the archives."

The picture had probably been taken in the forties, judging from his double-breasted jacket with its wide lapels. He's seated at a desk which may have been in his office at Booker T. Washington High School, because a large brass bell that he carried and reputedly slung at undisciplined students is on the crowded desk with his mallet.

The introductory information said that he had married Ernestine on 12 July 1918 and she bore him two sons, Wilson and Ernest. As it didn't mention my father but said that Grandfather

had served in the First World War as a chaplain ranked as a lieutenant, I immediately sat down and started calculating how many
months fell between the time he had married, when the war had
ended on 11 November 1918, and when my father was conceived.

My expression may have looked troubled, because I suddenly
wondered if there was some doubt about my father being
Grandfather's son. Luckily, Jim Johnson didn't know what I was
thinking. He offered to bring all the archives and disappeared long
enough for me to read the rest of the pamphlet.

Most of what it told me, about my grandfather being active in
the Urban League, the YMCA, and the YWCA were things I
knew. Though I hadn't known that he was the first black to serve
on the Tennessee Draft Board, that wasn't relevant to what I
wanted to know about his life with Ernestine. I was also worried
about how much of the information might have been wrong since
it said that he'd started teaching in 1925 and I knew that he'd
taught Ernestine who must have been his student before they married in 1918.

When Jim Johnson produced several cardboard file boxes I
decided to check the one with the news clippings, which were
neatly arranged in a book. Flipping it open at random to a page, it
was eerie that I had turned to my father's obituary dated 25 August
1956. Ernestine would have spent twenty-seven years at Bolivar by
then.

The bold print on the piece read DEATH ENTERS FAMILY, HOLD
LAST RITES FOR DR. BLAIR T. HUNT JR. It said he was the thirty-
seven-year-old son of Professor Blair T. Hunt, principal of Booker
T. Washington High. And although it said that he died on a
Wednesday night, 15 August, it didn't mention suicide. It was a
black newspaper and said that he was one of the nation's few
Negro psychiatrists. What shocked me was the picture of a smiling
bride in a white dress to whom he'd been married for only six
weeks when he died.

The Memphis Public Library was an odd place to discover that
my father had remarried before he died. The room I was sitting in

felt intimate, like there should have been a telephone at hand, so that I could ring somebody with the news. I sat with my head resting on my hand, staring at the picture of the young woman who was my father's widow: Roberta Quinn of Baltimore, pretty, pale, and smiling.

I jotted her name in my notebook as Jim Johnson popped his head around the door to say, "Finding what you need?"

I had only been there for half an hour and already I'd seen one piece of information that threw a question mark over my father's birthright and another that said he had had a wife I knew nothing about.

It was conceivable that his bride was pregnant when he died. Maybe I wasn't my father's only child.

The boxes which Jim had given me took up most of the table where I sat, so when he slipped back in the room with some small thick books for me to look at, he invited me to another table.

"These are Memphis city directories. Everybody who was living here is listed, along with whoever was living in the household with them. Schools are also listed along with the individual teachers who worked there. These go back to the twenties. But I can go back earlier than that if you want."

His southern accent was thin, and he made a point of looking directly at me when he spoke. I wondered if the shock of finding that my father had remarried registered in my face. I suddenly felt as if I looked abnormal. "I'd like to find out who was teaching with my grandfather in 1918."

Jim said, "Hang on," and rushed out of the room. The book that he brought back told me that Alzora Haste had taught with Grandfather at Kortrecht High School, and having heard O'Ferrell mention her as being one of his old teachers at Booker T. High, I hoped she might still be alive.

MY MOTEL ROOM WAS HOT. I sat on the bed cradling the phone and couldn't believe that Miss Haste's number was in the telephone directory. She answered on the fourth ring.

"Miss Alzora Haste?" I asked with hesitation.

"Who are you and what do you want?" She sounded old and petulant.

"I'm Blair T. Hunt's granddaughter. I've come to Memphis to visit his widow, Ernestine, and I noticed in the city directories at the library that you taught with him at Kortrecht . . . "

"Blair T. Hunt's granddaughter? What color are you?"

I held back a laugh. "Dark brown," I said, a little defiantly.

"And what's your hair like?"

It seemed impossible. Did anybody have the nerve to ask such questions in 1993?

"Kinky," I said, to provoke.

"Well, that doesn't sound right. He was a light-skinned man with nice hair."

I hadn't phoned to argue, so I pushed on. "As you were teaching at Kortrecht in 1918, I assume you knew my grandmother, who I think graduated that year." I was unsure.

Miss Haste didn't address my question. Since she was about to turn ninety-five, I was prepared for her to be incoherent, but she was precise when she answered.

"Just after the Civil War, there were a lot of mulattoes. We had five races. Now I'm dark with a flat nose, but I held myself; I was a strutter. I was a high-steppin' woman."

"Do you remember Beatrice Cartman?" I asked, still pursuing Ernestine's story. "I'm told that Beatrice Cartman had been vying for him while he courted Ernestine."

"I don't know anything about that and I don't want to talk now. This world is a terrible place and it hurts to see the things that go on. I don't like to watch the news. This world is Sodom and Gomorrah and it hurts me to be—"

"Excuse me, Miss Haste," I interrupted, "you may be the only person living that can help me. Would it be possible for me to come over and talk to you?"

"When?"

"Whenever you'd like. I'll come immediately if you want," I said, feeling my luck had changed.

"I don't want to see you."

"Wouldn't you like to meet Blair T. Hunt's granddaughter?"

I liked her for saying no.

"You sound like a wonderful woman, and I would love to spend a few minutes with you," I begged, wondering if the fact that she didn't want to talk about Beatrice Cartman meant there was something to talk about. "Miss Haste, I could come after lunch or tomorrow morning." At that moment I believed I was talking to the only person in the world who had a strand of information about Ernestine.

"I've had enough, I'm ready to go. It hurts me to see all the terrible things in this Sodom and Gomorrah."

"Aren't you excited that you'll be ninety-five soon?"

"I was born August fifteenth." Her birthday was the anniversary of my father's suicide.

I didn't know what to say. "I live in France," I began. "It's peaceful. Cows roam the meadows and I roam the lanes and I never watch the news. In fact I don't watch television," I added, hoping that would warm her to me.

"A pedigree and a cur . . . a cur was as dear to us as a pedigree," she said, but I wasn't sure why. Was she still reflecting on race or had this something to do with Sodom and Gomorrah? "When we fed them, we fed them both the same." Her voice was light and quivered with age. I knew that I was missing something by not seeing the expression on her face as she spoke. Did she look Nigerian or Ghanaian? That she described herself as dark with a flat nose said that she had been a victim of prejudice about her looks but I didn't expect her to talk specifically about it.

"What did you teach, Miss Haste?"

"English. I love poetry. It makes me happy."

"I love poetry too. Shall I come over and read you some?"

"I don't want to see you."

"But I'm dark." I laughed, trying to make that a bond we shared.

"I was a strutter, I could hold my head high."

"I would bring you flowers—" I told her before she suddenly broke into song.

> *"Are you from heaven?*
> *My glad heart sings.*
> *Are you an angel,*
> *Where are your wings?*
> *Who have you come for,*
> *Were you meant for me?"*

The high notes were beyond her reach, but she sang with sweet conviction and the old-fashioned melody wouldn't leave me.

THE GUARDIAN

WHENEVER I ASKED PEOPLE WHO KNEW my grandfather to name someone who knew him intimately, Harry Mae Simons was always mentioned. As he was surrounded by young women, both his teachers and students, I imagined that there might easily have been other women in his life—but no one was named. It seemed pointless to ask Harry Mae, but she and I had other things that we could talk about, so I invited her to breakfast.

She was behind the wheel of an old, black car when she pulled into the motel parking lot. I didn't realize at first that it was the same car in which she had collected Karis and me back in '77 with Grandfather as her front-seat passenger. It was over fifteen years old, one of those long American tanks that slips and slides on the road but doesn't seem to grip it. Harry Mae said, "Your grandaddy bought that for me and I'll never get rid of it."

She had come for breakfast in high heels. As she was about to turn eighty-four, it was remarkable that she could still totter about in them. She hadn't changed much since I'd met her the first time, although she'd probably lost twenty pounds. She could have passed for sixty-five and knew it.

My concern for Ernestine made me resist Harry Mae's charms. She may have been my grandfather's greatest joy, but I kept reminding myself that their liaison could have been the reason Grandfather had no interest in seeking Ernestine's release from Bolivar.

Harry Mae herself regularly talked about her forty-seven happy years with him. Counting back, it meant that they had been together since 1931, or not long after Ernestine was committed to Western State. He was at La Rose School then, and Harry Mae met him when she was a student teacher there. Her family lived in the house on Hastings Street which was to become his home within a couple of years of her training under him. Although she claimed that she had arrived as a student teacher at the school knowing nothing about him, I would have thought that he already had an impressive reputation in Memphis. Perhaps women saw him as an available bachelor since it's apparent that nobody talked about his wife in the state mental hospital or his three sons in Boston.

I was careful about what I said at breakfast. We had gone to the nearby restaurant where I'd bought Ernestine's rocking chair in 1991 and where I'd taken Harry Mae that same year. To concentrate on the huge breakfast menu was easier than discussing facts which troubled me. On my grandmother's behalf, I thought it was unacceptable that Grandfather's mistress had become her guardian.

It was a clear morning when we organized ourselves at a table at the back of the restaurant near the windows. Mock lanterns hung from the ceiling and the rocking chairs with the checkerboard set up between them were still near the open fireplace. Harry Mae's pink chiffon scarf was tied loosely around her neck—with her silver hair in a neat bun, she looked like a schoolmistress.

As I already knew her appointment as principal of La Rose School occurred when Grandfather was promoted from that post to the high school, I assumed his being a boarder in her house had something to do with her appointment. She had been teaching for only a few years.

I didn't like her to talk about Ernestine, because Harry Mae never visited her. Essie Mae had explained it. "Miss Simons say she scared of Miss Hunt. But what's there to be scared of?" If Harry Mae had no first-hand experience with Ernestine, then anything she said about her was hearsay.

She had said Ernestine's condition was hereditary, but since I'd met no one who claimed to know who Ernestine's father was, the implication was that hereditary insanity had come from Mattie's side of the family. When I asked Harry Mae to be specific, she couldn't be. None of the Hooks family knew of any of Mattie's relatives with mental illness.

Harry Mae was younger than my grandfather and as a young woman she might have accepted without question anything she heard from him. Keeping her age in mind, I suspected that her attitude toward mental illness was based on old mores. The way she painted the past suggested that my father and his brothers were regular visitors to Memphis. But that wasn't true; they never visited during their childhood and Grandfather helped none of them through college. But I listened politely when Harry Mae said, "Your father was too worried about his mother. He was just a boy in his teens and he would sit there poring over books about dementia praecox. He wanted to know everything about it."

Dementia praecox was the term once used in America for schizophrenia.

Harry Mae's tone was assured. It was understandable that she didn't like to be challenged. Not only had she been an elementary school principal, but she had been the companion of a powerful man; as Grandfather's silent partner, she would have commanded respect. But she was from another age, and I didn't pretend to understand her.

She ordered a large breakfast including biscuits and grits which she nibbled and I tried to imagine her as the young woman my grandfather had fallen in love with. She would have been handsome and her color would have been an asset. Lemoyne College where she had studied was the local college for black students. Her family didn't live in what had been called the "silk stocking" district where Grandfather's parents had been given a house by the family that had owned his father as a slave.

I was surprised that she admitted that Grandfather had come to her graduation from Lemoyne with a gift. It would have been 1931 and Ernestine would have been in her early thirties while Harry Mae was twenty-two.

Speaking about my father and his brothers, she said, "The boys took me aside and told me that they wanted me to talk to their father. . . . I remember them coming into the dining room and saying, 'You'll have to speak to our father, because we don't want to have to go out and see our mother again.' He used to expect that of them whenever they came out to visit during the summers. It was Wilson that did the talking because your father was shy. Wilson was always good with words, whereas your father kept things to himself."

My uncle remembers only one trip to the South, when he had been working in Florida as a bellhop and visited his father on his return journey home.

— MEDICAL RECORDS

AT BOLIVAR NOBODY PARKING in front of the building that housed medical records could miss the sign which read ROLL UP YOUR CAR WINDOWS AND LOCK YOUR DOORS. I stayed in the car and kept my eye on several male patients who milled about the entrance. Two of them stared at me, and when one made peculiar noises and started flailing his arms, beating back the invisible, I looked behind me hoping to spot a guard or other employee. But all I saw was a very fat man on a swing under a nearby tree. A deathly silence clung like a shroud to everything, and I was relieved when a young woman in jeans made her way past the car. Her gait was confident and so was her smile as she waved and said, "Hi. Weren't you here yesterday talking to Bobby and Ella? I remember all that hair of yours." Her name tag said SOCIAL SERVICES: CARLA. Bobby and Ella. Is that what the two were called?

"I'm meeting them here at twelve," I said and explained why I wanted to talk to them.

Carla said, "What you need is Medical Records."

Following her into the building, I felt safe for the first time since I'd driven through the entrance on the main road. There was something haunting about the emptiness of the grounds. No signs of joy, few signs of human life; even the trees looked morose hovering over the narrow lanes which linked the various buildings.

Carla's friendly hello to several people she passed didn't lift the atmosphere inside. To a couple she said, "I need permission to take this woman to Medical Records," and she got it.

The brown-haired woman wore glasses, a smile, and trousers.

"My grandmother was here most of her life," I said, glancing at the pale walls painted soothing hospital green. They looked impenetrable. But there were no signs of atrocities and no sounds of torture. Tall windows overlooked orderly, peaceful grounds. But instruments of restraint must have been as commonplace here as the typewriters on the desks of the brown-haired woman and her blue-eyed co-worker.

The blue eyes searched my black ones for clues.

"Listen, my grandmother's ninety-five."

"Hon, I can't just give you her file. You've got to fill out forms and she must have a guardian. I can't help you until I have the guardian's signature."

Although they may not have been, I felt as if all eyes in the room were on me, as my expression changed. The blue eyes stared hard at me. That trust which I thought they had shared with mine had become official detachment.

Harry Mae Simons was Ernestine's guardian. My grandfather had lived in her house for forty-seven of the fifty-odd years that my grandmother had been in the asylum. Something about Harry Mae's sweetness made my face squinch up any time I thought about her.

The blue-eyed clerk stood up with an air of dismissal. She'd given me the medical records application form and had other things on her mind. Possibly, lunch was at the top of her list.

"How long does it take to get records?"

"Once I get the form back, I can let you see what we've got. How long ago did you say she was here?"

"Twelve years."

"We probably still have something on her. Maybe in the other building. Anyway, I've got to go . . . good luck."

Bolivar, as the institution was referred to, was opened before Freud and Jung, Melanie Klein, R. D. Laing, and others had developed theories which penetrated the ignorance surrounding depression and neuroses, personality disorders and psychoses, at a time when the deaf were thought to be mentally deficient and postpartum depression had not yet been recognized.

On leaving, I tiptoed down the dimly lit passages leading to the elevator. The building was practically deserted and the thought that someone deranged might be lurking in any corner made me nervous. But my mind wanted to go back to 1929 to see Ernestine walking that corridor, a pretty young woman separated from her three little sons. Had she also been terrified by the sound of her footsteps clicking on this tiled floor?

I wasn't fooled. Despite the pristine lawns, things too grotesque to imagine had almost certainly occurred in that building. Like Ernestine having all her teeth removed. I eyed each passage, asking myself if that was where the padded cells had been.

⟶☙ JACKIE IN DUNN

IT WAS HARD TO WATCH. Inch by inch, inch by inch, his feet crept forward. The pale, unshaven old man with sunken eyes moved so slowly it seemed he had stopped near the nurses' station, but he was only turning around to head back to where he came from. Were all the patients here geriatrics? Is this where Ernestine had been? I wondered, as I asked somebody where I'd find Jackie.

I'd been admitted through a solid metal door with a small window meshed with chicken wire. I'd slipped in with someone returning from lunch. This was the Dunn building.

When I found Jackie she invited me into her office and I asked if she remembered Ernestine.

"Ernestine," she said with a headmistress's tone. "Of course I knew her. I was the one who placed her at Covington."

"But she's not at Covington. She's in a place in Memphis." Did I dare say it was substandard or would that put Jackie on guard? If her welcoming smile was meant to suggest that she was harmless, her long standing with the institution implied that she had seen it at its worst—and remained.

Whatever else she knew about Ernestine, maybe she knew my grandmother had had visitors, I suggested.

"Oh, that happens a lot. People come here and are forgotten. Even now it happens, but in the old days it happened a lot. Families would forget, although the first Sunday in every month was family day and people would come and bring the children. But there was always somebody who had nobody. . . . Of course I remember Ernestine. She kept to herself. She'd sit out when the weather was nice, but never fussed and never asked for anything."

"Was she violent?"

"No, no," Jackie said, giving it a moment's thought. "No . . . we all have our little upsets, but no, she was one of our quiet ones. There used to be 2400 patients here. There are only 387 now, and some of the wings have been torn down. Why, this place has been here over a century, and it was completely self-sufficient. Had its own water supply, livestock, and vegetable gardens. This was an industry, and everybody working here worked a twelve-hour day with one day off. My parents had a little apartment, but most people working here lived two or sometimes three to a room. But 2400 was too many. The place was only built to take a thousand."

When Ernestine had resided there, considering the acceptance of racism back then, the black wards were probably like tombs. I didn't think I should ask any pointed questions—I didn't want to endanger my chance of getting Ernestine's records.

"She kept to herself." That hadn't changed. Even at the nursing home, my grandmother was a loner locked into or out of her past.

Jackie's office was on the ground floor and behind her desk was a large window which overlooked grass, trees, even a few flowers. Why did it look as inviting as a picturesque corner of a country lane? And should I have been so willing to accept Jackie's cordial interest in my search for information about Ernestine? If there was something hidden how would I find it? I wondered, as Jackie invited three workers into her office and said, "This is Ernestine Hunt's granddaughter. Didn't you work with Ernestine?"

All of them managed to appear interested in my quest to discover what had happened to Ernestine, but none knew anything specific about her. Whether she had worked or made any friends, whether she had had a hobby . . . I would have been grateful for the smallest scrap of information but all I heard was that Ernestine kept to herself.

After this disappointment I was more eager than ever to talk to the woman in glasses who had asked me to return at noon but hadn't appeared—but I didn't know what to think when the reason I was given for her not keeping our date was that she was dead.

"Dead?" I said, when a young brown-skinned receptionist told me the news with tear-filled eyes. I was suddenly afraid. It was like something out of a movie; I'd been snooping for information about Ernestine and a woman who'd been ready to go out of her way to give it to me was reportedly dead. I didn't want to believe it—but I couldn't help thinking that she might have intended to tell me something that somebody didn't want her to talk about. Having come to Memphis thinking that malice could have played a part in what happened to Ernestine, I wondered if the information I wanted was more damning than I had expected.

The tearful receptionist said, "We're all shocked. She just dropped down dead in the supermarket. A heart attack."

When I got back to the motel and told Annabelle, her eyes bulged. "Holy shit!" she said.

 PEANUTS

My uncle remembers seeing his mother without teeth for the first time as a teenager when Ernestine would still have been in her thirties. Dentistry was brutal then and I hate to think how painful she must have found it to have had all her teeth removed. How much blood? How much screaming? How long did it take her to recover from the trauma? Did they hold her or tie her down and was she conscious when it happened? But most important, was it necessary?

Ernestine speaks with difficulty. Without teeth it's not easy for her to enunciate and if she had any pride in the sound of her voice, becoming toothless at an uncommonly young age may have silenced her, stopped her wanting to speak since she could no longer be easily understood.

Essie Mae said, "She can eat most things, but you gotta cut up the meat. . . . She probably been chewing on them gums for a long time."

When I asked my grandmother if she wanted something from the supermarket, as often as not she'd say peanuts, and Essie Mae would bark, "Miss Hunt, you can't eat no peanuts."

"But maybe she's longing for them," I'd say.

"That may be, but she can't have none. Maybe you can get her some peanut butter." Turning to Ernestine, Essie Mae would say, "How about some peanut butter?"

No reply. Silence, even from her eyes.

"Grandma, you *really* want peanuts?" I asked, staring at her for clues as one would search the face of a child with an ailment it couldn't describe.

"Miss Hunt don't want no peanuts. She just said that to be saying something."

Maybe Essie Mae was right, but I hated the fact that whatever Ernestine said could be disputed by anybody and she was always wrong, so I said, "Come on. We'll go to the supermarket and you can choose anything you want."

I expected her to be overwhelmed by ordinary situations and I didn't know what she would make of the supermarket: the packages and lighting, strangers pushing metal carts up and down aisles stacked with colorful cans and boxes designed to be attention-grabbing. But none of it changed her expression as she walked beside me pushing an empty cart. She wanted nothing and we abandoned the store to get her some soft ice cream from McDonald's.

"Here's what we'll do," I told her as though she was listening. "First we'll get you some ice cream, then you can come to my motel and hang out. Watch TV, or take a bath, because there's absolutely no need to rush you back to Mrs. Cummings's, because you won't miss a thing if you never go back."

I thought she'd miss Essie Mae, but I didn't add that.

Watching Ernestine slide into the bucket seat of my rented car, I wondered if it was my duty to kidnap her. She was more mine than anybody's since nobody else wanted to claim her and I couldn't think what the nursing home offered apart from Essie Mae.

⟋⟍ ROBERTA QUINN

"WHO'S ROBERTA QUINN?" I asked O'Ferrell, thinking back to my discovery in the library of my father's second wife.

"Oh, Lord. Who are you chasing now?" The Nelsons' collection of chiming clocks hadn't struck eight yet. O'Ferrell poured his bourbon over a couple of chunks of ice while Anne prepared dinner as if she wasn't tired after nursing in a midtown medical center all day. She looked up from the vegetables she was chopping.

"Did you call Harry Mae?" She and Anne were in a women's club together despite the big gap in their ages.

"No. The woman I want to speak to is Roberta Quinn. She was

from Baltimore and is probably your age. Surely you know somebody in Baltimore?"

The Nelsons were social; they belonged to fraternities and
sororities, and my father's obituary suggested that Roberta Quinn
would have been the sort of woman some of their friends would
know. If she and my father had been newly wed when he committed suicide, she had information I needed.

I rang a detective friend in Los Angeles and asked how I should
begin tracing Roberta Quinn. He said I needed more than a name,
but I had no address and knew no one who might know her
except my uncle, whom I was afraid to call. Ernestine was his
mother. Didn't that make her more his than mine? In case my resurrecting her upset him, I didn't want to ring him. There must, I
thought, be some other way of finding Roberta Quinn.

﹏ᢙ MISS DORA

SEEING DORA TODD RUN UP THE STAIRS in her white loafers made
me tired. She was nearly ninety but looked sixty-five, even with
her snow-white hair which grew into long sideburns along her
dark cheeks.

O'Ferrell had said Miss Todd knew as much about Grandfather
as Harry Mae, so I arrived hoping she could tell me something
about his relationship with Ernestine.

"Did you realize he had a wife?" I asked, after looking at a group
shot on her living room wall which included him. He had been
photographed at a retirement dinner and she was seated nearby.

"Of course. Everybody knew he had a wife. But nobody talked about it."

"Why?"

"He was a wonderful man, your grandfather—and the way he could talk, the way he carried himself. Such stature for a big man."

"He was small, wasn't he?"

Miss Dora Todd laughed. She beamed as though he'd just strutted into her living room standing six feet tall. So I didn't dare disagree with her, but even his three sons were small men.

Like other homes I'd been to in Memphis, Miss Todd had Christmas decorations displayed, although it was May. On the mantel were garlands of tinsel. She was Catholic and above the seat where I was sitting was a picture of her meeting the Pope. She wasn't the only retired teacher in Memphis who had taught under Grandfather, but having been told she knew him so well I had expected her to tell me something about his relationship with Ernestine. But maybe he didn't have one.

─🙠 GIVING BIRTH

"MY GRANDMOTHER GREW UP IN MEMPHIS. She can't be the only person living who's black and over ninety. Somebody must remember her, O'Ferrell!"

He was examining the large box of mixed doughnuts which his son Vincent had laid on the kitchen counter.

Vincent, an American Airlines pilot in town for the day, said, "Birth certificates and death certificates have all kinds of pertinent information, and the department is near where you plan to shop."

So that afternoon, before taking Ernestine to look for shoes, we went to the Department of Vital Statistics, and I requested her three sons' birth certificates.

Ernestine gave birth for the first time on 25 August 1919. She was twenty-one, her husband was thirty-one, and the address they gave was 895 Gune Avenue. The delivering doctor was C. E. Craigen and the baby was named after his father, Blair T. Hunt. Her second son, Wilson, was born thirteen months later and her third, Ernest, in November of 1921. She was then living with her husband and children at 799 Mississippi Boulevard.

In photographs taken with her first child, she looks happy standing outside a house with the baby in her arms. But pictures lie, and maybe birth certificates do too, because on no map of Memphis including old ones at the library could I find Gune Avenue. Was there some reason for a false address?

Ernestine had all the answers, but could supply none of them. Had she suffered postpartum depression after having three births in close succession? How did her behavior change?

While we had been waiting for the birth certificates, Ernestine had sat in a chair against the wall with her head down and both hands clasped together. She looked at no one who came into or left the small office in which clerks sat on the other side of a high counter where applications for certificates could be filled out. Her left eye was bloodshot and had been since I'd arrived in Memphis. Her shoes badly needed replacing and her dress had been washed so often the fabric was faded. A man greeted her when he sat in a chair beside hers and she didn't respond. To those who don't sense from her posture that she is withdrawn, she must look normal.

Helping her up from the chair, I guided her out into the heat of another May afternoon. The information on the three birth certificates didn't provide much but it raised some questions. The possibility she had suffered from nothing worse than postpartum depression weighed upon me as I read through them. Did it matter *why* she had been interned? She was ninety-five years old and nothing which I had yet uncovered about her past could change it or affect her future, but perhaps it could affect somebody else's. I continued to think that Ernestine's abandonment and long-term incarceration were indications of what may have happened to thousands of others. Her years at Bolivar had given my grandfather the right to say his wife suffered from hereditary insanity. In 1977, when I'd heard him say it, I didn't challenge him, because she wasn't mine to defend. But that was changing. Every time I brushed her hair or wiped ice cream from her mouth she became more mine.

THE CHURCH BY THE RIVER

ON MY FIRST SUNDAY IN MEMPHIS, Anne and O'Ferrell invited me to bring Ernestine to their Unitarian Universalist church called the Church by the River. Considering the role that the Unitarian Universalists had in my finding Ernestine through O'Ferrell, I felt it was appropriate to take her there. I knew little about their beliefs except that intellectuals like Thoreau and Emerson had supported it. It was non-Christian.

The Church by the River was very modern and mostly made of glass. There was no smell of frankincense, no stained-glass windows, and no religious symbolism. The congregation, all white except for Anne and O'Ferrell, had a floor-to-ceiling view of the muddy Mississippi. Seated on benches descending to the pulpit, I

felt as if I were in a theater. I sat Ernestine near the aisle in case she
decided to give a performance of her own during the service. She
wasn't prone to outbursts, yet if she wanted to laugh there was no
controlling her. But there was a cool stillness in the church which
was peaceful and perhaps she was sensitive to the atmosphere.

When we had arrived, a man shook her hand and asked her to
sign the visitors' book, which I did for both of us. Having followed
Anne and O'Ferrell there along the freeway, we were early and settled into a large reception area where the congregation mingled,
drinking coffee and eating cookies. It was the most public place I'd
taken Ernestine and I wasn't sure if she was alarmed by seeing so
many white faces gathered. I told her we were in a church, but did
she believe me?

I guarded her on a sofa and was nervous about what she might
say or do, having heard from Harry Mae that she had a violent
history, but people shared their smiles easily. The congregation was
young and middle-class. Anne and O'Ferrell said they had joined
it after the civil rights movement of the sixties when there was
racial tension in the city. They were quiet and sober in church,
dressed in their Sunday best, and greeted several fellow church
members who entered from the glass doors some few steps
behind us.

The service would last forty-five minutes and I doubted that
Ernestine could remain seated there for that long. She had laughed
twice soon after we sat down, and in case she began to cackle during the sermon, I had already decided which door we could leave
by to cause the least disturbance.

O'Ferrell was a church officer and had spoken to some of the
members earlier in the week to ensure that the minister knew
Ernestine might need to leave in the middle of his sermon. As
couples and families seated themselves around the church, it began
to feel more like we were gathering for a parent–teachers meeting
in a classy suburb.

Ernestine was wearing a navy skirt I'd sent her the previous
Christmas and a dark pink blazer that Essie Mae found in the

closet at the nursing home and said belonged to no one in particular. It was O'Ferrell who had said that she should only be taken
to the church where Grandfather had been minister if she had a
fancy outfit. "Those folks turn out on Sunday," he had warned
when I asked if he thought she would be welcomed there.

When the church choir stood in their purple robes behind us,
Ernestine turned as the organ began and the male and female
voices rose. There was a rustling as the congregation collected their
hymnbooks and stood to sing, but Anne eyed me to indicate that
Ernestine could remain seated. Hoping she would feel part of the
group and not become bored, I helped her to her feet. I had never
heard the song that was being sung as the congregation joined the
choir, with O'Ferrell sounding like the Mississippi itself singing.

Ernestine looked toward the river and with her head lifted she
attempted to join in, making a minute squeak like a baby chick.
Anne heard it and turned to me smiling as Ernestine made a second fleeting attempt before dropping her head and sinking back
into her silence.

Fifteen minutes later we were standing in the parking lot. There
had been no outburst and she might have sat quietly throughout
the entire service, but it seemed right to leave when we did.

"Grandma, would you like to go home or do you want to go to
your cousins?" I asked.

"Let's go to my cousins, hon," she said. Hearing a complete sentence from her was startling. But who did she think her cousins
were? I had never mentioned Julia Hooks or her sisters Mildred
and Bessie to Ernestine, but with the May sun upon us, I drove her
to their place.

It was after midday when I rang Julia's bell and she was leaning
on a cane when she opened the door. I had rung her once since
my arrival from London and knew she wanted to see my grandmother.

Julia already had her champagne-blond wig in place and her
makeup on. Her eyes and voice registered shock. "My goodness!
This is Ernestine!"

Was it so unexpected that my grandmother wasn't frothing at the mouth? She was as well groomed that afternoon as Julia. When offered a large chair, Ernestine perched herself on the edge of it and crossed her legs demurely. With her hands clasped in her lap, they hardly jerked.

Her "hello" required coaxing but she said no more when I added, "Julia's your cousin. She's your Aunt Bessie's granddaughter."

Julia wore a smile. "I didn't think she'd look so well. She's got such a neat figure and you've got her dressed so cute."

There was no telling what could stir Ernestine's memory but neither hearing Julia talk about Mattie's house on Mississippi Boulevard nor taking her into the living room to see the chair upon which her child had once been photographed produced any effect. But the artificial Christmas tree caught her attention. Laden with colored balls and heavy tinsel, it might have made her think it was Christmas.

THE SHOES AND SOME GUYS

SITTING IN THE PASSENGER SEAT, Ernestine was being her usual self. Silent and flexible, she never made me feel that I was a blight on her old age, and I did all I could to make her more active and comfortable. If she hated the excursions I took her on, she hadn't the ability to complain and endured them all with good grace— except getting strapped into her seatbelt.

That particular afternoon I'd taken her to the Midtown Mall, the main shopping area. I had hoped to find shoes for her and take her for a ride on the new trolleys designed to look like ones she might have ridden during her childhood. Streams of people were out shopping or rushing to grab lunch from the sandwich shops that catered to the midtown office workers.

Ernestine looked bright when I finally found a parking space and said, "We're here, Grandma, and we can undo that seatbelt." It was a pleasure to release her. I always wondered if the sense of restraint it gave her reminded her of some horrifying asylum experience.

That she was limber enough to get in and out of the car unaided continued to amaze me, and having opened the passenger door, I waited for her to step out. But a male voice yelled, "Hey! What ch'you doing letting that old lady get out the car by herself?" He was short and grinning and accompanied by two others. They were black and in their twenties and I knew they wanted something but I wasn't sure what. Smelling liquor on the talker, I scanned the gutter for a weapon as he addressed Ernestine.

"Ma'am, you want some help? See, I wasn't raised to just stand back and watch no old lady get out a car while I'm standing here looking. Know what I'm saying?"

Of course Ernestine said nothing, but I was sorry she wasn't moving faster.

"Thanks but no thanks," I told him, unsure if we were about to be mugged.

With three men shadowing us and the car, I felt unable to protect her but said, "Take your time, Grandma."

"Grandma!" shouted the one with the liquor breath. "This pretty woman ain't old enough to be no grandmother! I was about ready to ask her if her and me could go out on a date."

Ernestine took no notice of him and her nonchalance read like disdain as she hoisted herself from the seat.

The three men were decently dressed and I hoped we weren't going to be attacked in broad daylight. The short one's sneakers

were new and when he begged a dollar off me I said, "Let's pretend that I didn't hear you say that."

My voice must have irritated him, because he strolled off angrily
with his buddies, shouting, "I got a job!"

This was a poor start for our afternoon excursion and things did
not improve. In store after store, I would sit Ernestine down, undo
her broken laces, remove her worn-out shoes to free her badly
misshapen feet, to be shown shoes that she couldn't get over her
bunions and hammertoes. Every pair of shoes she was given she
sniffed inside and out—maybe she'd had secondhand ones at the
asylum. Desperate to replace her wedgies, I hadn't taken account
of her age. We'd tried five shops before she staggered in the street.

"Oh, my God, Grandma, are you okay?" I asked, though I was
afraid she wasn't. The thought of her suffering a cardiac arrest for
the sake of new shoes made me ashamed of myself. "I'll take you
back home right now, all right?" I promised, but we were at least
five long blocks from the car. I saw neither taxis nor public phones
and I was about to suggest that we sit on the sidewalk when I
heard, "Hey, Grandmommy! Looking good!"

It was the little drunk with one of his buddies. "Y'all still shopping?" he asked.

"Please. Not now," I told him. "She's exhausted and I'm worried
that I won't get her back to the car." Feeling desperate, I would
have explained our problem to anybody.

"Let me carry her!"

"You can't carry her."

"Yes, I can. I do it all the time. I work in an old folks' home and
I have to carry one of them somewhere practically every day.
Come on, let me carry her."

He walked beside us as we crept along with the sun in our eyes.
Ernestine, normally sure-footed, stumbled twice.

"Grandma, my God," I said with my heart pounding with fear
that I'd killed her for a pair of shoes, "do you think you'd better sit
on the curb?"

"Poor little old thing," said the short one, which made me feel more guilty. "Let me carry her. I'm telling you I do it all the time and she ain't got no weight on her." Bending, he tried to look her in the eyes. "Want me to carry you, Miss Grandma? You do, don't you?"

"No, she doesn't. Just leave her," I said, but I was reluctant to chase him away entirely. If he intended to snatch my bag, he wasn't going to get much, because after encountering him earlier at the parked car I'd put my cash in my shoe.

His taller friend walked on my right side, smoking a cigarette and saying no more than Ernestine, who said nothing. If she'd taken in either of them, she showed no sign of it, and I was conscious of how antisocial she seemed in the presence of two people who knew nothing about her. But what preyed on my mind was that I might have killed her for a pair of shoes.

The short guy gave me his employment history to reassure me that he'd handled enough elderly people to carry Ernestine to the car, and I didn't want to say that he didn't seem sober enough to get himself there. He was determined to try and said, pointing to his friend, "How about if she holds on to me and him? He used to work with old folks too. . . . Anyway, what you need for her is a wheel-chair, but since we ain't got one, you best let me carry her."

While he begged, I studied my grandmother's face to see if she could manage another step, as the two who had joined us greeted people they knew who I feared might join our slow procession. But his chatter eased my fears and when we were within sight of the car, I thanked God.

"Just a few more steps," I told Ernestine, who plodded along. Did she remember who I was? Did she understand that I didn't know the two men who'd joined us? She was always an enigma to me.

When the short one said, "Leave her with us and you go get the car," I wondered if I dared. I would have never forgiven myself had she died from exhaustion, but I would have been equally guilty had she been whisked off by two men. America is stranger than fiction and I decided not to risk it, even though he repeated, "Let me carry her. You want me to, don't you, Miss Grandma, Miss Pretty Thing?"

His familiarity was my fault, because I had answered questions about myself and been relieved to have company as we trekked along the mall. But his calling Ernestine "pretty thing" zapped me back to reality.

"It's only a little farther, Grandma," I said but she was silent. I held her arm as we moved on.

The car was an oven, and I needed to air it out before we got in, but I was so relieved that we had reached it. I wondered how much money I would need to tip our escorts for the interest they'd shown.

Ernestine seemed more remote than usual and I wondered if she felt uncomfortable, excluded even. With her head slightly bowed and her shoulders hunched, her fingers began to dance, although she tried to control them by clasping her hands together. She was standing by the passenger door with the two guys beside her, as I rolled down the window on the driver's side. That's when I saw the little guy scoop her into his arms like she was his bride. But he grimaced and his knees buckled like a weightlifter hoisting five hundred pounds of cold steel. I had visions of him collapsing and I gagged my scream as I saw my grandmother's eyes flash with terror and her body stiffen. While she made no sound her expression cried *Help* but I was too far away to do more than yell, "Put her down! You stupid . . . put her down!" I rushed to grab her before they both fell. It was painful to see that even when filled with terror, she was unable to call out.

"I didn't hurt her." He laughed.

Would she ever trust me again? Did she know the men weren't my friends? "I'm sorry, Grandma," I begged. But she said nothing.

THE TALL WOMAN IN MEDICAL RECORDS handed me a wad of papers three inches thick and said, "You're lucky. Some old records have been put on microfilm, and personal letters get thrown out. But I had a quick look through your grandmother's file. Looks like everything's there. Want some coffee?"

I was tempted to say yes, but did accepting hospitality mean I owed something to the hospital? The five women in Medical Records were white and I didn't trust them. Which of them was a racist? I asked myself, studying their faces as best as I could while standing there with my briefcase in one hand and Ernestine's heavy medical file in the other.

"There are some doughnuts too," said the tall woman. So not only did I feel suspicious but I felt guilty as well. She was being nice but I was trapped by the South's history. Maybe a Jewish tourist in modern Germany could identify with my problem. When your race has been abused and maligned, it might be possible to forgive but never to forget.

I'd driven out of Memphis so early that it didn't feel like I'd brushed my teeth that morning, which made it easy to decline the doughnut, but I was grateful for the coffee—and for the records.

"Start at the back first. You can use that desk," said the tall woman.

"I'll be here all day."

Not only was I given a large desk with a swivel chair; she returned with a jar of paper clips. "Clip these to anything you want copied."

"I can get copies?" Coffee, doughnuts, *and* a copy service? Could they read my mind? Did they know that I intended to write about Ernestine?

"Well, I don't have time to copy all of it, but I can do quite a few. Not right away, but how long you plan to be in Memphis?"

The office wasn't getting direct sunlight; with big windows overlooking the well-tended grounds of the hospital, it was only vaguely dismal, but the furniture was dated. Probably it hadn't been refurnished since the fifties, and maybe that's why I stood there all too conscious of the race war which had been fought in the South throughout my childhood.

I was standing in a hospital which had been racially segregated for most of the years that Ernestine had been there, and the tall woman who was my age and whose southern accent told me that she'd grown up in the South would have been aware throughout her childhood, as I had been, that "Negroes" were demanding equal rights when nobody in power was prepared to concede them. Was she as suspicious of me as I was of her, but more practiced at hiding it? I dared be honest with her.

"I'm here for another couple of weeks."

She smiled. "Oh, we've got loads of time."

Her tan made her light hair look lighter still and her blue eyes transparent. Her name was Imogen but she pronounced it Amojean and the desk she had offered was the one she'd been sitting at the first time I'd come to Medical Records asking for my grandmother's file. If she was as free of racism as she seemed, she was fortunate, because sitting there at her desk I suffered from the paranoia left over from an earlier time when she could have harmed me without recourse.

The earliest entries were at the back. The small woman wearing glasses at the desk two feet from mine heard me sigh as I read Ernestine's commitment order.

"Is it upsetting?" she asked.

"Perplexing. I thought my grandmother graduated from high school at least. But the earliest record says that she only finished fourth grade and that she was mentally deficient."

I didn't want to tell her that Ernestine saying during her commitment interview that she was "a white girl" was equally perplexing—but it was. Why would my grandmother have said that? I had never heard that she had ever claimed to be white, but perhaps in her confusion she couldn't equate how she looked with what race she was. I kept looking at the typed sheet of questions and answers which recorded what had taken place between Ernestine and the doctor who conducted the interview and I envisioned a young unprotected black female, confused, afraid, and accustomed to having no rights. How vulnerable did she feel? How desperate was she? Was she alert enough to know that if she was classified as white she would get better conditions and more help? Or was confusion about her racial identity part of her illness? The first time I saw Ernestine at the nursing home, I was surprised by how white she looked. Did her appearance cause an identity crisis at a time in American history when having African blood provoked so much racism?

The woman at the desk across from mine said, "All kinds of people used to end up here that didn't belong."

"She was committed on September ninth, 1929," I said, but I was still looking at the question and answer which had been categorized under hallucinations and delusions. The question was "Are you a Negro?" and her answer, "No, I'm a white girl."

Despite seeing it typed on her record, I didn't want to believe that my grandmother had tried to pass for white, because the implication was that she didn't want to be grouped with a people rooted in slavery.

My imagination worked overtime. Seeing written records frustrated me because the information available was so vague as to be inexplicable. For instance, why had she been committed with no family history and where was my grandfather, who would have been in his early forties that year and was already a principal and a pastor? There was no record of him being present or interviewed.

Although Western State Mental Health Institute, as Bolivar was formerly called, was a state hospital, patients' spouses were required to pay. The records suggested that my grandmother had arrived at the hospital alone.

None of it made sense, and with jet lag creeping over me as I sat in that office, my back to the window, I felt extremely down.

With hindsight, I knew that Ernestine's life had ended on 9 September 1929 when she was committed to Bolivar. During her oral examination on admission, she had complained of a headache and her answers indicated that she was confused. For example, having grown up in Memphis, she would have known that the Mississippi River ran through the city, but when asked this basic question, she couldn't answer.

Whereas the information in Ernestine's records was very disturbing, nothing in them indicated that she had undergone inhumane therapies such as shock treatment and frontal lobotomy which hospitals were experimenting with at the time.

The records were on the one hand unexpectedly complete, dating back to her committal, but at the same time I knew they contained grossly misleading information. That it was not known that she was a married woman with three young sons, nor that her husband was a leading black citizen, indicates the institution's ignorance about the most basic elements of her history. The false information that she managed only to complete fourth grade and was mentally deficient remained on her record for fifty-two years. Unless her graduation picture was a hoax and my grandfather had lied about her being his student, I assumed that Ernestine had finished high school. The only thing which was substantiated in her medical records was the length of time she had spent in the institution.

Bolivar was built on a tract of a Confederate general's 2500-acre plantation. It opened in 1890 with 119 males and 130 females admitted during its first year. Nashville already had a state asylum, as did Knoxville, built in 1840 and 1873 respectively.

Grains of Sand, Bolivar's official history, says that at the time it opened, Superintendent Dr. John P. Douglas "felt strongly that there should be facilities for the insane colored." Six years later he is quoted as saying that the new "colored section," already overcrowded, led to "unsanitary conditions." No specifics are cited, but the "coloreds" were placed in a building with tubercular patients.

Built to accommodate 300, Bolivar then housed 594 and overcrowding remained a major problem ten years later. *Grains of Sand* notes that treatment consisted of diet, discipline, occupation, and diversion. Work was therapy!

By 1918, Dr. Edwin Cooke, talking of his new position as superintendent, said that patients were sleeping on the floor. As the institution was segregated, it is more likely that black patients would have been sleeping on the floor while white patients occupied beds, rather than the reverse.

There was neither a social worker nor a dentist employed until 1929, the year Ernestine was committed. But by then the superintendent was rarely at Bolivar, because he was also the commissioner of the Department of Institutions. The Wall Street crash in October of that year affected the whole nation and the superintendent's biennial report of 1932–34 states, "Due to the dire financial difficulties of the state, we were confronted at the beginning of this administration with a decrease in appropriation from the previous biennium." Employees' salaries were cut by 20 to 50 percent.

During 1930 and 1931 there was only an 8.47 percent rate of recovery at Bolivar. Staff duties ranged from 78 to 91 hours per week. This information comes from the official history of the asylum. Did it reveal as much as it could have?

Ernestine was committed as a psychotic with mental deficiency. With an overworked, underpaid staff, what hope had she in the "colored section" of getting proper treatment? By 1938 there were 2000 patients and 200 staff and no doubt a stressful environment resulted. She was forty years old, her three children were in Boston over a thousand miles away, and she may have had no contact with her husband, since he had supplied no family history when she was admitted on 9 September 1929. She was effectively abandoned and highly vulnerable.

Were female patients protected at all or was she, as a "colored girl," particularly at risk? Could she have been sexually abused? The racism which prevailed in Tennessee at that time meant that even in the outside world all "colored girls" were unsafe. In a segregated asylum how probable was it that a defenseless blonde in a black ward would attract male attention from staff or other patients? Ernestine had said she was white during her first interview. Did she continue to say this while she was an inmate? How would those of her own race have reacted to her? She must have stood out from the rest and therefore been singled out for bullying.

If Ernestine felt betrayed or abandoned when her first days at Bolivar became months, how despondent must she have been in 1933 when the records show that her husband made several attempts to divorce her?

The words "patient" and "hospital" imply that medical care and treatment are available. From Ernestine's records and the pages of *Grains of Sand,* it appears that no real treatment was given.

For over fifty years the false information that her education ended in fourth grade and she was mentally deficient remained on her medical records. Social workers continued to rely upon her admission assessments, so her status as "mentally deficient" went unchallenged. The progress of psychiatry and psychiatric social work was never to benefit Ernestine. As late as 1979, her social-work case history still quoted the misinformation written about her during that short, ill-informed interview.

The most disturbing thing I read concerning her treatment took place after she'd been there more than two decades: despite her signature revealing that she was hardly able to sign her name, there it was on a permission form permitting the hospital to administer a drug known to cause permanent side effects. I had imagined that the involuntary jerking of her hands was a condition of her mental illness, but in fact it was more likely to be a side effect of that drug she'd been given many years before.

There's a museum on the second floor of the administration building. Collections of old photographs line the table in the center of the room. I went through them all hoping to spot Ernestine among the many group shots, but there were no pictures of the segregated wards.

I touched the long arms of a straitjacket and wondered how often Ernestine had worn one. It was heavier than I'd imagined, and the white fabric was coarse and densely woven so there was no give in it. It was lying next to an upright dental cabinet, and I looked at the terrible instruments, thinking about why and how all her teeth had been removed.

⟿ 799 MISSISSIPPI BOULEVARD

AT THE LIBRARY I WAS ABLE TO FIND OUT more information from the city directories and the U.S. census reports.

Although Julia Hooks referred to the house on Mississippi Boulevard as "Aunt Mattie's," in the 1920 census, Ernestine's husband, Blair, is registered as the head of the household, with his wife, Ernestine, and baby son, Blair Jr., living with him. Ernestine was twenty-two and pregnant with her second child. But Julia was correct in thinking that Mattie lived there, and perhaps her presence dominated the household. The census lists Mattie's age as thirty-nine. Actually she was forty-two; her new husband, Humphries Nevels, was only twenty-nine and this may have caused her to falsify her age. He was a Pullman porter registered as mulatto. Her daughter Roberta was thirteen. Information from the Memphis street directories and the U.S. census reports indicate that Mattie had lived at 895 Lane for over ten years and Ernestine and Blair were living there when their first child was born. Their

Blair T. Hunt Jr., my grandfather, was the son of slaves, Blair Hunt
and Emma Shouse. He became a highly respected member of the
Memphis community and a church leader.

(*Left*) Ernestine with Blair (*above*), her firstborn, whom she called B.T. She was nineteen or twenty when this picture of both of them was taken.

My grandfather was a chaplain, ranking as a lieutenant in the First World War. Stationed in France, he married Ernestine immediately after her graduation and before he went overseas.

(*Left*) Ernestine's graduation photograph from Ol'Kortrech High School.

My grandfather when he was principal of Booker T. Washington High in Memphis. He stayed in the South, while his sons went north to Boston to be brought up by Ernestine's mother, Mattie. (*See photo below right.*)

(*Above*) Wilson (*left*), Blair (*center*), Ernest (*right*) in Boston with Ernestine's half-sister, Roberta.

(*Right*) Ernestine's mother, Mattie, is seated in front of three of her sisters in Hyannis Port, Cape Cod.

My father went to Boys Latin in Boston and graduated at seventeen.

Wilson's high school graduation picture.

Ernest, youngest of the three brothers.

second and third sons were born at 799 Mississippi Boulevard.

Blair was back from France where he had been gassed, judging from his veteran's disability pension. He was teaching and had accepted an appointment as pastor of the new Mississippi Church.

It must have been an interesting household. Ernestine was closer in age to Mattie's young husband, and Mattie was closer to Blair's age. Did this create problems for any of them?

Was there tension between the mother and daughter in a situation where Ernestine's husband, being older and better educated than Humphries Nevels, was head of the household, and Ernestine was probably still controlled by Mattie?

Ernestine and Blair were still living on Mississippi Boulevard the following year when Ernest was born on 22 November. It's not certain that Mattie and her husband and daughter were still living there. But if they were, Ernestine might have been pleased to have the help and companionship of her mother and fourteen-year-old half-sister.

As a Pullman porter, Nevels would have been away often; in segregated Memphis, Mattie might have felt protected living in a house where at least one husband was ever-present.

⟋☙ THE LITTLE RUSSET BOY AND OTHERS

WHILE I CONTINUED TO TRY TO UNCOVER ERNESTINE'S PAST, she was always in my daily life. Despite my earlier attempts to replace her shoes, she was still wearing those white wedgies which had been new when I'd met her in 1991. They were no longer clean and white. The broken laces were knotted together and where the leather had been cut away to allow room for her disfigured feet, the shoes were fraying. In a cut-rate shoe store a male shopper said, when I put them on the counter, "They some sad-looking brogans."

There was only one clerk, and as soon as we walked into the store, I bought Ernestine some socks and put them on her so that she understood we had a reason to be there. The most common experience may have been new and inexplicable to her but when I sat her on a pine bench in the center of the store, she didn't seem either interested or disturbed by the towering display racks of shoes.

While I searched for a pair small enough for her, two teenaged mothers with toddlers entered and allowed their little boys to run up and down the three aisles. The largest had enormous black eyes and cinnamon-colored lashes that were as russet as his skin and closely cropped hair. When he spied Ernestine sitting silently on her own, he deserted his little friend and stopped to stare at her. Her eyes had been fixed upon the floor, but he caught her attention and they gazed intently at each other.

He'd been boisterous from the moment he'd entered the store, and I didn't know if she needed protection, so I watched from several feet away. Suppose he decides to hit her with a shoe, I was thinking as he inched toward her, his eyes fixed upon her as though he was calculating an attack.

But suddenly her hand grabbed his. "Hey, sugar," she chuckled, "you a sweet little boy!" She sounded so sassy and gay that it felt like an awakening that was permanent. She couldn't have been more welcoming had she bumped into her oldest friend.

The little boy didn't resist her grip. He stood fixed and looked at her with adult earnestness, leaning toward her until his mother snapped from the other end of the store, "What are you doing! Come over here!"

His brown baby-fat forearm looked velvety compared to Ernestine's pale, bony fingers ridged with veins. He didn't run to his mother's call, and having never seen Ernestine with a child I was as concerned for his safety as for hers, because they were both children. Fearing catastrophe, I inched my way nearer.

"That's a pretty little boy," Ernestine said, before he yanked his arm away and rushed off to pummel the aisles again in his plastic sandals.

Perhaps she still felt the loss of her own boys. Being around small children may have struck a chord in her and put her in touch with who she had been. That's why I took her one afternoon to the Union Avenue Baptist Church, which has two full-day nurseries for working mothers.

"Perhaps your grandmother would like to meet some of our four- and five-year-olds," said the administrator.

"Toddlers might be better."

They called the nursery the Child Enrichment Center and I had been taken there by Fred Hooks, nephew of Ben. It was a sharp contrast to the nursing home, starkly clean with colorful mobiles dangling from the ceiling and nursery tunes singing out from a music box. Color and light and sound made it as much a welcoming environment as the eight brown-skinned women of various ages who attended the six babies and nine toddlers. How would the residents at the nursing home have flourished, given as much attention?

Ernestine looked pretty in the secondhand clothes I had bought her, though they had cost only a few dollars. Her cheeks were pink with blusher and she was wearing lipstick and pearl earrings. Baby bouncers and harnesses, walkers, and low chairs for feeding were dotted about the two rooms, where some babies crawled and others sat on the laps of the women. Whether the contraptions puzzled her or not, Ernestine sat in a low rocker and looked at ease. Her left eye was still bloodshot and ironically the toddler most interested in standing by her was a boy of two with a swollen eye. For twenty minutes he hovered at her knees, showing her his play telephone and trying to climb on her. They didn't talk but they were gentle with each other. Winter and spring touching. A life ending, a life beginning.

THE TWENTY-THIRD PSALM

THE DAY WAS MILDER THAN USUAL. Sun poured over the crusty porch and warmed the air around us. In exchange for a pack of cigarettes fetched from the nearest store, Mama Tiny, a resident at the home, had loaned me her Bible. The print was larger than usual and the text modern. I sat Ernestine by my side, intending to read some passages to her. She had been a minister's wife, and the Bible would have played a role in their lives.

It was good to be outside, not in the house, not in the car, and I sat there thinking how happy Ernestine might have been sitting in my garden in France. I imagined her wandering from the front garden to the back and picking gooseberries. As I sat there with that Bible in my hands and asked her if there was anything in particular she wanted me to read, I dreamed of setting her free.

"No, hon," she said to my question.

So I chose the Twenty-third Psalm because it was a familiar one she would surely have known and recited. Her left shoulder was pressing against my right upper arm and I laughed under my breath, thinking what an odd picture we must have made on the dilapidated porch—Ernestine was so much the wren and I so much the raven—yet we were family.

"The Lord is my shepherd," I began, "I shall not want."

Ernestine shifted slightly and said, "I shall not want." Had I heard correctly? Had she managed those sounds? I looked at her out of the corner of my eye, but she was wrapped in more than her normal stillness. Her hands, clasped together, were still, her legs crossed.

But where was her attention?

Raising my voice a notch I went on. "He maketh me to lie down." I didn't dare lurch ahead for fear of losing her. But she followed with each word, cutting through the silence which held her captive. She had missed the first few words but none of the rest and this was as much a feat for her as a child in leg braces completing a hundred-yard dash.

How long had it been since Ernestine had repeated anything? When had she last trusted herself to mouth words like "anointest" and "pastures"? And when had she last trusted anyone to hear her speech muffled by the absence of her teeth?

"The Lord is my shepherd;
I shall not want.
He maketh me to lie down
In green pastures:
He leadeth me beside still waters.
He restoreth my soul:
He leadeth me in the paths of righteousness
For his name's sake.
And yet, though I walk through the valley
Of the shadow of death
I will fear no evil; for thou art with me,
Thy rod and thy staff they comfort me.
Thou prepareth a table before me
In the presence of mine enemies:
Thou anointest my head with oil:
My cup runneth over.

Surely goodness and graciousness
Shall follow me all the days of my life,
And I will dwell in the house
Of the Lord forever."

I had just heard a miracle. But there was no one to tell, and who would have cared? I was four thousand miles from home, and the wounded creature beside me was not an animal but a human being.

⟶ ᴇᴈ FANCY CLOTHES

"ESSIE MAE, DO YOU THINK SHE MIGHT BE SICKENING with something?"

"Miss Hunt, how you feel, hon?"

"All right."

Essie Mae and I were staring at Ernestine in the new clothes which I'd bought for her that afternoon. But she stood silently in the kitchen nook, looking down at her feet in gleaming white slippers. Maybe she needed to know why I fussed over her, but I still hadn't found the right moment to tell her who I was, although two years had passed since we first sat in that nook and she had kissed my father's baby picture.

"Grandma, want to put on your other new things?"

"Yeah, hon." Her shoulders were hunched and her eyes sad.

"Want a banana?"

"Yeah."

Essie Mae guided her toward the back room. "We all have our days. Can't nobody be a hundred percent every day. Ain't that right, hon?"

Ernestine said nothing and I removed her new clothes.

"Want a little nap?" I asked, half peeling her banana.

"Yeah. Um-hmmm." Her eyes told nothing.

Underneath Ernestine's new dress was a shabby handmade slip of coarse white cotton. Why was my grandmother living like this? I asked myself as I threw back the lightweight cover on her bed. But I could hear my mother's voice repeating something she had said two days before. "Why are you getting involved in that? She's not your family! What does Wilson say?"

I didn't know and was afraid to ask. And why *was* I getting involved?

"Want me to sing to you, Grandma?" I asked after settling her into bed.

"Yes, uh-huh."

I stroked her temple like my other grandmother had once stroked mine when I used to return home from nursery school. Essie Mae let out a sigh as she put Ernestine's new dress into its clear plastic cover. "Essie Mae, you don't have to fool with that. You've got more than enough to do."

It was nearly suppertime and she had to prepare it, set it out, and clear it away without help.

Ernestine's eye had been bloodshot for days, and while I didn't want to badger Essie Mae, I wanted something done about it. I sat on the edge of the bed feeling powerless. The sun was glaring outside but refused to peek into that ugly bedroom. Could you blame it? A ghetto nursing home housing too many people with too few employees. Sure I wanted Mrs. Cummings's business to get support from the community, but not at Ernestine's expense.

Before I'd finished a verse of the Brahms "Lullaby," her lashes fluttered and she fell asleep, stretched out like a board with her toes pointing to the ceiling and her arms by her sides.

CARLOTTA

BEEFY TRUCKERS IN JEANS, TEE-SHIRTS, and baseball caps talked to each other in a couple of doorways and I tried not to look their way as I headed for the motel's coin-op washing machine. Annabelle, the manager who had gone with me to Bolivar, called out from the level below, "Somebody phoned who says she knew your grandmother."

"Did you get her number?" I asked, running back down the stairs. It was nearly seven. Annabelle passed me a torn piece of paper with Carlotta Watson's number on it.

I'd tried ringing her a few times but always got the answering machine. She had taught at Booker T. Washington under Grandfather and I had been told she was over ninety. But when she answered my call from the motel that evening, her voice sounded too robust to belong to someone elderly.

"I've been out of town, otherwise I would have got back to you sooner." Her speech was more strident than most of the women I had talked to and her words spilled out quickly.

I had asked so many people if they had known Ernestine and been disappointed so many times that I was discounting Miss Watson's claim to have known her. I said, "You were a friend of my grandfather's?"

"I also knew your grandmother. We graduated together."

I held back a holler. It was light outside. Big trucks rattled up and down the road and one drove into the parking lot screeching its brakes. With the curtains in my room drawn, I had tapped out Miss Watson's number in semi-darkness, but what she had to say deserved light and I yanked open the drapes.

"You knew Ernestine?"

"She was a beautiful girl, and smart. In fact I think she was either class valedictorian or salutatorian."

"Salutatorian?"

"That's second best but she may have been first. The thing I recall about her best was that when we sent out our graduation announcements, Ernestine included her wedding invitations."

Was it acceptable back then for a schoolgirl to marry her teacher? Had she and Grandfather openly courted or did it come as a surprise to Ernestine's classmates that she and Blair T. Hunt were to marry?

Unable to see Miss Watson, I didn't broach these questions but asked, "Did you go to the wedding?"

"Who, me?" She roared. "I was a nobody. Nothing but a little dark country girl!"

Dark and country? Would that have stopped Ernestine from associating with her? I tried to imagine this woman's face. How African did she look and what had made it anathema to social status?

"You're the first person I've spoken to who knew Ernestine before she went to Bolivar. Her medical records say she was mentally deficient."

"Shoot! Now do you think Blair T. Hunt would have married some poor girl that was mentally deficient?" Miss Watson laughed. "Ernestine was brilliant. And I'll tell you what. If you come over here, I'll see if we can get Mamie Toler on the phone. She graduated the same year we did. Mamie will tell you that Ernestine was a beautiful girl and brilliant. And not stuck up either . . . she was popular and nice to everybody—everybody. She was blond, had hair to her waist. That's why he wanted her. She was a great girl. A great catch."

"So how did she end up at Bolivar?" I asked.

"You come over here and we can talk all you want."

Had I finally met someone who would be unafraid to talk openly about my grandfather? That this woman had known him as her teacher and also taught with him was as encouraging as her enthusiasm for Ernestine.

"You know your way around Memphis?" she asked. "I'm on Park. Not on the fancy side of town, but I've been married a few times and I got a big house and couldn't want for more. Been everywhere I wanted to go and I still go. Best time to come is Sunday."

Our meeting couldn't have come soon enough for me, and when I arrived at her house after she'd been to church she showed me into a living room of chairs covered in handmade patchwork quilts. She was ninety-four and had been living alone for some years. An exercise bike stood beside a sideboard in her dining room. It was an outdated model but the pedals still went around.

"I get stiff and have to work out on that thing sometimes. . . . I guess I sit on it every day. But shoot, that ain't nothing."

"Mrs. Watson—"

"Call me Carlotta," she interrupted, her dark eyes never shifting, "because I'm too young for you to call me Mrs. Watson and it's Steward Watson anyway."

Carlotta is as difficult to describe as a flower. Slim and tall for her generation, she was a dark walnut color. She had a round nose with flared nostrils and smiling lips so that her healthy teeth showed. Her energy was red, her laugh a sensuous perfume that clung to every room even when she was silent. She had a deep openness as pure as soil. Being in her presence reminded me of Ernestine's potential. My grandmother was a long-lasting as Carlotta, but what had deprived her of being all she could have been? Was it mental illness or just being burnt out by the asylum system?

Carlotta took me into her office off the bedroom of her bungalow. A computer was switched off. Did she use it?

"I still write an article now and then and do some broadcasting." She laughed, scratching hair which was duckling fluff, white with strands of gray.

Her portrait hung on the wall behind the computer. "That's when I was married to the second one. Or no . . . maybe that was the third." She giggled. "But you ain't nothing but a flatterer. Come on now. You're here to talk about your grandmother." Her hand pulling me into the living room was as muscular as I was about to discover her memory to be. "Somewhere in this house I have our graduation announcement. But I looked and looked. . . . Anyway, I think I can recall everybody that graduated with us. Now there was Esquire Buckner, and Mamie." She named several more. "And one thing I'll never forget. The girls used to hold artificial flowers when they received their diplomas, but Ernestine had a dozen roses. I don't think I had ever seen anything like them. I guess they came from him." She was referring to Grandfather.

"Was it a surprise when she sent out wedding invitations?"

"Oh, yes," said Carlotta as she headed for the telephone. An apron splattered with various stains covered her old blue tracksuit and the velvet slippers on her feet were tied on with a ribbon running right around the sole. She tried tapping out a number several times before she got a reply.

"Mamie," Carlotta yelled, "Mamie! Yes, I'm back. But listen. I've got somebody here. Blair T. Hunt's granddaughter. And she wants to know something about Ernestine. You remember Ernestine, don't you?" Carlotta's shouting suggested that Mamie was hard of hearing. "Now listen, Mamie, this child is trying to find out something about her grandmother. They told her at Bolivar that Ernestine was mentally deficient. Yes . . . that's what I told her."

Inviting me to speak to Mamie, who was in Greensboro, Mississippi, Carlotta said, "Mamie married a doctor. She and I keep in touch."

Mrs. Toler's voice was a gentle swing. "Oh, my," she said about Ernestine, "she was a mother's dream. An ideal woman in every way. Very smart. *Very.* She was brilliant, a brilliant student. Quiet spoken, and everybody liked her. I think she was valedictorian. She was friendly with everybody. Like I say, an ideal woman."

Carlotta explained that only white students went through to the twelfth grade. "We finished in the eleventh and you could go straight from school to teaching."

"My grandmother was a teacher," I said, repeating what I'd heard from my cousin Alan.

"You couldn't be married and teach. Not back then."

"And you think she married right away?"

"Oh, I'm *sure* of that."

"Were you surprised when you heard that she was in Bolivar?"

"I was sorry to hear it."

"What do you think may have happened?"

"I heard it was insanity in the genes."

—⌒⌒ THE ZOO

OUTINGS WITH ERNESTINE RANGED FROM TRIPS to McDonald's to car rides, shopping trips, and even the occasional visit to Anne and O'Ferrell's. But I didn't expect anything to be as exciting for her as our trip to the Memphis Zoo.

Ernestine looked relaxed in the wheelchair rented from the ticket office, leaning on one arm with her legs crossed as we passed the giraffes and I pushed her up the path leading to the hippopotamus enclosure. She was wearing her best secondhand dress, a mock antique, with a longish skirt and lace collar. She even had her pearl earrings on, so it was puzzling when a small, sunburned girl stopped dead as we passed to yell, "Look, Mommy! Look at the old, old man!"

We pressed on in the heat and a faint drizzle, which had started when we left the new lions' den. It was a small zoo and, since it was late in the afternoon, was hardly crowded. People seemed more interested in the food concessions than in seeing the animals.

Essie Mae had said that my grandmother loved the zoo, but I saw no sign of it as I pushed her from one exotic animal to the next. "See the zebras, Grandma?" I shouted down at her, trying to make an occasion out of the visit.

She didn't fall asleep but her expression was solemn, especially when we reached the hippopotamus with her baby. The iron fences separating the animals from the onlookers were like prison bars and I watched Ernestine looking at the hippopotamus with sad eyes while children and their parents giggled and pointed to her left and right, in front of her and behind her. What was she thinking? Did she identify with that caged mother? Had she been in rooms with bars on the windows?

The child who had called her an old man held her mother's hand tightly and simply stared when we passed her on our way out.

THE LUNCHTIME SERMON

ESSIE MAE'S LAUGHTER SPLASHED THE GRIMY WALLS in the hallway as she followed us from the bathroom to the kitchen nook, saying, "If somebody had told me that you could get some tights to fit Miss Hunt's little legs, I wouldn't have believed 'em!"

"Think she'll be all right in the slippers?" I asked, as I pulled a lipstick out of the makeup bag on the table.

"They fine," claimed Essie Mae, though we both knew they were not designed for street wear. "But I wouldn't walk her through no grass, 'cause they ain't gonna stay white for long."

Ernestine puckered her lips when she saw the rust-red lipstick and Essie Mae howled. "Lord, Miss Hunt, you know how to let her put that lipstick on you, don't you! And look at your little earrings." The tiny fake pearls were clustered to resemble grapes on a vine.

In her dull pink dress with the knee-length floral jacket, Ernestine looked as out of place in the kitchen nook as Katharine Hepburn and it was sad that there was no full-length mirror that she could see herself in.

It hadn't seemed wise to buy her a hat, and I was hoping that since the service was taking place at lunchtime, there would be other women at the Mississippi Boulevard Church who would arrive bareheaded. Besides, Ernestine's healthy silver mane was her glory, especially that day, when I'd washed it and styled it with a borrowed hair dryer.

When Essie Mae rushed ahead of us to open the screen door, she couldn't have been more excited if Ernestine had been a teenager going to her first prom. But Ernestine was as poker-faced as a drill sergeant and when I strapped her seatbelt on, I wondered if I was making a mistake in taking her to a place where she might be as much on display as that hippopotamus we'd seen at the zoo. Did it matter? She needed help. Maybe she had to endure people's curiosity to get it.

In the doorway of a large hall the smell of fried chicken was more intense than the din of voices, and gripping her arm I put two ten-dollar bills on the table to buy our entrance tickets. A man wearing a broad smile said, "This is Elder Hunt's widow, isn't it?"

"Would you like to say good afternoon, Grandma?"

She managed to look at him but didn't acknowledge that he'd extended his hand. Surprisingly she blurted, "How do you do!" People were coming in and rushing past to join the lines at the buffet tables where elderly ladies helped to serve them, and Ernestine looked from him to them.

He continued to smile. "We're honored that you could join us today."

It would have been reasonable for him to expect more of a response from her, because she looked normal. But when he said that he had worked with Grandfather at the church for many years, I assumed he knew Ernestine had spent most of her life at Bolivar. He was a member of the church board and returned my ten-dollar bills. "We can't allow you to pay."

Two women posted at a buffet table heard him and scurried over to hug Ernestine. She didn't resist them, but their enthusiasm was more overpowering than their unexpected embrace.

"Oh, my," said the taller, whose straightened hair was drawn back in a bun, "we heard that Elder Hunt's wife was coming, but we didn't believe it. This *is* her, isn't it?"

Ernestine's silence must have been contagious, because they fell silent until the second one felt easier and said, "We've waited years for this. We really have, and my husband's not going to believe he missed you. How *are* you?"

Before I could say anything, Ernestine had replied herself. "Fine, thanks," she said, to my astonishment. Was she about to have an awakening? Twice within a few minutes she had responded to two strangers while the noise in the room rose and surrounded her: voices, metal spoons serving food from metal pans, balloons of loud laughter, male and female, the whimper of one baby, all blending with the scent of chicken competing with the smell of ribs.

Ernestine was still wrapped in one woman's arms and while she looked sedate in her new clothes, I wondered how unpredictable she was. Even Essie Mae admitted that she would occasionally curse everybody and everything, and I didn't want this to be the afternoon for it, so I pried her from the woman's hold and was relieved to be shown two seats at a long table where no one else was yet sitting.

"We'll get you whatever you want. You stay here in the dining room and we'll bring you a tray," said our guide.

The dining room held a few hundred, and one section was filling up with people. Many looked like young professionals, especially the men in their suits and ties who entered smiling with a briefcase in one hand and an aluminum food tray in the other. One, who sat only a table away, had skin as dark as the richest soil. His gold-rimmed glasses glistened in sharp contrast and he stared at Ernestine. Could his black eyes not see that her blue ones had seen suffering, or was he searching for the hints of Africa which he probably expected to see in the faces of that congregation?

My grandmother was the oldest person there, but maybe the woman who joined us at the table imagined herself to be. She announced she was eighty-four as she nibbled a chicken leg and fell asleep after a few bites, with her chin resting upon her bosom.

Attendants in the hall moved about inconspicuously, offering napkins and thin polyethylene bibs which even some of the smartest-looking women there had tied around themselves to pro-tect their clothing from the greasy meats. But they looked silly, and not wanting Ernestine to look like that I resisted tying one around her neck.

The mountain of home-cooked food that was set before her was probably more delicious than any she'd been served since she'd been put away, and she ate like someone starving. Yet perhaps it was less hunger than memory that prompted her eating. The candied sweet potatoes and overcooked green beans boiled with pork rind may have tasted like the food her mother had cooked. Maybe she longed to scoop up the rice and gravy with her fingers and smear it over her face, or wished that she had her teeth so that she could bite into the crusty chicken.

"Grandma, take your time," I begged, hoping that people wouldn't think she was starving. "Can't you see there's tons to eat?" She spooned hunks of sweet potato into her mouth. Maybe that was as close as she gets to bliss.

Our table had remained empty apart from the eighty-four-year-old, who snored now and again. So we sat shrouded in Ernestine's usual silence and I wondered if I would ever get her to speak.

"Is the chicken good, Grandma?"

"Yeah, hon."

"Would you like to have some peaches for dessert?"

"Yeah."

Perhaps Ernestine sensed that the atmosphere was light-years away from her grim bedroom at the nursing home. When had she last sat down in a room filled with happy people? The faces were alight as they talked, laughed, ate, and called greetings to each other from one table to the next. The eyes which studied her could only see who she was that day, but how much had she contributed to all of us being there? How much had she struggled or given up in 1921, when the church had been conceived, which made it possible for it to become more than a dream?

Only two years after her marriage to Blair T. Hunt, he was asked to become minister of the newly formed church. He was teaching at Kortrecht and Ernestine probably had two babies by then, while she and her husband were living at 799 Mississippi Boulevard, possibly with her mother, her young stepfather, and her thirteen-year-old half-sister. But she had no idea as she sat smashing small bits of chicken between her gums that this gathering had grown out of that church which she had served as its first minister's wife.

"Grandma, take your time, and don't swallow the chicken whole—you'll choke." She had her eye on the bowl of canned peaches. I didn't understand how she had found room in her small stomach for so much.

A few feet away from us was a raised platform. On it stood the podium with a microphone, and when a male soloist took his place to the right and was joined by a pianist, I became excited. When had Ernestine last heard live music? I reached for her hand in her lap, as she stared up at the singer and burst out laughing. Not a loud, penetrating laugh, but one I wasn't sure was controllable. "Grandma, Grandma . . . do you want to taste those peaches?"

Ernestine slid back into her silence as I spooned slippery orange segments into her mouth. Was it time to leave? What if she took a laughing fit while Reverend Jackson was giving his sermon?

Everything had gone so smoothly—but perhaps the singer's voice as he raced up and down gospel scales excited something in her. My mind stumbled over the options as I held her hand, fed her peaches, and tried to decide if that laughter of hers was a passing moment or the beginning of a performance of her own. If anyone was looking at us, I didn't know, because I dared not look up. Staring from Ernestine's face to that of the old woman next to her, I held my breath.

The long rows of dining tables were arranged so that people could see and eat, and most of them had a clear view of Ernestine because we'd been seated near the podium. It was time to slip away but I didn't know how, so I started praying until the music stopped and Reverend Jackson stepped onto the podium to a rush of applause.

"Clap, Grandma. Clap," I said, hoping that she might release some energy, but maybe it was the peaches which calmed her.

Essie Mae was standing in the doorway of the nursing home when we returned. "Miss Hunt, you had a good time?"

"She's been a trouper," I said. "And like you told me the first time you spoke to me, 'Couldn't nobody ask her to be no better.' The minister introduced her to the congregation and they clapped and when he asked who present was over eighty-five, she was the only one who raised her hand."

Essie Mae said, "Miss Hunt, look at you in them slippers. You had a good time, I bet . . . did she eat good?"

"Like she was starving."

The Mississippi Boulevard Church had become one of the largest and wealthiest in Memphis. Grandfather was its founding father and had presided over services for four decades. It seemed odd that the church had no role in Ernestine's present life. But perhaps it was down to what Reverend Jackson had said when we first met—that the family didn't want it. However, as Elder Hunt's widow, she was still its first lady.

ETHYL VINSON

"OH, ERNESTINE WAS A PRETTY GIRL. Blue eyes and blond hair that hung way down her back and we were all upset when she married that old man . . . the whole neighborhood, because we were all proud of her, although I was more her sister's age," said Ethyl Vinson, after showing me pictures of her mother, who looked as white as Ernestine.

When Mrs. Vinson had answered her door, I tried to imagine her in the fifties when her pale skin made her a good catch. Her husband, a dentist, had been much darker. He had created the Cotton Makers Jubilee, an annual parade which featured a queen who reigned for a year, traveling the country as a diplomat. Among the photographs was one of these Cotton Queens with Vice-President Nixon when he served under Eisenhower.

How many homes had I entered which displayed plastic flowers and had plastic covers protecting living room furniture which no one sat on? I had returned to the culture of my childhood and strangers like Ethyl Vinson seemed familiar, though as a little dark-skinned girl I might not have been accepted by them until they found out my father had been a doctor.

How many strangers had I talked to in my searches who wanted to tell me what a wonderful man Ernestine's husband had been? Even the cleaner at my motel gave him credit for her brother's success. But Ethyl Vinson had reservations about him.

I asked, "Can you recall any reason why anybody would have been upset about their marriage?"

"No," said Mrs. Vinson, "it was more his age. He was an *old* man."

"Well, he wasn't that old. He was only thirty."

"I don't know anything about that. All I remember is that we were upset. And she could have married anybody, she was that nice and that pretty."

After lunch, Mrs. Vinson offered to show me the neighborhood where her family and Ernestine's had lived. In north Memphis, it was at Air and Lane, not far from the neighborhood in which Grandfather had lived with Harry Mae Simons during forty-seven of the years Ernestine was at Bolivar. Explaining that Ernestine had lived at what was 895 Lane with her mother, Mrs. Vinson solved the mystery related to my father's birth certificate. Surely 895 Gune Street had been 895 Lane, and perhaps the reason Ernestine and her husband were living there had something to do with his being in the First World War.

Whatever the neighborhood had looked like back then, Mrs. Vinson apologized for it that May of 1993. It was a run-down back street in a north Memphis ghetto. The fading billboard overlooking the location where Ernestine had lived with her mother and sister was the only colorful thing on the block, and pointing across from it, Mrs. Vinson said, "That was the back door of our place. This area was nice back then. Nice people lived here and it was pleasant."

It was hard to imagine. That afternoon not a soul passed the corner. The sun had scorched the grass below the freeway where houses had once been, and cans, bottles, and fast-food containers littered it. In Ernestine's day, there would have been shotgun houses, the sort which allowed you to look from the front door straight through to the back one. But those had been replaced by better houses and rougher residents.

Mrs. Vinson reminisced. "Sure I remember Ernestine, how can I forget? She was so beautiful. When my sister was born, I can remember my mother asking what should we name her. My daddy was lying on the floor and I was bouncing up and down against his leg, and I think I was the one that said, "Why don't we name her after Miss Mattie's daughter, Ernestine?" And we did. . . . We were in and out of each other's place, although I was more her sister's age. . . . It was Ernestine who taught me my alphabet. I can still see her now coming through the kitchen door." If only Mrs. Vinson could have painted my grandmother's laughter or expressed a few of her dreams. "Their mother used to sew," she said, "and my mother sewed too, so they shared patterns. But otherwise Miss Mattie would have probably kept to herself."

Mrs. Vinson got back into my car where Ernestine's faded plaid dress was folded on the backseat. Beside it was a container of baby powder which I kept on hand to powder her with.

⎯⎯☙ BEALE STREET

THE TALL SIGN AT 533 BEALE STREET SAID THE HUNT-PHELAN HOUSE. Having heard that Grandfather's father had been a slave in a house still standing on Beale, I imagined this was it and parked the car. It was late morning and no one was walking, although a few cafés at the other end of the street probably had some blues spilling out from loudspeakers to attract tourists. Beale Street is known as the home of the blues, but there was no sign of that at number 533.

The house was surrounded by a high fence trimmed with barbed wire, but it didn't look worthy of protection. Set far back from the street and obscured by a few trees, it was being renovated. Plastic sheets covered two second-story windows and, had a third not been open, I would have assumed the building was deserted. Gray paint peeled off the pillars either side of the porch. It was hard to imagine how it would have looked when it was maintained by slaves.

I wanted it to be grander and was disappointed that it looked no more exceptional than a large London house with a gravel drive.

Admittedly there was a good deal of land considering that it was in the heart of midtown Memphis, but it evoked nothing of the antebellum South for me as I peered through the hedge. But when a man driving a miniature tractor appeared in the distance, I yelled, "Sir, may I take a picture of your house? I think my great-grand-father was a slave here."

The man was from slave stock too, which is probably the reason he opened the gate. I entered smiling because, however shabby the estate, some of my forebears both black and white might have lived there, and shook the man's hand. His name was Tony and he was an employee.

"You should have come yesterday," he said. "Even the major was here, and I was wearing a tux and serving. They turning this place into a museum."

The grounds were an unlikely place to have invited guests. The hedges needed trimming, the lawn had more bare patches than grass, and no flowers grew. From where I stood, the house looked ghostly and I still wasn't certain that my great-grandfather had anything to do with it.

"Who lives here?" I asked.

I felt uncomfortable, although I might have had a right to be there snapping shots of the house as I tiptoed closer to it. Before Tony could answer I heard footsteps on the gravel walk but dared not look up. Was I being allowed to trespass? Tony made excuses for me. "Her grandfather used to work here," he said as he climbed onto his little tractor. The man he addressed was lanky and had a long stride, and guessing where he was from I would have said New Orleans, because he was an odd mix of mahogany skin and curly black hair. As old as he was, he was still handsome despite some missing teeth.

"No," I said. "I think my *great*-grandfather was a slave here. My grandfather was Blair T. Hunt." For older Memphians Grandfather's name was a calling card, and there was always the possibility that someone knew something about him that I needed to know for Ernestine's benefit.

The lanky man removed his baseball cap and scratched his head, before staring me down. Maybe he didn't believe me. He said, "Blair T. Hunt came to Mr. George's funeral." The way he said "Mr." almost sounded like "master."

"Mr. George?" Was that a Christian or a family name?

"Mr. Steve's brother," replied Tony, pointing over his shoulder to the windows on the second floor of the house. I gathered Mr. Steve was up there and wondered why anybody would choose to be in that crumbling house.

Tony said, "This here's Jesse. He's been working here way longer than me."

"Thirty-five years," Jesse said. "I been seeing after Mr. Steve all that time."

Jesse's clothes suggested that he worked inside the house and out. His boss was in his late eighties, a dying recluse who had already passed the management of the renovations on to his cousin, William B. Day. I didn't have to ask if they were white, but as Mr. Steve's last name was Phelan, I wondered about the Hunt connection. Perhaps my grandfather's attending the funeral was more than civic duty, but neither Jesse nor Tony knew much about the history of the house.

"They had slaves here, I know that. But it's Billy that can tell you all that stuff."

"Is he here?"

"No," said Tony, "but his phone number's out there on that sign." He pointed to the one by the exit.

I didn't want to waste time chasing my grandfather's history when Ernestine's was still a riddle, but I half convinced myself that my grandfather's story would shed light on hers. So later that afternoon, I rang Day and his mother answered. When she drifted off to call him, shouting "Billy, pick up the phone!" prejudice stung me like a bee. Why was I ringing a family of rednecks? I asked myself. They were descendants of people who had enslaved at least one of my forebears. But maybe we shared a bloodline, whether I liked it or not.

Thinking about my grandfather's pale skin and European features, I recalled a picture of his mother, who was born a slave and was half German Jew. For Grandfather to look as he did, his father must have had mixed blood too, but there was probably no way of tracing it.

William B. Day was so polite and interested in having me look over the house that I was guarded. He hadn't known my grandfather but said, "Some of his father's furniture is still here. I know we've got a few pieces."

My great-grandfather, Ernestine's father-in-law, was also named Blair T. Hunt. He had been a carpenter and had lived with his family at 693 Linden Avenue, which was a block away from the Hunt–Phelan house, and he had played more of a role in Ernestine's tragedy than I then realized.

Arriving for my appointed visit the following Saturday, I found the gate locked. Even the postman said that he knew of no bell so I went to the busy end of Beale Street to ring Day and was surprised to get his answering machine.

It was thanks to Jesse that I finally got in and was greeted by William B. Day at the kitchen door. In his baseball cap, tee-shirt, and jeans, he looked so like my cousin Alan, I laughed. It wasn't just his eyebrows and cheeks, it was the slant of his eyes. He was in his twenties and his handshake was friendly. But I suddenly couldn't understand why I wanted to see that house or meet anyone whose forebears had owned mine. Or begat them?

Day said, "I'm Billy. Aren't you early?"

"Our appointment was at two."

Billy's eighty-seven-year-old cousin, Stephen Phelan, was upstairs and I didn't expect to be introduced. His house indicated that he was a devout recluse and his age suggested that he wouldn't consider me an equal.

Before the Civil War when my great-grandfather had been a slave here, the Hunts had owned 2500 slaves and the property had stretched to Alabama. That's what I was thinking about when Billy showed me through to an entrance hall where a carved hatstand stood by the front door. Seven dusty hats hung on the pegs. "Your great-grandfather made that," Billy said. I wanted to be proud of the carved wooden piece, but my stomach churned and I didn't know why.

Billy guided me through the dusty rooms, where original floorboards rotten with age and furniture faded with time reminded me only of a period when people could be bought and sold.

I looked at Billy and thought about Ernestine while he showed me a marble-topped round table in the library where Ulysses S. Grant had laid out his maps to plot the Battle of Vicksburg when he occupied the house for some months during the Civil War. It had been fought so long ago, yet Ernestine, at ninety-five, represented one life still marked by slavery's legacy.

How was my family related to that house, those owners? We would never know. All that's certain is that we carry their name.

THE CENSUS REPORT

ERNESTINE HAS NO BIRTH CERTIFICATE. That's not unusual. There were no birth certificates for blacks born as she was in Roanoke, Virginia, before the turn of the century. It's unknown why Mattie had left her home in Huntsville, Alabama. Her maternal grandmother lived there, but she could have gone to Roanoke looking for work—mining in the area attracted migrant workers.

The thirteenth census of the United States, taken in 1910, gives some information about the household Ernestine was growing up in as of 15 April of that year. Although Ernestine gave her maiden name as Martin on her children's birth certificates, her family name on the census was recorded as Jacobs, as were her mother's and little sister Roberta's. Ernestine was eleven years old and attending school. She could read and write.

The family was living in rented accommodation at 546 Concord Avenue on a segregated street in Memphis. Mattie, who was thirty-two and head of the household, was a widow. One of her younger sisters, Cora Lewis, was living with them. Cora was a nineteen-year-old saleslady working in a coffee store. Mattie and Cora's father was born in Alabama, their mother in Virginia.

Mattie had given birth to only two children and both of them were living, Roberta being three and born in Tennessee. There was an eight-year difference between Ernestine and her half-sister and the same between Ernestine and her young Aunt Cora, who had missed only one week's work the previous year. She could read and write, as could Mattie, who was a seamstress working for a private family. Although one of Mattie's daughters was born in Virginia and the other in Tennessee, both their fathers were born in Alabama.

Under the heading of personal description, everyone had to state their color or race as black, white, or mulatto. Mattie, Cora, and Roberta are listed as black, Ernestine as mulatto.

They were living next door to the Robinson family, who were at 546½. Lafayette and his wife, Ada, had two daughters, Willie and Mansie, who were ten and nine and may have been playmates of Ernestine's. Since the girls and their parents are listed as mulattoes, perhaps the family was as pale as Ernestine. In fact, there was an equal number of blacks and mulattoes included on Mattie's page in the census report.

It's unlikely that many asked to whom Ernestine owed her blue eyes. The older neighbors, including Lafayette Robinson, would have been born slaves, like their parents; everyone who featured on Mattie's page had had both parents born in southern states, Alabama being the most common. With slavery being part of their families' pasts, the reality of miscegenation was as familiar to them as the social-class system related to looking European, which produced rhymes like:

> *If you're light you're right,*
> *If you're brown you'll get around,*
> *But if you're black, step back.*

Who Ernestine's father was is an unanswered question. She obviously looks as she does because conditions of slavery made the sexual abuse of slaves legal and common.

Having a blonde blue-eyed daughter is something my Uncle Wilson says that Mattie (who raised him) was proud of. Perhaps it enhanced her social status and made her feel better about her image in the mirror and her relationship to her paler siblings and parents, but it was also a reminder that she was socially their inferior.

⟶ MISS ROSA ROBINSON

ROSA ROBINSON'S BITE-SIZE HOUSE with its immaculate white porch swing was half a block from Ernestine. It was out of place on Englewood Street, and maybe Miss Robinson was too. She was a teacher who had taught under my grandfather at Booker T. Washington. Though she looked too thin to walk even with the help of her Zimmer frame, at eighty-eight she maintained her independence despite a recent operation. When I went to talk with her she wanted to recall her cruises and adventures, her journeys to Europe and South America, but I was there to talk about

Ernestine. She didn't tell me she had heard I was asking questions about my grandfather, but since I had approached others like her who had taught under him, I sensed she knew my reasons when I rang requesting an appointment.

Her living room was airy, and unlike other homes I'd been in, decorated sparingly and with a hint of style. A touch of light blue here, faint peach there against white. It showed that she had spent time out of the neighborhood, out of Memphis.

The short, dark wig she was wearing looked wrong against her pale skin. It had dropped too low on her forehead and made her face look even thinner and paler than it was. She had small teeth and large gums, but probably she had once been handsome by any standards.

"I knew your grandmother. Her sister Roberta and I played with cut-out dolls and skated together. We were probably too big for playing with dolls, but we did. I can see us now on the steps of Miss Jacobs's house." By Miss Jacobs, she was referring to Ernestine's mother, Mattie. Walter Jacobs was her husband and Roberta's father. Miss Robinson went on. "She was a lovely woman, Miss Jacobs. Not that I knew her to speak to, but I used to play with Roberta. And then when my sister Johnny married, Ernestine's little boy was the ring bearer at the wedding." She was talking about my father, who must have been three, because her sister married in 1922.

Miss Robinson couldn't recall if Ernestine had attended the wedding, but it seemed unlikely that she would have allowed her three-year-old to be part of the ceremony without being there herself.

Grandfather had been principal at the high school where she taught. Couldn't she remember the wife of a man that she worked with most of her life?

"Ernestine was very beautiful. I remember that."

It seemed peculiar that all of black Memphis seemed to have been impressed by Grandfather but didn't gossip about his private life.

"Did anyone know that he had a wife up at Bolivar?" I asked.

Miss Robinson's slow delivery didn't alter after my implied accusation, but she drew her fleecy pink robe tighter about her and shifted in her chair.

"*I* knew she was there," she said, as if she didn't mind telling me but didn't want it repeated. "In fact, I saw her there. Some of my club members would go out and visit the patients and take little things and put on shows. And once I asked to see your grandmother. But she didn't seem to know me, and when I went in, she was lying on the bed. . . . It didn't look like Ernestine. She was just lying on the bed."

"Was she in a room by herself?"

Miss Robinson nodded and looked away as though trying to recall the day. "And what was strange," she said, as if my grandmother's image had just come into focus, "is that her hair was black. You see . . . well, Ernestine had always had blond hair. Blond hair and blue eyes."

Others had said that Ernestine had blond hair. It was a fact that I was less conscious of when I had gone to Bolivar to inspect my grandmother's medical records. But sitting there in Miss Robinson's pristine living room, I recalled seeing a small ID photo of Ernestine in which her hair looked extremely dark. Perhaps the institution's hairdresser had been experimenting on her, but the way Miss Robinson had related the fact was disturbingly mysterious.

It was just one more question which Ernestine couldn't answer.

ALZORA HASTE AGAIN

THE INTENSIVE CARE UNIT OF BAPTIST MEMORIAL HOSPITAL wasn't the place to ask Alzora Haste what she remembered about

Ernestine and Grandfather. I was visiting because Dora Todd had phoned to say Alzora had been rushed there.

I arrived with flowers although Miss Todd had warned me that they weren't allowed. She and I sat side by side in the waiting room, watching the clock, anxious for the visiting hour to begin. She eyed the collection of Emily Dickinson poetry and said, "Alzora's not going to be able to read."

Maybe holding the book would be enough for an old woman dying. I remembered her saying, "The world loves the wrong things" and was still confused about why she had mentioned the pedigree and the cur.

She was frailer than I expected. Standing at her bedside with Dora Todd behind me, I stroked the polar-white hair at Alzora's temple and wanted to say, You're not so black. You should see the Africans who sell belts and sunglasses outside the Eiffel Tower. But instead I said, "Miss Haste, I'm Blair T. Hunt's granddaughter. I phoned you. Remember?"

"Why did you bring me here!" she yelped. "And why is your hair all over your eyes? Pull it back so I can see your face!"

Her own was round, the cheekbones glacial, and her black eyes were clouded with age. Plastic tubes inserted in her nostrils made it impossible to imagine what this wrinkled spinster once looked like when she had been a high-steppin' woman. I wound my hair into a knot.

"That's better," she said, raising her hand as if to give a benediction.

I showed her the flowers and the book.

"Oh, read me something. I like Emily Dickinson."

"Do you have a favorite?"

Her voice was honey, sweet, and thick enough to scoop with a spoon. In her day she had been a manipulator. "My precious, any one will be fine. But *why* did you bring me to this awful place?"

The hospital was modern, immaculately clean, and her cubicle in the intensive care unit was identical to the others on this ward where the lights were dim and all the visitors spoke in whispers.

Dora Todd had been there the day before and, planning to return the following day, she let me stand closer to the bed. I touched Alzora's hand. Hands that had done work? Or had she come into the world with sturdy fingers and a broad palm? Though she looked very weak, her grip was strong and as I read some poetry to her, she suddenly started to sing, "Are you from heaven. . . ?"

Watching her lips to anticipate the words, I sang along. It was easy to love and hate the South which had shaped her. I thought about her childhood, thought about the extra effort it took her to hold her head up because she had been dark with a flat nose.

 # LEAVING

"DON'T YOU LOOK BEAUTIFUL, GRANDMA!"

Ernestine stared hard at her image in the mirror, as if seeing her wrinkled face for the first time. Did she understand that she had aged? With lipstick and a touch of rouge and her hair styled, she looked better than usual.

"The corner of your eye is bloodshot," I said, in case she wondered why it was red, "but you still look wonderful."

I stood behind her in the dingy overhead light of the nursing home bathroom while she angled her face in the mirror, pursing her lips and squinting. Was she trying to recall her youthful face, or did she not understand why she was a mask of wrinkles?

Ernestine turned from the mirror and laughed before turning back to grab her cheek and twist it viciously.

"Oh, no, Grandma. Don't! You'll hurt yourself!" I pulled her hand away and rubbed her cheek. "You mustn't hurt yourself."

Her brief cackle cleared the air after I had spoiled her fun and she looked back into the glass with a knowingness that was eerie. I wasn't ashamed of her history of so-called lunacy but at times I couldn't believe in it. I wanted to recover that pretty young girl in the graduation photograph. To allow Ernestine to see herself in a flattering light, in a mirror where shadows didn't hood her eyes or dull her complexion, seemed important.

It was Memorial Day, the day before my departure for Boston, and I had already begun trying to distance myself from her, saving my hugs and doing nothing to draw her any closer to me. It was as if this old woman had become my child. I knew she wouldn't understand why I was leaving her behind.

Essie Mae had said again, "After that first time you come to Memphis, Miss Hunt used to stand by that door just looking and looking. And I'd say, "She looking for that little ol' red car. Looking for her granddaughter." She would just be looking and looking."

"But Essie Mae, how can I explain to her that I live too far away to take her with me?"

"Don't try."

"But she'll think I've deserted her. She'll think—"

Essie Mae shook her head. Sometimes I believed that she saw my grandmother as a sweet but empty shell.

"Essie Mae, now don't forget how she sat on the edge of her bed a few days ago and she repeated the Twenty-third Psalm. I told you she could and you didn't believe it until you heard it with your own ears."

Ernestine was sitting in the rocking chair I'd bought her. Her legs were crossed and her hands though clasped were jerking slightly. "Come on, Grandma," I called to her. We were going to Walgreen's, where I planned to buy some sodas and cakes and other treats so that the residents could have a Memorial Day party.

But despite the fancy napkins and paper plates and cups, nobody knew *how* to have a party. The card table was set out in the mid-

During the Civil War Memphis fell early into the hands of the Union Army. The Hunt Phelan House was occupied by Union soldiers. Ulysses S. Grant was based there when he developed his strategy for the victory at Vicksburg.

(*Above*) The Hunt Phelan House photographed in 1993 before its restoration.

(*Right*) Emma Shouse, mother of my grandfather. She was born a slave in Kentucky and upon her marriage to Blair Hunt Sr., who had been a slave at Hunt Phelan House, they were given a home on Linden Street as a wedding gift.

(*Above*) Ernestine and I visited O'Ferrell and Anne Nelson who had been responsible for finding her.

(*Left*) Ernestine being embraced by Carlotta Watson who had been in her graduating class at Ol'Kortrech High School.

The administration building at Western State Hospital.

Couches repaired with electrical tape; an old TV with poor reception; the sitting room at the home was not a welcoming place.

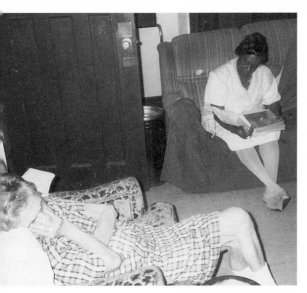

(*Left*) While Lula Mae flips through the family album I gave Ernestine in 1991, my grandmother sleeps in the secondhand easy chair I bought from a garage sale in June 1993.

(*Below*) Having groomed my grandmother for an outing to visit a nursery school...Ernestine with Essie Mae Dukes, the first person I spoke to who knew my grandmother well.

My daughter, Karis Hunt Jagger, who drove from New Haven to see
Ernestine after completing her junior year at Yale in 1991.

dle of the room and the atmosphere was as flat as any ordinary lunchtime. It was like throwing a party for children who had never been to one. All the residents were quiet and maybe a little uncertain as they received their party rations.

I was due to go to Elmwood Cemetery with Dora Todd to visit my grandfather's grave, but I had decided against taking Ernestine, because I still wasn't certain that she understood that her husband was dead. That morning I'd been to the florist to buy flowers to place at his headstone. I had planned to buy fresh ones, but the florist insisted that plastic was the norm, recommending some artificial carnations.

It disturbed me that my grandmother wasn't to be buried with Grandfather. Perhaps that was for Harry Mae's benefit, though I hadn't asked her.

Grandfather's headstone was gray and his name was carved above that of his parents. Dora Todd stood aside while I placed the white plastic roses before it. I thought about what would happen when Ernestine died. O'Ferrell Nelson regularly asked about this and I'd huff, "It's more important that I make the effort to see her while she's living. I can't afford to come to Memphis when she dies." But how she was to be buried mattered more to me than I admitted.

Ernestine seemed groggy later that evening when I returned to the nursing home. Essie Mae had changed shifts with Lula Mae, who was sitting on the sofa watching TV.

"Has my grandmother had her supper?" I asked.

"They won't need supper tonight. They already had something." Lula Mae was talking about the few party treats.

"All they had was some cake and potato chips and cookies. Don't tell me they're going to miss supper because of that!"

Ernestine was unsure on her feet and stumbled as I guided her out to the car. Fortunately when we got to O'Ferrell and Anne's they had beef and chicken left over from their afternoon barbecue. We crumbled it up so that Ernestine could chew it.

I knew she received substandard care, despite Essie Mae's goodwill, and nothing I said would change it. In fact, I was sure any complaints would jeopardize the way my grandmother was treated.

When I left her back at the home she was wearing a flannel nightgown I'd bought her at Schwab's and had been keeping in the car. The brown floral quilt and pillows I'd bought her were on her bed. I tried to keep my distance, knowing that the following morning I would have to say my goodbyes, and I didn't want to cry as I had in 1991.

Once Essie Mae had said, "One of these days, you gon' be sitting over there in France and look up, and me and Miss Hunt's gon' be coming through your front door." I wanted to believe it.

5

Boston

MASSACHUSETTS

AFTER TWENTY DAYS IN MEMPHIS I arrived in Boston on the first of June 1993 and rang my Uncle Wilson from a public phone on Route 1. I knew he and Dorothea would find it strange that I had chosen a hotel in Saugus when they had a guest room.

"Saugus!" said Dorothea. "Oh, my, why stay so far north? Well, if you change your mind, you know there's a bed here for you."

Next I rang my cousin Alan, whose phone call to me in France had begun my search for our grandmother. He had once told me that Ernestine had first been committed to an asylum near Boston, and that was why I had come north.

The traffic on Route 1 made it difficult to hear, but I couldn't mistake the lack of interest in his voice when I spoke about Ernestine. He hadn't yet seen her and I wanted him to explain why.

"Let's meet," I said. "I'm only here for a week, and I have a lot to do, because Ernestine's records at Bolivar show nothing about her being sent there from a Massachusetts asylum."

"Well, she was," said Alan. "My father's always said that she was committed here and the authorities sent her back to Tennessee when they found out she had a husband there."

Facts and fiction. Myths and lies. Had my three weeks in Memphis drawn me closer to understanding what had happened to Ernestine? And what did Boston have to help me color in great missing scenes of her history? If it was true that she had first been committed in Massachusetts, why did her records from Western State omit this information?

—🙢 More His Than Mine

"THERE WAS NO INDICATION FROM HER MEDICAL records at Bolivar that she'd been committed to any other asylum," I told Wilson. Dorothea and Wilson Jr. were sitting with us at the kitchen table.

"But I remember going to see her at Foxboro." He was adamant.

"Foxboro?"

"The state asylum here in Massachusetts. My grandmother took us there to see her more than once. We would go on Sundays."

I tried to picture Ernestine as her son Wilson sat opposite me. The similarities between them were obvious: the same strong, healthy hair, the large but perfectly formed ears. But his eyes were dark and hadn't seen his mother since boyhood. Visiting her at Bolivar must have been all the more disturbing when he saw her toothless for the first time. The shape of her face would have changed dramatically: cheeks sunken, lips shriveled, chin prominent. She must have looked grotesque compared to the beautiful mother he would have remembered.

As a psychotherapist, Wilson listened to other people's problems. But who listened to his? I wondered, as we sat in his Brookline home not far from where John F. Kennedy had spent his boyhood. It was a prosperous district and my uncle's home displayed moderate good taste. The cane-back suite in his living room had belonged to Mattie when she lived at 3 Harold Park, where she raised Ernestine's sons. And although I couldn't remember his bedroom, I doubted that he could have slept in the conditions his mother currently endured.

We sat in his white kitchen with its glistening copper ornaments on one wall. Would Ernestine ever sit there? Her son had no intention of visiting her, and he hardly responded to descriptions of things she had said or done while I had been with her in the previous weeks. He listened to the story of Ernestine and of my finding her sons' birth certificates. I kept referring to her as "your mother," and I felt as if I'd been nosing into his business when I nervously produced the three certificates.

Passing him his own, I mumbled, "I've also got my father's and Ernest's if you'd like to see them. A doctor named Craigen delivered all of you."

I added that just to say something, because the kitchen was so quiet while he finished his bowl of salad. Like his mother, he has an air of still water about him, and when he suddenly spoke, his voice barely disturbed the calm of that room.

It must have been irritating to have a niece he hardly knew dipping into matters that he probably felt she had nothing to do with. But if he was annoyed that I was prying, he didn't say so, and his quiet good manners were more difficult to read than even those of a tight-lipped Englishman. His eyes told me nothing as he accepted his birth certificate and I tried to make conversation about that half sheet of paper embossed with Tennessee's seal.

"I was lucky to get it," I recalled, "because you're only allowed to apply for your own birth certificate. But your mother was with me, so I claimed they were for some research I was doing about her life."

Wilson's plump fingers adjusted his glasses and he raised his thick white eyebrows to peruse the documents. Only thirty hours earlier I been standing with Ernestine in her gloomy bedroom. She had that odd, musty smell which I had begun to think was the

stench of melancholy. It wasn't overpowering but it lingered like
the stalest perfume.

Today Ernestine was old but no longer grotesque, and if he
remembered her as she was an inmate at Bolivar, I wanted him to
see that his mother was no longer that mental patient. Yet the conditions of her life now were equally sad.

My uncle was the kind of man who wouldn't allow his wife to
do dishes if she cooked. He helped his grandchildren with their
homework and never raised his hand or his voice against anyone.
It was strange that his mother remained abandoned, though he was
the epitome of the family man.

I told him I planned to drive to Foxboro the following day and
took it as a positive sign when he brought out a map to plot my
route. Maybe it was merely the helpful gesture of a polite host, but
I sensed it was more. Maybe he wanted me to find out what had
really happened to Ernestine; perhaps he had his own doubts that
her long years in an asylum ward had been necessary.

 WILL

SEVEN WAS EARLY FOR DINNER, so when the waitress showed us
to a table, my cousin Will and I seemed to be the first guests in
the restaurant. He'd agreed we could meet as soon as he finished
work, but maybe he was already regretting it, because he released
a deep sigh after sliding on to the bench seat. The shades in the
room had been drawn and dimmed carriage lights on the walls
created an evening atmosphere, although it was still bright out-

side on the Brookline streets clogged with rush-hour traffic.

Will knew we were there to talk about Ernestine, because although his brother Alan and I had spoken about her, Will, the elder, had avoided the issue. But she was his grandmother too; it could have been thanks to her that he had such attractive gray-green eyes. They were avoiding mine as he glanced over the menu and said, "I don't think it's as easy for him as he makes it look." Obviously he was talking about his father. "He keeps a lot to himself. And it's not just Ernestine. There was Blair's suicide and Ernest's murder . . . and their childhood."

I'd almost forgotten about Ernest, the youngest of Ernestine's sons, who had never moved from the apartment in Roxbury where Mattie had raised the three boys. Ernest, a bachelor lawyer, was in that Roxbury apartment in Boston's ghetto when he was strangled in August 1970. Wilson, then based in upstate New York, had had to identify the body, which had not been found for some days after the murder; it was badly decomposed, and it was Wilson rather than the police who had noticed something tied around his brother's neck.

Will had good reason to be concerned about his father's well-being. But was it good enough to justify abandoning Ernestine?

The waitress brought the wine but it wasn't easy to think of a lighthearted toast, so we drank to our children, Will's two, Alan's son, and my daughter. Maybe it was for them that I wanted to prove that Ernestine did not suffer from genetic illness. I asked Will about Mattie, whom he had known during his early childhood.

"Suppose her identity problems were at the bottom of her daughter's illness. Mattie, being the only dark child among her thirteen brothers and sisters, might have encountered abuse both within the family and without. She would have been reminded from the cradle that she was not as good as her fairer brothers and sisters. And if she resented it, giving birth to a blond blue-eyed daughter must have increased her problems."

"But my father says that Mattie was proud of having a blond blue-eyed child."

"But why was that a thing to be proud of, and how often was she accused of giving birth to a white man's baby, when that would have been seen as scandalous at that time?"

If Mattie had been teased, jeered at, and set apart because of her skin color, it wouldn't have helped her to understand why she was so much darker than the rest of her family if her mother's reported explanation for it was "a buzzard laid you and the sun hatched you." In fact that would have increased Mattie's childhood confusion and made her feel deserving of contempt. But even had someone been able to explain that she was a genetic throwback, looking more like her African forebears than her European ones, Mattie might have continued to envy her fairer family, given the times she lived through.

Or perhaps Ernestine resented having a dark-skinned mother?

Will sipped his glass of white wine as people trickled into the restaurant, their whispers blending with the background music. He had recently turned fifty and had still not lived for as many years as our grandmother had been institutionalized. Maybe he saw abandoning her as a way of protecting himself. Otherwise, what was his excuse for not seeing her?

Even in the somber light, Will's complexion glowed. He was a shade of pale pine which accentuated his graying hair and pallid eyes. Did he wonder why I was dark brown or did he assume that I was a throwback like my great-grandmother Mattie?

Will said, "The thing I remember best about her was her cane and her parrot and the fact that it seemed as if her daughter was afraid of her, cowed and afraid to speak up for herself."

The only picture I'd ever seen of Mattie was the one which I'd shown Ernestine to which she made no response.

_⌒⊙ TITICUT FOLLIES

A DOCUMENTARY FILMMAKER NAMED Frederick Wiseman who
was based in Cambridge near Harvard loaned me his office copy
of a documentary called *Titicut Follies,* which he'd shot in a
Massachusetts mental institution in the sixties. The state government had banned it from being televised for twenty-five years, so
it had only recently been shown.

I was eager to see it because people in Memphis and Boston had
recommended it, though none so highly as Sheila LaForge, who
had been introduced to me by film director and actress Mai
Zetterling. Although I'd met Sheila in London before leaving for
Memphis she'd told me that I not only had to see Wiseman's film
but I also had to see Concord, the town where she lived in
Massachusetts. It seemed unlikely then that I would find time to
visit her, but as it turned out, she was the only person who offered
to let me use her VCR to see the documentary. It's not recommended viewing for 9 A.M. on a Saturday morning, but it was
important for me to see it.

Despite having visited the institution at Bolivar, I felt that I
knew nothing about daily life for patients in asylums. Books I'd
read about it weren't graphic and even Erving Goffman's definitive
study *Asylums* didn't expose me as much as *Titicut Follies* to the
harrowing environment of a mental hospital.

Wiseman's film was shot in a men's wing during a period when
the hospital staff were preparing and performing their Christmas
show for the patients.

While I sat in the orderly comfort of Sheila's living room
watching the film, it was impossible not to relate it to my grandmother, especially since I'd heard and read that Bolivar was not
well equipped, well run, or properly staffed to treat its excess pop-
ulation. That the footage was in black and white may have added
to its bleakness, but I was sure that a television viewing didn't con-

vey the harshness of the actual environment, and when patients shouted or cried out, I could reduce the sound on the TV.

Patients were degraded in subtle ways. To see one stripped naked in a grimly bare cell while he was provoked by members of the staff may not seem a torture, but I felt for that man as he was being teased and taunted. It indicated the total power which the orderlies had over the patients. Recalling Bolivar, I thought of how many years Ernestine had spent in that place and how she must have encountered more than one unreasonable orderly in her time.

I hadn't considered how stressful upon one another the personalities of patients could be until I watched Wiseman's footage of the men in their recreation yard acting out their fantasies and neuroses in a confined space. To hear patients ranting, to see them rocking and pacing, angry or intimidated, while grouped together was more disturbing than anything that Hollywood has tried to manufacture in films. *One Flew Over the Cuckoo's Nest* couldn't begin to capture the shocking circumstances which Wiseman's documentary revealed. For instance, to see one man being held down to be force-fed by a tube thrust down his throat may have been to see him murdered. His final appearance in the film was as a corpse in the hospital morgue.

One young patient who had been transferred to the institution from prison begged to be returned to prison again, because he said that the environment was causing him so much emotional distress. He appealed not only to the psychiatrist but to a release board, saying that to be around so many disturbed people left him feeling tormented. He seemed more rational than the people who were in charge of him but his request to be returned to prison was denied. So was his appeal to have his medication reduced; the appeal board called for an increase in his tranquilizers.

Sheila had seen the film before, and I don't know how she had the stomach to watch it again; sometimes I had to turn away from the screen. What was as disturbing as watching the men herded together in a debilitating environment was seeing staff who

seemed emotionally ill equipped to cope with patients with psychological problems.

A prison for the insane is what *Titicut Follies* depicted, and all I
could think about while I watched it was Ernestine, small, defenseless, and abandoned at Bolivar for most of her life.

⟋⟋Ꭹ FOXBORO

DRIVING THROUGH THE ENTRANCE I BECAME EXCITED. This was
the place where Ernestine's hospitalization began and I hoped that
here the mystery of why she was put away would be clarified. It
was 6:50 A.M. and the only sign of life was a night-light shining
over a doorway. There were no cars in the parking lot and my heart
sank as I drove from one building to the next. Long sun-scorched
grass and boarded-up windows told me the place had been closed
down but I refused to believe that I had driven all that way for
nothing.

The institution was a series of industrial-looking brick buildings
and a slab over the only one with a Victorian-styled entrance said
FOXBORO STATE HOSPITAL. Some distance away were some wood-
frame houses, apparently derelict, which had probably been staff
quarters or administration residences. Surrounded by the abandoned buildings I felt wary and anxious and wondered how
Ernestine must have felt being left here in the twenties.

As I cruised slowly around the back of the three-story buildings,
I saw a scruffy Alsatian scratching himself beside what might have
been a work shed. As an old van was parked beside it, I rolled

down my window and yelled, "Anybody home?" When an elderly man appeared from behind the shed door, I hoped I wasn't putting myself at risk. He wore a cap and a blue maintenance uniform and as he sauntered over to my car I could see *Art* stitched in red on his breast pocket. He didn't return my smile and I suddenly remembered what color I was. How must I have looked to him sitting in my shiny red rented car? Did he see the fear suddenly cloud my expression? I asked myself, What the hell are you doing alone in this godforsaken place? but what came out of my mouth was, "Good morning, sir, my grandmother was admitted here back in the twenties, I think, and I'm looking for anybody who can tell me something about the place."

He had big, beefy hands like some of the farmers in my village. His eyes studied mine and I kept smiling. Whatever he was thinking, he said, "They closed this place down in '75. Decided to go into this de-institutionalization program. But up until then, it was a fully fledged operating mental institution. They said these places were warehouses, weren't humane, and all this stuff and they decided to put people out in smaller community-based units, like in nursing homes and places like that . . . on October thirtieth all the patients were outa here, and they just locked the doors an' walked away. And then in '77 they reopened it as a place for retarded citizens, because Wrentham State School, which is who we work for now, had a court decree where they had to upgrade the whole institution. So what they did, these buildings were in pretty good condition back then, so we reopened some of them and put the place back operating again.

"So they brought the clients here and we set the kitchen up and they stayed 'til '81–82. Then they went back to Wrentham and we kept the Dexter building opened. You know, that new building across the street. We had retarded citizens in there until just a month or so ago."

For somebody dressed like a maintenance man, he had a comprehensive knowledge of the hospital's history, and I was relieved that he knew where the old records would have been put.

"All the old records went outa here. But the BMH has to keep them, so they put them over at Grafton; now they're probably keepin' them in Boston."

Art explained that he'd worked at Foxboro for forty years. "I had about every job in the place. Started as a ward attendant."

I asked what Foxboro had been like when he started.

"It wasn't a nice place. Forty years ago it was the smallest institution in the state and we had fourteen hundred patients here. Don't forget—you didn't have Thorazine, you didn't have Mellaril, you didn't have any of these drugs they use today. I mean, this was a tough place to work."

"Why?"

"Because these people weren't . . . how can I put it gracefully? They were insane! I mean, there were people here who would kill you at the drop of a hat."

"So how did you cope? Weren't you young?"

"I was. I was eighteen years old, just outa high school. You watched how the old-timers handled it and then you fell into it."

"Were you afraid?" I asked. But I was also thinking about Ernestine and what chance she had of getting well when some of her caregivers were only high school graduates, eighteen with no life experience and as frightened of the patients as the patients might have been of them or each other.

"Yeah, I was afraid! Back then I was. But you get over it."

I wondered if, like Bolivar, Foxboro was the main employer in the small town.

"Oh, yeah. Back then you worked here or you worked at the Foxboro Company. They make gauges and measuring devices and that for industries. Steam heaters."

While we talked the dog sat scratching beside the shed and two scraggly cats appeared from out of nowhere. They stared in our direction and seemed to be examining Art and me as we talked under a clear blue sky. I had stepped out of the car the moment Art ceased to seem forbidding. He had eyes as blue as the sky and a manner as open as the father in the TV series *The Waltons*. I pre-

tended not to notice that as we talked a strange-looking man leaning on one crutch had emerged from the shed. It was difficult at a
distance to gauge his age, because his body told me he was old, but
he was wearing jeans, a tee-shirt, and a baseball cap which even
from a distance couldn't hide the fact that he had no hair.

It was hard to believe that I was in Massachusetts. The derelict
buildings spoke of the North, but there was something midwest-
ern about the look of the shed and the animals and the old man
with his single crutch.

I wanted the old man to join us, but Art said, "Oh, he won't talk
to you. He won't talk to nobody."

Had the man heard him? Is that why he hobbled toward us and
started talking nonstop? But the picture he painted of Foxboro was
a rest home where patients picnicked and danced.

"My grandmother lived up the street, and I had an uncle who
was down here, was an alcoholic. See, this place was a home for
inebriates—they put alcoholics in here. My Uncle John, my grandmother's brother, was here. He froze to death down here, working
outside in the wintertime. They had a few people here that they
couldn't control. Then it got to be, any town with anybody that
they couldn't control, they'd bring 'em down here. Sign 'em in.
And that's where they stayed. And they were *happy* here. Oh, they
had everything here! They had dances, they had parties, they had
bus trips. Christmas, Thanksgiving, they'd put on big feeds! They
used to take 'em to the beach."

"Did most of them have visitors?"

"No, most of them did not. In the summertime, if somebody
came to visit, a big crowd would gather around them."

"You make it sound like a lot of fun," I said, taking in his tee-
shirt, which depicted two characters dancing and had SEX printed
in boldface.

Art interrupted meekly. "It wasn't all fun and games here. It's like
thinkin' back to the army. You only remember the good times."
Obviously he didn't like to disagree with his friend, but each time
the man with the crutch lunged into another example of how

wonderful things had been for the patients, Art's eyes searched the ground. Finally he interrupted to say softly, "There were bad times. People got hurt here. Johnny Moynihan had his right eye knocked out."

"Some guy got killed here!" Art's friend suddenly recalled.

"Employees got hurt here," Art said, as he remembered back to a time when the only requirement for working on the wards was that you be eighteen.

But Art's friend disagreed. He remembered when they had employed sixteen- and seventeen-year-olds.

Art didn't want to be dour. "I'll tell you one thing about this place. It was a self-sustaining city. We could generate our own electricity. We bought water off the town, but we had our own farm, raised our own vegetables."

I wanted to understand why both Bolivar and Foxboro had operated in this way.

"For one thing, it gave the patients something to do. Get 'em off the wards. Get 'em out hoeing potatoes . . . and they loved doing it, they loved working on the farm."

Art's friend interrupted. "The patients ran the place. What they had is people that supervised patients, and the patients did the work. We even had patients run machinery. They used to run lawn mowers, sewing machines, and up in the industrial shop they used to repair. Make tables. Chairs. And they run the orchards. . . . We had apples, peaches, strawberries."

He didn't say whether the work was voluntary or obligatory or whether the patients received proper wages.

"When I started working here," said Art, "the only thing they bought as far as staples was flour 'n' sugar."

"Were you happy working here?" I asked the one with the crutch.

"Back then you weren't protected like you are today. We didn't have unions. If they didn't like you, they fired you."

Neither man had been employed at Foxboro during the time when Ernestine had been there and they couldn't agree on which buildings had existed in the twenties, although they did agree about which ward had housed the violent patients.

"It was nothing for them to bust out a window and take a piece of glass and cut themselves," said Art's friend.

"And if a woman was violent?" I asked.

"They'd put a restraint on her. Most of the patients were abusive to themselves."

Art said, "When we first came here we had two guys, I can't think of their names, and all they did was work eight hours a day, forty hours a week, putting windows in."

Mesh over the windows seemed the obvious solution, I thought, but he said, "They had wire glass and they found out with the wire glass, they got cut worse. They'd put their fists right through the wire glass."

TAUNTON

MRS. WILSON RETURNED FROM THE FILE CABINET shaking her head and fingering her beads. "If she hasn't got a file card, she was never here. And I looked under Ernestine Hunt, Martin, and Nevels, and there's nothing."

Who to believe? Mrs. Wilson, who said Ernestine had never been at Foxboro; or my uncle, who sat across from me at his dinner table that evening and said, "My mother was there. . . . I can remember visiting her once and she was wearing a coat and the wind was blowing her hair."

Was I asking him to recall memories he needed to forget or

didn't want to speak about in front of Dorothea and Wilson Jr., who were present?

That morning at Foxboro, Art and his friend had told me that someone among the small staff in the administration building might know where the old hospital records were stored. The offices in Foxboro State Hospital were outdated and a Ghanaian social worker sitting behind a big desk did all she could by telephone to inquire at various hospitals, asking if they warehoused old Foxboro records.

"My grandmother's name is Ernestine Hunt but perhaps she was registered under another name," I told her. "Martin or Jacobs had been her maiden name. The family says she became ill in Massachusetts, was hospitalized here, but when the authorities discovered that she had a husband in Tennessee, she was sent to the state hospital there."

Thirty-five miles from Foxboro was Taunton State Hospital, which I was told held the Foxboro records and, heading there without an appointment, I knew there was a possibility I wouldn't be allowed on the grounds.

Ernestine had a name, an address, and a family. But where was her history? Would her mother have been able to explain why Ernestine, "an ideal woman," a "brilliant" student, would spend her life in asylums? And could her father's history have shed light upon Ernestine's?

I drove to Taunton with images of my grandmother playing in my mind. I could see her in her paltry red plaid dress standing in her bedroom during my visit in '91. I'd bought her a rocking chair and she clapped her hands when she saw me and yelled, "Hi!" Moments like these bound me to her.

Taunton was a large town and the mental hospital wasn't its main employer, so no one I asked could direct me to it. But it wasn't hard to find though it was hidden behind a high stone wall like the one I'd imagined would have surrounded Bolivar.

It was nearly three o'clock by the time I was offered a seat in

Mrs. Wilson's office; she was in charge of medical records. My experience at Bolivar made me hopeful as I reeled off my grandmother's particulars, and while I was uncertain how much information I could get from her Foxboro records, I didn't expect Mrs. Wilson to tell me Ernestine had never been a Foxboro patient. She said, "Have you tried Liederman in Boston?"

"Are you positive she wasn't at Foxboro?"

"Every patient ever admitted has a file card. She hasn't."

⎯⎯⎯ WITCHCRAFT

I HAD BEGUN TO FEEL LIKE A DISPLACED PERSON and although my hotel room in Saugus was an improvement over my room in the Econo Lodge, I missed the friends I'd made in Memphis, so I called O'Ferrell two mornings in a row.

"Have you seen your uncle?" he asked.

"Yep."

"And?"

"And what?" I didn't want anybody to know everything, and as much as I loved O'Ferrell, I wasn't sure to whom he might gossip. I don't know why I cared, but I did. And I didn't want him to know my plans: I was going to Salem, scene of the infamous witch trials of 1692, because I had a feeling that old attitudes toward mental illness were left over from our fears of demonic possession.

I drove there with a sense of purpose and rushed into the Essex Institute with a pen and pad as though that historical tragedy could throw some light on my grandmother's life. I was searching for any reason why my religious grandfather might have abandoned Ernestine. I didn't want to believe that she suffered from incurable insanity, so I yanked and pulled at straws. And perhaps I did come across something which clarified the purpose of my search for her past. A tour guide who gave me an hour of his time told me to buy a book by Chadwick Hansen called *Witchcraft at Salem.* It begins: "The purpose of this book is to try to set straight the record of the witchcraft phenomena at Salem, Massachusetts, in the year 1692, about which much has been written and much misunderstood. . . . It seemed serious reconsideration of them was in order."

That was how I felt about Ernestine. A serious reconsideration of her history was in order, a setting straight of the record. Relying on repeated gossip or inadequate, unschooled attitudes wasn't good enough. But I had nothing to support my feelings, except the fact that she was neither violent as reported nor incapable of recognizing anyone.

CONCORD

AT DAWN THAT SATURDAY, I DROVE THIRTY-ODD MILES northwest of Boston to Concord, a small town famous for its role in the American Revolution. After I saw Sheila, she had insisted that I look around and had said, "If you haven't been here before, it's a must-see. The Minutemen were here and Paul Revere. So were Ralph Waldo Emerson and Thoreau."

By midday a few groups of tourists were milling about the town square. One lot was German, another was Danish. They stood gazing up at the gleaming courthouse. Like most of the houses in Concord, it had been built of wood in the eighteenth century and enhanced the feeling that the community which was solid and "olde New England," took its role in history to heart.

Patriotism, rooted in Concord, was the source of its tourist industry. The American flag was stationed outside several houses as well as businesses lining the main streets where tended front gardens and immaculate sidewalks made the community seem as self-conscious as a Disney theme park.

As I stood in the center of town, clusters of tourists passed with their heads in colorful guidebooks like the one Sheila had given me. The American history which it painted extolled the courage and ingenuity of the early settlers and even corrected a few long-standing myths, so that in Concord I discovered that Paul Revere never completed his ride there to announce that the British were coming. Not only had this small village supported the Minutemen and their arsenal during the Revolution, but by the nineteenth century it was home to several of America's foremost transcendental philosophers including Emerson, Thoreau, and Bronson Alcott. Nineteenth-century novelists Louisa May Alcott, renowned for *Little Women,* and Nathaniel Hawthorne, who scandalized society with *The Scarlet Letter,* also made Concord their base. But it was Henry David Thoreau who immortalized the local pond and surrounding wood with *Walden,* the study of his reclusive experiment. A century later, his essay "On the Duty of Civil Disobedience" inspired Mohandas Gandhi and Dr. Martin Luther King. Thoreau had written it after he went to jail for refusing to pay taxes, which he said supported the war with Mexico and indirectly supported slavery. Understandably, the town was proud of its liberal forebears and could even boast that it had been a station of the underground railroad, a chain of hideaways from the South to the North which sheltered slaves on the road to freedom.

Nonetheless, standing opposite the courthouse I saw no other blacks in town. I probably looked less like I belonged than the German and Danish tourists, who hadn't had Paul Revere's heroism drummed into them as children. Discovering that he had never ridden into Concord to alert the Minutemen meant nothing to them, but it reminded me that so much of what I'd been taught as history was America's sophisticated public relations job to attract immigrants. Nobody explained that its high ideals of freedom and democracy were financed by generations of hostages providing free labor. Ironically, it was the marriage of freedom and slavery that made America rich. Not that I expected Concord's guidebook to mention it; the community which had been a force in the growth of Unitarianism may only have felt comfortable dispelling *small* myths.

I was suddenly angry with myself for being there. What did Concord have to do with Ernestine apart from its link with the Unitarian Church that was indirectly responsible for my finding her? I certainly couldn't expect the guidebooks to reveal that some of the great men in the community may have sordidly exploited slave women, thereby producing children whom they not only disclaimed but abandoned.

It's unlikely that Ernestine ever looked in the mirror and equated her blue eyes and blond hair with raped slaves, penetrated by men who worked them like animals but also reproduced through them, just as it's hard to look in a mirror and understand that the features which were considered the most sought after, like fair skin, smooth hair, and pale eyes, are the features passed to us through men who raped our mothers.

Buried in Concord Cemetery is an African slave named John Jack who died in March 1773, age sixty. Tourists take rubbings of his gravestone, which says among other things, "Tho he lived in a land of liberty, he lived a slave. . . . Death the grand tyrant gave him his final emancipation and set him on a footing with kings." America's war for independence hadn't begun when John Jack died. It would be three years thence before the Declaration of Independence would be penned with the classic American myth, "We hold these truths to be self evident, that all men are created equal," and nearly a hundred years thence when Abraham Lincoln would write the Gettysburg Address, which began, "Fourscore and seven years ago our fathers brought forth on this continent a new nation, conceived in liberty and dedicated to the proposition that all men are created equal."

—❦ Boston Psychiatric

TUESDAY AFTERNOON. ONLY TWO DAYS LEFT to fill in the huge blanks in Ernestine's history. The ease of getting her records from Bolivar made me hopeful that some Massachusetts hospital retained information about her commitment. I continued to think that she had been placed in a Massachusetts asylum first, because what motive could Wilson have for insisting on this if it were not true?

His wife had visited the local photographic developers with me before lunch and we had looked together at the pictures I had taken of Ernestine in the nursing home in Memphis. She seemed a little shocked by the conditions in the place and understood why I was concerned, but she said nothing to Wilson when we got back to their house.

Several people had said that anyone committed in the area in which Mattie had been living would have gone to Boston Psychiatric, so I needed to go there. When I told Dorothea my plan she told her husband, "Wilson, why don't you put on your jacket and go with her. She'll never find her way to Boston Psychiatric alone."

It wasn't far but the one-way system in the center of town made getting to it difficult. I was uncomfortable with my uncle in the car, because I still sensed that he didn't want to get involved with his mother's past.

Before we'd left the house, I'd rung the hospital and spoken to Vicky MacNamara in Medical Records. But when we reached her office, she presented us with a piece of paper explaining why no patients' records were available without a lawyer's permission.

"Are you saying that you can't tell us whether my grandmother was ever a patient?" I asked angrily.

My uncle's approach was more gentle, but even he couldn't change the official rules, which were part of the state's health code.

"Lawyers cost money. And why should a lawyer have rights to information that a patient's family is denied?"

Official rules rendered pointless any attempt at argument, and, as we walked down the stairs, I expected that I would leave Boston without proof that Ernestine had ever been hospitalized there.

 LETTERS

WILSON MUST HAVE HATED BEING TOLD he was wrong when he knew he was right. But only he knew that he had proof of his convictions. I wanted to believe that his memories of visiting his mother at Foxboro were real, and when he had said, "I remember she was wearing a coat and the wind was blowing her hair," I could almost see Ernestine in her mid-twenties standing in the grounds as her mother approached with the three little boys. But Wilson's memory was possibly a figment of his imagination, or so I thought.

Dorothea sat opposite me at the kitchen table and watched him
open the refrigerator. We had just been discussing our frustrating
attempts to gain any information about Ernestine's having been in
any of the Massachusetts asylums. Dorothea seemed more eager
than my uncle to discuss Ernestine's medical records from Bolivar.

"Did you know that Grandfather had tried to divorce her?" I
asked.

Wilson didn't answer. He placed the milk on the table and sat
down. Was he angry that I wouldn't let the matter rest? If my
obsession with her disturbed him, he managed to hide it. For his
sake I wanted to talk about Grandfather's absence when Ernestine
was committed.

"Don't you think it was odd that he didn't come forward to
provide information about her background?"

Dorothea and I waited for Wilson's answer but instead of reply-
ing he excused himself and went upstairs.

I had spent seven days in Boston. They seemed wasted, and as I
sat there with a sunbeam warming my forearm, it seemed that the
only thing achieved was convincing Dorothea and Wilson that it
was wrong for Harry Mae to be Ernestine's guardian. That he had
rung Harry Mae to tell her he wanted me to replace her was as
much as I thought I could expect from him. But when he returned
to the kitchen he handed me three letters and disappeared again.

The letterhead on the first read, THE COMMONWEALTH OF MASS-
ACHUSETTS DEPARTMENT OF MENTAL DISEASES. It was dated 20
March 1925 and came from the office of the superintendent of
Foxboro State Hospital. Addressed to my grandfather, it concerned
Ernestine, a reply to his of the 15th. The Superintendent, Albert C.
Thomas, M.D., wrote that Ernestine had been sent to Foxboro on
3 March from Boston Psychiatric Hospital. He said: "She has been
rather restless, excitable, and very unstable. She has very many
bizarre ideas as to certain acts which she claims to have committed before coming to the hospital." Among them was Ernestine's
assertion that she had consumed her mother and was carrying her
about in her body. The superintendent also wrote: "She informed

us that it is impossible for her to keep up with her husband as he was in the habit of dressing himself up in girl's clothes and walking the streets." He concluded that it was too soon to predict how long her attack would last and "what the hope is in the way of improvement or recovery."

Passing the letter to Dorothea, I said, "Did you know Wilson had this?"

"I don't know what he keeps," she replied.

The second letter to Grandfather from the superintendent was dated 20 June and said that Ernestine was still having delusions and hearing imaginary voices. He wrote: "She shows no insight into her condition and does not realize that the ideas she entertains are all wrong." His final paragraph states: "Regarding her recovery, we would say that it is a little bit early to make any definite statement, but judging from her present condition and the progress she has made thus far, we do not believe it looks very encouraging."

Grandfather might have been unable to leave his teaching post when Ernestine was committed, or perhaps he couldn't afford the journey.

By 30 November 1925, Grandfather had received a third letter from Foxboro, which stated that Ernestine was doing a little better on the ward. "She is able to occupy herself, is more tidy in her personal appearance, and is helping with the work on the ward. We hope for further improvement but it is doubtful whether she will ever be quite well mentally."

Ernestine had been at the asylum for eight months, and while the words "patient," "hospital," "ward" evoke the image of a healthy, caring environment, it is important to remember the Massachusetts asylum in *Titicut Follies* and the patient who said that the environment and the treatment were making him feel worse.

The letters were yellow with age. Placing them on the kitchen table, I tried to picture Ernestine, a young mother and wife who had traveled to Boston from Memphis with her three sons, leaving her husband behind. Why hadn't he traveled with them? Might Ernestine have gone to Boston to seek help from her mother, or had her mental condition made it impossible for her to remain at home with the children while her husband worked?

The Foxboro letters clarified several things. Ernestine was first committed in Boston at the hospital Wilson and I had visited in search of her records. She had spent nearly a year in asylums by the time she was twenty-seven. Her behavior was abnormal, although it's unclear what caused her to be committed, and while her husband did not travel from Memphis to visit her, he remained in touch with the hospital.

Wilson brought a fourth letter to the kitchen. The letter, dated 23 January 1926, had the same heading as the other three and was also signed by the superintendent.

Having seen Ernestine's Bolivar records, I imagined that her commitment there in 1929 marked the end of her free life, but her imprisonment had begun in Massachusetts, where her condition was described as hopeless. The final letter concludes: "As to the cause of her mental breakdown, there is no evidence of any blood disease or other physical cause, and it would seem that her mental abnormality had been coming on insidiously for a long time and is an expression of her inherited personality."

 MYTHS

RACHEL'S EARRINGS JERKED WITH HER HEAD as she swayed back and forth, balancing her giant slice of pizza on one hand. She is my cousin Will's younger child and is very confident, though only seven. The pizza box was open on my Uncle Wilson's kitchen table and she hovered as near to it as her brother, David, and Alan's son, Valente. I had to take a flight to London that afternoon and it seemed that I had seen too little of them because I had been pre-occupied with Ernestine's story.

I asked all three, "Did you see the picture of your great-grand-mother which I left here?" I was referring to the framed enlarge-ment of Ernestine in the pink floral dress which she'd worn to lunch at the Massachusetts Boulevard Church. The picture was still sitting on Wilson's desk in the living room. I thought it was a good sign that he hadn't moved it.

"You mean the picture of Ernestine?" said Rachel. It sounded odd to hear her name from a child's lips.

I said, "I've been spending time with her in Memphis and although she's just a tiny thing, she might be the bravest person I know."

The three children were ready to listen. Valente took another bite of pizza and stared intently at me. It was tempting to get Ernestine's picture and place it on the table by the pizza box as I said, "You'd like her. She's as gentle as a lamb, and as quiet as a mouse, although I've been told that sometimes she gets mad and cusses and swears. But usually she doesn't bother to say anything at all. She's like the Lone Ranger and keeps to herself."

These were Wilson's grandchildren, and in case he didn't want them to know too much about his mother, I stopped there. But I felt Ernestine's great-grandchildren could have been important to her. Karis proved it a few months later when she went to Memphis on Billy Day's invitation to work with him on converting the Beale Street house into a museum. She took an apartment in mid-town Memphis and made visits to Ernestine over that three-month period. I didn't get much of a report from my daughter about their relationship, but it was good to know that Ernestine had family with her. Once Karis rang to say, "I took her to see *The Three Musketeers,* but I was worried that I'd overdone it. She looked worn out when I got her back to the home."

6

Los Angeles/
Silver Spring

ROBERTA QUINN

IF I FELT RESPONSIBLE FOR ERNESTINE because she was my father's mother, I also became acutely aware of how little I'd known him. To discover from a news clipping in the Memphis library that Blair had had a second wife distressed me. What other information about him had my mother failed to tell me and what did I need to know?

The name of my father's second wife, Roberta Quinn, played upon me. I imagined that she not only knew why he took his life but whether he had been diagnosed as having a problem which was hereditary.

I had asked several people, including my Uncle Wilson, if there was a logical way to trace Roberta Quinn's whereabouts, but none of them had any advice. During December of 1993, while in Los Angeles, I even sought help from a detective friend. His advice, since I had no more than Roberta's name, was to get more information about her from Wilson. But I still imagined that Ernestine wasn't my business and that delving into her life and my father's was irritating to my uncle. To question him seemed disrespectful; having asked him in June of '93 if he knew how to find Roberta, I was reluctant to probe him again. He'd told me that she'd remarried and probably lived abroad, because her husband was in the diplomatic corps.

Every phone call to him in Boston was a long and expensive transatlantic charge from England or France, so I was more apt to ring him from LA. Usually Dorothea would join him on the line and she always seemed encouraging when I asked Wilson questions that I sensed he was reluctant to answer.

It was Dorothea who reminded Wilson during one of my calls that he had a dentist friend who lived on Cape Cod who had kept in touch with Roberta. My heart leapt when I heard that, but I asked casually, "You couldn't give me his number, could you?"

My uncle didn't openly decline but neither did he give me his friend's number, suggesting that he would contact him himself.

For six months, since my trip to Memphis and Boston, I'd been frustrated by all the unanswered questions about Ernestine. Perhaps my father had told her why his mother had taken him and his two brothers to Boston; maybe she had ideas of her own about how his mother's illness related to his choosing psychiatry as a profession.

In the hope of spending some time with my daughter, I was in Los Angeles in December 1993. I was house-sitting for a friend and had arrived with my typewriter and an even greater determination to find my father's widow. The ranch-style house I was staying in was perched on a Bel Air hillside overlooking LA. It was as isolated as my French home and gave me too much time to think about Ernestine and the unhealthy conditions in which she was living almost two thousand miles away.

Two and a half years had passed since I'd found her, complained about her circumstances, and tried to encourage the family to improve her conditions. But only Karis took an interest; Alan, having originally involved me, had still not been to visit our grandmother.

My cautious requests to my uncle to track down Roberta's number finally produced a result one December night. I was in the living room looking out of the huge window, which gave a sprawling view of the millions of lights that LA became after dark. It was still warm, and the scent of the lavender growing at the front of the house slipped in through the open door. When Wilson said, "I've got Roberta's number," I felt a rush of excitement and guilt. I felt like a child with a crowbar prying open another sealed room I was not supposed to enter. All I had really set out to discover was why

Ernestine had been forced to spend fifty-two years in an asylum. But I could hear my mother saying, "That's not your family!"

I was sure that I had alienated Wilson—talk between us was polite rather than friendly. To recover my grandmother I was losing her son, who remained my most solid connection to Blair, my father. But it seemed that all of us would benefit from uncovering the truth about what had happened to Ernestine, and finding Roberta Quinn gave me a rush of hope that Ernestine's story might shape up as neatly as a detective novel rather than remain an unsolvable mystery.

My father's widow. Even the concept seemed strange. I had imagined my mother was his only wife, but I was about to talk with someone who had known him intimately before he chose to die, someone who probably heard stories about his childhood.

I managed to sound confident when I said, "Hello, I hope you won't mind my calling, I'm Blair's daughter," but I was gripping the receiver tightly and my jaws were set.

"Oh, my!" said a slightly girlish southern lilt with dusky undertones. Her "Oh, my's" were punctuated with bubbling laughter, as though my call was her unexpected magnum of Dom Pérignon and she wanted to take great swigs of anything I had to say.

I imagined her as a wispy woman who watched her figure, played canasta, and liked to shop. Her accent sounded as frivolous as the name of her town, Silver Spring, Maryland. But as we talked I discovered she was in her sixties, was employed as a psychiatric social worker in Washington, and lived alone. Her second marriage, which ended in divorce, had produced two now-grown-up children and years of travel abroad, because her husband had indeed been in the diplomatic service. Roberta was so positive about my quest for Ernestine that I relaxed.

"Oooohh," she cried, "your father would be so happy! He became a psychiatrist so that he could help that poor woman." My growing anxiety that I was delving into something that was none of my business eased as she said, "He worried so about her. To think that she's alive after all these years!"

Thousands of miles stretched between us. We were in the same country but she was almost as far from me as my cousin had been when he phoned me in France in 1991 to say that Ernestine might be alive. A phone conversation seemed inadequate. She also felt this, and said, "You've got to come see me. We've got so much to talk about and." Words of goodwill spilled out. She was excited to hear that I was writing about Ernestine.

I said, "I think color has a lot to do with the dysfunction in our family. . . . You know Ernestine's mother was dark-skinned, one of fourteen children and the only dark one. That may have caused her to have all kinds of difficulties growing up, leading to her emotional problems."

"I know she wasn't nice to your father."

"Did you know her?"

"No. She had a numbers racket, didn't she?"

"She was a numbers runner, I think," I said; although I wasn't certain about her role, Wilson had told me that Mattie had earned her income in the numbers racket.

Our conversation jumped from Mattie to my grandfather.

"He came to our wedding," Roberta said. "That was the first time I'd met him, and he looked at me and gasped. He said, "Daughter, you take my breath away. You look just like my poor, dear sick wife.""

I wanted to ask Roberta why she had never been in touch with me, but it was too soon. Her invitation to visit was more than I expected.

"Oh, please try to come. I could take a few days off. We have a lot to talk about."

My ticket to Los Angeles had been in exchange for my house-sitting, and I couldn't afford a journey to Maryland or a trip to Memphis to see Ernestine again. Nonetheless, Roberta had planted a seed of hope and when, shortly afterward, a job offer from the BBC in London promised to take me to Philadelphia, within only two hours away from Silver Spring, I accepted and agreed to an overnight stay with Roberta.

The name Silver Spring, Maryland, brought to mind rolling green hills, cherry blossoms, and white picket fences. I thought of apple pies cooling on window ledges, but Roberta's apartment complex was square and brick and looked no more quaint than a fifties housing development. Drizzling rain which dulled the mid-January sky was less gruesome than the snow and ice crippling other parts of the East Coast, but as I stood behind Roberta while she fiddled with her key, I had to admit she also was different from what I had expected. Her saying that my grandfather had compared her to Ernestine had led me to visualize somebody frailer, with lighter skin.

There was no mistaking that Roberta was black, although her complexion was fair and her hair was light brown. She looked like a younger version of Ethyl Vinson, who had remembered Ernestine living opposite her, and had Roberta not been wearing such a big smile when she met me at the airport, I probably would have passed her by in search of a whiter-looking woman. I had flown overnight with a stopover in Chicago and I was almost too tired to talk when we finally settled into the living room of her two-bedroom apartment, which had pictures by black artists on its walls.

I had come for information and may well have been less curious about her life than she was about mine, but we liked each other immediately and the openness we'd established during our first phone call was obviously going to develop further. What we had in common was not only my father but also that we had spent time outside America. She had felt liberated, living abroad when her children were small.

It didn't disturb her that I thought something as simple as skin color might have played a large part in my family's problems. That Ernestine looked as "white" or European as she did and that her mother, Mattie, may have had a complex about her own dark color were views which Roberta was prepared to discuss as openly as she talked about my father's death. She was the first person I'd met who shared my notion that variations in skin color within the family might have caused Mattie to have identity problems which resulted in her being unkind.

Roberta talked about Blair's position at Harvard. She was sure that, being black, he would have been socially excluded. Yet it was possible he was often mistaken for white.

At the time of his death my father had only known an America which was more prejudiced, more divided, than it had become when Roberta and I sat at her mahogany dining table talking. She had outlived him by decades and, whereas I could only imagine him as the young father that I remembered, his widow was older and wiser than she'd been as his wife. She had been in her twenties when they married, studying for her master's degree in sociology at Boston University. They'd met on a double date. She'd been with his brother Ernest and Blair was with another girl. At a dance, Blair and Roberta gravitated toward each other, finding their original partners frivolous.

In her sixties, Roberta was still a handsome woman, but it was obvious that her round face had been pretty when she was young and that her blue-gray eyes and pale peach complexion would have singled her out as a beauty among those of our race when such factors were the most desirable.

She laughed a lot and swore a little and the time that she'd spent living in Saudi Arabia and France made her feel we had something in common. But she was a social woman, and, like O'Ferrell and Anne Nelson, was part of a network of sororities and fraternities, a lifestyle alien to me. I had never thought of my father as being part of such a group, but since he had married Roberta, perhaps he was.

Roberta had been divorced in her forties. Her small apartment with its white walls covered by paintings she'd collected for years felt as if it belonged to a bachelor woman, and the cheese that had gone bad in the fridge hinted that domesticity wasn't important to her.

She was tearful when she talked about my father, and I tried to imagine how traumatic it must have been for her to have married someone who committed suicide within six weeks of pledging himself to a future with her.

"Your Uncle Ernest had put him out after he was released from the hospital, because Blair went to their place in Roxbury and tore the wires out of the walls. He'd been given shock treatment in the hospital and was afraid of wires." I had vaguely known that my father had had a nervous breakdown but no one had said that he'd had shock treatment.

Despite psychiatric social work being her occupation, she wasn't able to tell me what symptoms had caused him to be confined, but she said, "They put him in the same hospital that he'd worked in, and when they took him into the ward one of the patients told Blair, 'Hey, Doc, you're one of us now.' "

Roberta jumped excitedly from stories about her youth to questions about mine, to musing about literature and travel, motherhood and womanhood. As she'd been married for hardly more than a month to Blair and had raised a family since then, I didn't think she was being evasive, I merely thought that she'd forgotten that episode in her life or had made efforts to put it behind her.

She fixed us some eggs and we sat eating with the winter sun coming through her front window. Slight traffic noise from outside reminded me that we were at street level. The fact of my getting there from Los Angeles, that I'd finally found someone who had not only known my father but had loved him, had filled me with great expectations that my meeting with Roberta would at least solve the mystery of his illness and how it related to Ernestine. So a flat feeling of anticlimax was starting to creep over me, a dull sadness that Roberta couldn't say, Your father said such and such about his mother's condition.

If I'd been expecting too much, Roberta suddenly offered more than I had hoped for when she produced an envelope which included information about my father's burial arrangements. There was a drawing of his simple headstone and the deed for his cemetery plot. Since Wilson had said that he couldn't recall where my father had been buried, I had never visited his grave, which

Roberta said was in Mount Hope Cemetery in Boston. She also said, "Of course, when he died, I thought that I would want to be buried with him, so I bought two plots side by side. I have the papers for them and would like to give you the other plot if you'd like to have it."

Knowing that Ernestine would not be buried with my grandfather, I said, "It would be wonderful if my grandmother could rest beside my father."

We know so little about death, about the spirit. Is it possible that two souls resting side by side are comforted in an afterworld?

I wanted to hug her and said, "Maybe it would be important for both of them. Ernestine recognized his baby picture the very first time I showed it to her. She calls him Bee Tee." While I held the drawing of my father's headstone, Roberta pointed to it, saying, "There's room there for Ernestine's name and a short dedication."

I felt that I'd achieved something on my grandmother's behalf, but I knew that both Harry Mae Simons and my uncle would have to agree to Ernestine's being buried beside Blair.

Roberta repeated something she'd said during our first phone call. "I bet your father's standing over your shoulder, darlin', because he worried about his mother and became a psychiatrist because he wanted to help her."

But she and I both knew that Ernestine would have been in Bolivar for over twenty years by the time he qualified.

I said, "His mother was in a segregated institution. As a Negro psychiatrist what hope would he have had of gaining access to her in that backwoods asylum? Surely he would have caused resentment by the mere fact that he was a black psychiatrist educated in the North. And by 1950, Ernestine had been in that place for over two decades. Even if she hadn't been incurably ill when she was committed, the abuse she'd suffered all those years would have probably damaged her beyond repair."

It was easy to talk to Roberta. Her certainty that my father would have wanted me to find his mother made me feel easier about upsetting my uncle and Harry Mae Simons, both of whom

might have resented my contact with her, although neither had
said so directly.

Roberta agreed with my theory that Ernestine's mother's dark
skin may have been at the root of emotional problems which
affected subsequent generations.

"If Mattie felt an outcast growing up," I said, "because she was
so much darker than her brothers and sisters, then giving birth to
Ernestine drove her further into feeling inferior or bitter because
she was dark."

"Color has made so many people crazy," said Roberta. "You
know, we're the most prejudiced people in the world."

She was referring to African Americans and to the caste system
we had inherited through slavery, which made us value any resem-
blance to those who had such complete power over us. As we
move further away from slavery, we try to forget certain factors
imposed on us. But obviously a slave's trade value was affected by
how the slave appealed to the buyer; and how handsome the slave
appeared was based upon the buyer's beauty standards. Thus
Ernestine would have been seen as more beautiful and more
socially acceptable than her mother, and Mattie would have been
less valuable than her sisters and brothers.

By evening, Roberta and I had settled in her small study, which
had once been her son's bedroom. An alcove was lined with books,
and lamplight cast a warm glow across a small chaise set at an
angle. I sat on the floor surrounded by the family photographs she
eagerly showed me of her daughter, her son, and his daughter.

I was aware of the clock ticking and knew that we were running out of time, because I had only come for an overnight stay, so
I asked if she had pictures of Blair and hoped that photographs
would jog her memory about him.

The small black-and-white snapshots of their wedding looked
as if they'd been taken with a Brownie camera, because they
showed little detail—the white was too stark and the black too
dense. It had been a small wedding but Blair was in a white dinner jacket and Roberta wore a gown and veil. Some letters which

she found in a shoebox had been written by him to her mother. They made me sad, because they were apologies for his being late in repaying her for the flowers. I imagined him as a struggling young doctor, recently hospitalized, who was trying to cope with the expense of a wedding. I read and reread each letter, written only a couple of months before his suicide, while Roberta described him as gentle and kind. I couldn't get her to recall any particular incidents and imagined that she was keeping her harsher memories to herself.

"My father must have told you something about his childhood," I begged.

"Once he told me that Mattie—he called her Gran—had tried to send him to school in a dress. She was punishing him, but I can't remember if he said what for. . . . He said she was cruel, mean, and ignorant, and he said he had tried to run away with his brothers when they were small."

I tried to bear in mind Roberta's age. It had been generous of her to have me in her home at all. I had arrived to dig up a past that she had every right to want to forget. Nonetheless, she said a few words about his suicide.

"Where were you living?" I asked.

"In Cambridge," she said. "We had a little apartment. But we were ahead of our time. We were living together before we got married because of Ernest putting Blair out after he snatched all the electric wires from the walls."

"Had anything happened, anything special which made him—"

Roberta interrupted me. "He had received an incomplete on a paper that he was writing, and that upset him."

"My mother told me that he was very distressed, that shock treatment had affected his memory. Maybe he saw the incomplete as a sign that his mind was permanently damaged?"

"His body was still warm when I found him," Roberta said. "But it was already too late. The paramedics came, but it was already too late."

There had been such light in her pale eyes when she'd greeted me eight hours earlier at the airport. But they clouded over as she spoke, sitting on the floor across from me, surrounded by pictures of the past.

"He took all those pills. And I think what upset him was that incomplete."

I got chills when she reminisced about their first date, because he had taken her to Walden Pond. I said, "Roberta, that's kind of spooky, because when I was in Boston six months ago trying to find out about what had happened to Ernestine, I ended up going to Concord. I felt guilty about it then because it seemed like a waste of time. But of course Walden Pond is there."

"Mark my words," Roberta said. "That man is at your elbow."

I thought about that morning in Concord when I had traveled so far to see the video of *Titicut Follies,* and I remembered how often I'd asked myself why I was there. I laughed and said to Roberta, "You think he wanted me there? Think he wanted me to visit Concord?"

"Who knows? The Unitarians were big there."

"I know. I went to Ralph Waldo Emerson's house."

"Emerson was Unitarian—so was your father. He even got me to join the church and I never left it."

I was shocked. "My father was a Unitarian?"

"Absolutely. We went to their big church in Boston. On Beacon Hill."

"Have I told you that Ernestine was found because of a Unitarian convention? Well, Unitarian Universalists."

Roberta smiled. "That's us. But what did that have to do with your grandmother?"

"A man from Memphis named O'Ferrell Nelson was running for a national office and his promotional handout said that he had gone to my grandfather's high school in Memphis. Somehow, he and my cousin Alan got to talking and he said that not only had he known Grandfather but he'd seen our grandmother."

Roberta said, "Oooohh. Now you know Blair's up there just working! Mark my words! He proposed to me at Walden Pond."

Her voice was rising. "He proposed to me there," she squealed. On our first date! He was so different from the other guys I knew. Can you imagine? He drove me to Walden Pond—what is it, thirty miles from where we were living? That's where he asked me if I thought a person could know right away that he was in love with somebody."

I thought about my grandfather telling her that she looked like Ernestine and wondered if my father had been attracted to her because of it.

Whatever Roberta was keeping to herself, she had shared some of her memories with me, and she gave me a beautiful picture of Blair, a head shot, from his graduation from Boys Latin High School in Boston. But it was the cemetery plot she'd given Ernestine which made me sleep better in Roberta's study that night.

She also gave me the name of a black female psychiatrist named Frances Bonner who had been treating my father before his death. But as I curled up on the sofa and dozed off, I recalled that Roberta had said that while he was in hospital under Dr. Finestein's care he received shock treatment. Then she added that the damned doctor had sent her a bill for it after Blair had died.

7

France

DR. BONNER

MORE THAN A YEAR HAD PASSED since that June '93 when I'd knelt beside Ernestine in her new rocker and kissed her goodbye. I didn't expect to see her again. I had other members of my family, like my mother, to think about and money was low. I couldn't plan a return to Memphis.

Back in France I kept thinking about Ernestine. I didn't believe that hereditary insanity was the reason she'd spent fifty-two years at Bolivar. Nor did I relate my father's emotional disturbance directly with hers, because even Ernestine's committal may have created deep-seated problems for him, which he was able to suppress until he became an adult. Anytime I'd tell someone about her they'd relate some other horror story that they'd heard about someone else's misspent years in an asylum. I spent sleepless nights going over her sketchy past and convinced myself that I had a duty to restore her history. Her story was all that I could give her.

Occasionally Roberta would ring from Baltimore and give me some encouragement. Her southern accent was evangelical. She had a skill for raising hopes and would say things like, "Keeping secrets in families is the main cause of dysfunction in them. All people's energy goes into keeping something hidden." Or we'd talk about how looking European or not looking European enough had undermined the unity in black families as well as in the black community and debate whether this had played a role in Ernestine's family life.

Whenever Roberta said, "Girl, your father is at your side. He's up there dancing, happy that you've taken interest in your grandmother," I felt more compelled to delve into Ernestine's life. And when Roberta told me that Dr. Bonner, who had been one of Blair's psychiatrists, was still alive and in Boston, I knew I had to contact her.

I didn't know how frail my father's myth was for me and wasn't aware of the role it had played in my life. Maybe my subconscious knew and that's why I was nervous about ringing his psychiatrist. Hereditary insanity was the charge against Ernestine; had a similar diagnosis hung over him, and did I want to know if it was hanging over me? Over Karis? Over my cousins and their children?

Roberta was certain that Dr. Bonner was alive, because the doctor had been a speaker at Roberta's black female college in North Carolina. She gave me a name and number to call in the college's administration office, but it took a frustrating week of leaving messages for the doctor before I discovered I'd been given a wrong Boston number. The night I got the right one, my French village was sleeping and the black night was dense with stars.

I was in bed. A candle lit the room. Ernestine was on my mind. I was trying to recall that strange pungent scent of hers. I could see the thin spread of dark hairs on her bony calves. But I could only recall her face in profile, when her jaw was tense and her mouth was twitching uncontrollably. Her cap of thick gray hair was as clear as the blue plaid dress which I'd finally brought away as proof that she had been poorly clothed. These images played chase in my head when Dr. Bonner answered her telephone.

I had never been truly interested in why my father killed himself. It wasn't going to change my life, although it had added a dramatic note. I didn't need sordid details.

"Dr. Bonner?" I asked. "I'm sorry to ring you at home. . . ."

I was as apologetic as somebody who'd reached a wrong number. She was breathing into her receiver, and the connection between us was so good that it was impossible to remember that almost four thousand miles stretched between us. I hoped my transatlantic accent would certify that I wasn't a faker, a pretender to the crown of the gifted Harvard graduate who had been my father.

"I'm sorry to trouble you," I began with diffidence, "but I believe my father was a patient of yours in the fifties. I'm ringing from France."

I told her my name and said that Blair had committed suicide when I was a child but I had recently found his mother and hoped that Dr. Bonner might remember something about him which would lead to a better understanding of his mother's history.

With the French doors open, I could hear the leaves of the large walnut tree brushing the side of the house when Dr. Bonner spoke. Her voice was taut, thin; she sounded emaciated, a little haughty, and gave me nothing to like, but I wasn't looking for friendship, I was seeking information. I said, "I was given your name by my father's widow, who now lives in Maryland."

The stars were twinkling over my house but night hadn't yet fallen in Boston. I was prepared to accept that Dr. Bonner had had thousands of patients during her career and had forgotten Blair. But she needed no prompting after I mentioned his name.

"I remember Dr. Hunt." She said it as a statement which insinuated nothing but that fact. But it was odd to hear my father referred to as "Dr. Hunt." Her voice told me at once that I was talking to someone who was going to give me no more than she wanted to. I felt as if I'd disturbed a dowager duchess.

Roberta had been so encouraging about my contacting Dr. Bonner that I hadn't prepared myself to face my father's psychiatrist as an opponent. I tried to remember that I was calling someone in America, a litigious arena where doctors are sued regularly for what in Europe seem quite bizarre reasons. That I'd mentioned Blair's suicide may have been the reason she seemed guarded, or maybe I wasn't giving enough consideration to her age.

I sat up in bed and flicked on the bedside lamp. It stirred the sleeping flies. As they buzzed about the beamed ceiling I had an image of my father in an easy chair, his hairy forearms exposed in a white shirt with the sleeves rolled up. His head is back, his smooth hair hardly ruffled, his clear glasses in place. I see a pale woman's hand lifting his limp hand to check his pulse. But he has none.

An owl hooted a few times and yanked me back to my purpose in phoning Dr. Bonner. I said, "My grandmother is ninety-six. Perhaps you may recall that my father's mother was in a mental institution. I realize it may not be proper to talk about a patient but it would help if you could tell me something about him."

She said curtly, "I knew nothing about his having a daughter."

My heart stopped and then started to race. I felt like a fool. Was it possible that my father hadn't cared enough about me to mention me to his psychiatrist? As a child, I'd suspected that maybe I was too dark to be loved by him and his fair-skinned family, but I'd long since cast off that possibility. Had I spent two years fretting over my father's mother when he hadn't cared enough about me to tell his psychiatrist that he had a child?

Rather than open a can of worms in my own psyche, I laughed and said, "I can assure you that I'm Blair T. Hunt's daughter, Dr. Bonner. I was ten when he died, living in Philadelphia, where I was raised by my mother and her family."

Dr. Bonner made no reply. I thought about my phone bill. I could hear her breathing. I didn't know this woman but she had to have been exceptional, because black female psychiatrists are a rarity and must have been even rarer back in the fifties. But who she was had nothing to do with how much information I was going to get out of her. Maybe she'd said enough. I was a little wiser.

Wounded, but wiser.

There was no point in continuing the conversation. I said my thank-you and goodbye and wondered what Dr. Bonner was thinking when she hung up the telephone. She and Blair had been two of the very few black psychiatrists at the time. Even if the Negro press hadn't reported his death as suicide, *she* knew that he'd taken his life. That she'd treated a man without fully knowing his personal history—that he'd been married to my mother and had a child—wasn't going to become my problem unless I allowed it to.

I rang Roberta. She said, "Well, *I* knew about you. Blair told me he had a little girl. . . . You just keep on doing what you're doing. This world is full of secrets and you writing about what happened to Ernestine could help somebody else."

Assuming that while he was ill Blair had talked about his past, I thought Dr. Bonner should have known more about his feelings toward his mother than anyone else. But then again, perhaps I was still caught in the trap of thinking that mental hospitals provided more care and psychiatric treatment than they did. I had visions of Blair in quiet therapy sessions, but perhaps he never had any. Shock treatment was possibly the best his hospital offered.

It was hard to keep in mind how different times had been when he suffered, when he died. Being a Negro meant that his life counted for less. For all I knew that may have been the fact that drove him crazy.

THE GRAVE

ALTHOUGH ROBERTA HAD SAID THAT THE EMPTY PLOT beside my father's at Mount Hope Cemetery could become Ernestine's, transferring the deed required paperwork. Roberta had to notify the parks commission in Boston that Ernestine was to be buried there. When she sent me the official confirmation from the Boston mayor's office that this had been done, I rushed off copies to my Uncle Wilson and Harry Mae—she was still guardian and he was next of kin, and they had the legal power to decide where my grandmother would be buried.

It seemed possible that Ernestine would be happy to know that she was going to rest next to her son. Had she resisted death until she was assigned a suitable resting place. Although I phoned every few weeks, I did all the talking. She only spoke if Essie Mae coaxed her, and even then a flat "hello" was all I'd get.

Neither Wilson nor Harry Mae responded to my letter about the grave. I didn't bother to write again; it seemed pointless. But I couldn't understand why they weren't relieved that Ernestine could rest beside her son, since Grandfather had made no provision for her to be buried in his grand Memphis plot.

Alan had the answer. I hadn't heard from him in over a year, and he still hadn't been to visit Ernestine. Three years had slipped by since his phone call to me to say that she was possibly alive. But when he called in July of 1994 to say that he was going to try to visit her that summer, I asked if he'd heard that she'd been given a cemetery plot next to Blair's.

Alan's voice was as soft and reflective as always. I could imagine that he hadn't changed, that he still had his heavy black beard and dark-rimmed glasses and was probably dressed in a plaid shirt and overalls. Studying for the Unitarian Universalist ministry should have enhanced his interest in the traditions related to death.

I said, "How people get buried matters, don't you think?" It seemed to me that something good had finally happened for Ernestine when she was given the plot next to Blair's.

"I think my father doesn't understand why you bother to care about something like that."

"What happens when Ernestine dies is relevant. If it isn't, then why hasn't your father or Harry Mae confirmed that Ernestine can be buried beside her son?"

Some days I was worn down by the family's indifference to Ernestine, and other days it incensed me. But my life had to carry on either way.

An acting assignment took me to England and I settled back in my Folkestone base, where I had gone that summer of 1991 to collect the copy of my father's baby picture to give to Ernestine.

8

Folkestone

↶ Out of the Blue

IT WAS A FREEZING NOVEMBER NIGHT IN FOLKESTONE. Gale-force winds whistled and shook the house. My flat occupied the top two floors of the building; I listened to the windows rattling and hoped the weather wasn't destroying my place in France—work and major surgery kept me from returning there. So did the use of free office space in a large local travel firm which organized holidays for people over fifty and also produced a magazine for the aged. I had declined an offer to write for it until I was asked to write about Ernestine, whom I ranted about from time to time, obsessed as I was with her plight. When the magazine editor, Paul Bach, had listened to the story of her kissing my father's baby picture, he said, "We would fly you to Memphis."

By the time I left his office, he was also ready to fly Ernestine back to England with Essie Mae if I could convince Essie Mae to come. I had never really considered getting Ernestine out of Memphis, but once the idea took hold, I was spinning.

I could hear Essie Mae telling me after my second visit to Memphis, "One of these days, you gon' be sitting over there in France and look up, and me and Miss Hunt's gon' be coming through your front door." I could see her gap-tooth smile and hear her laugh and wondered if in her wildest dreams she ever really believed that she could cut herself free from that job at the nursing home.

The orange flame from the fire cast a gold light on the white walls and I flicked through my Filofax to *H* for my uncle's phone number. Without his approval, I had no hope of bringing Ernestine to England or giving her a home.

The obstacles which faced me, such as getting my grandmother a passport and convincing Essie Mae to come with her, seemed manageable if I had someone I could depend on in Memphis, and there was only one person to call: Fred Hooks, who was Ben and Julia's nephew. I'd met him during my second trip to Memphis in May of 1993. He was a couple of years older than I was, and we agreed about most things. Memphis hadn't been the only place he had lived; as a captain in the army he'd even done time in Vietnam. As a property assessor, he was used to dealing with people, and having been raised by his aunts Julia, Mildred, and Bessie, to whom O'Ferrell had introduced me, I suspected that Fred could manage elderly women.

If lions could speak they would probably have Fred's bass voice. With his smooth brown skin and curly gray hair, he was movie star material, and his unaffected good manners added to his charm. The first time I'd met him, I phoned Julia Hooks to congratulate her on how well he'd been raised. He didn't let his cunning show, but hearing him talk about how he'd been chosen for officers' training told me he didn't miss chances.

That he'd met Ernestine and appreciated my worries about her living conditions increased my conviction that he was the person who could help me get her a passport, and in truth, when he heard my news, he seemed as excited as I was about the prospect of her coming to live with me.

Then I rang Essie Mae Dukes at home. We'd spoken on the phone often over the past three and a half years, when I'd call to check on Ernestine's progress. But I don't think Essie Mae ever expected me to offer her a trip to Europe. She was single and unattached with a grown son. Her nephew Ricky, who was in his late twenties, shared her small rented bungalow, which was a block from the nursing home.

Ricky was the nearest thing I'd ever seen to a black cowboy. He was ebony, with a round face and long black sideburns. The first time I'd met him, he was wearing cowboy boots and a cowpoke's hat with his jeans slung low. It was inconceivable that he couldn't manage without Essie Mae, but when I rang her I thought it might be worry about him that would convince her not to come.

"I've got two places, and you could have your own bedroom in both of them," I told her. I always tried to talk like Essie Mae when I was speaking to her, and I wondered what she would think if she heard me with my English friends, but that was the only thing I could think of which might have made her uncomfortable. I added, "Essie Mae, you could try it for a few months, and if you didn't like it, you could go home."

I was sitting cross-legged on the floor in front of the fire. The glass of wine I was drinking was within arm's reach and I took a swig of it when Essie Mae said she'd be glad to come, but her enthusiasm had slipped when I checked in with her two days later.

"Hon, I'm right behind you a hundred percent. I really, really am . . . and like I say, I been right behind you from the first. But Miss Hunt done changed since you was last here. She ain't strong like she was. . . . But then if the doctor say she can go over there, I'm right behind you. But I don't think she can make it."

I had images of some official doctor for the nursing home listening to Ernestine's heartbeat and proclaiming her unfit to travel as a ruse to keep her there. Essie Mae had said more than once in the time that I'd known her that Ernestine was a high-paying guest, so I didn't think the owner wanted to see my grandmother leave.

"Essie Mae," I said, "there's nothing taxing about a plane journey. And if it makes you feel better, I'll take my grandmother for a checkup when I get there. But I need to know if you still want to come."

To have my grandmother without Essie Mae wouldn't have been impossible, but when and how to take on Ernestine would be a different consideration if she wasn't traveling with Essie Mae, who knew her habits.

Essie Mae said eagerly, "Don't get me wrong. I'm behind what you're trying to do, one hundred percent. One hundred."

"But what about you? Will you come with us?"

"I said I would. 'Cause Miss Hunt's my baby. *My* baby. And if she's going somewhere, I'm goin' too!"

I was worried that Essie Mae hadn't thought the whole operation through. "And you're sure that you can just up and leave your house?"

"What I got to stay for? I can be out of here in a couple days."

⟶⟍ MEMPHIS BOUND

DARKNESS MADE THE EARLY MORNING CHILL GROTESQUE. The gulls were still sleeping, as was everyone else who lived in the crescent, and there were no signs that Christmas was five days away. Rough winds had whistled while I was packing, but by the time I hauled the suitcase down to the car, the air was still and the sea was quiet. To drive to the airport before dawn meant I'd miss the commuter traffic heading for London, but there was no other consolation for being out at that hour.

I needed to hold a picture of Ernestine in my head to remind myself why I was making this journey to retrieve her. I visualized the dirty sleeping bag covering the sofa at the nursing home and my grandmother slumped upon it, wearing a sad plaid housedress with her emaciated legs exposed in ankle socks. She had often been in that position, with her hands clasped together and tucked between her knees. It was important to recall the thin cover on her bed and the torn cotton slip she wore the first time I put her down for a nap. Without this memory play my trip made no sense, because these days grandmothers are expendable.

Somehow three hundred dollars would have to cover my ten-day stay. It was a lot more than I had been carrying the first time I flew to Memphis to find Ernestine—and this time I was also carrying plane tickets for her and Essie Mae.

9

Memphis

~~ THE SHOCK

FRED HOOKS STEPPED OUT OF HIS TOYOTA clutching a Federal Express envelope containing documents needed for Ernestine's and Essie Mae's passport applications. It was barely light enough to make out his green snakeskin cowboy boots; I hadn't noticed them while we were in the restaurant, but having just arrived from Folkestone that afternoon, my senses were numb.

I'd already visited Ernestine after dropping my bags at Anne and O'Ferrell's. Dinner with Fred, to get an update on his progress with the passports, should have been my last appointment, but he'd insisted that we go to the nursing home to get Essie Mae's signature and I'd followed him there in my rented car. I'd lost count of how many hours had passed since I'd driven out of Folkestone. My burning eyes told me to go to bed.

Darkness was creeping in fast as Fred and I stood beside my car whispering. The street was empty and the lights in the nursing home seemed to be out. Fred had worked hard to get the passport pictures taken and had difficulty getting Harry Mae to the post office, where she had to sign as my grandmother's guardian, so I was letting him take the lead, but standing in the dimming light I said, "Fred, we're too late. Look at the house. No lights are on."

There was a slight chill in the air, but compared to England it wasn't cold. Fred stuck one hand in the pocket of his suede jacket and tucked the envelope under his arm. He was already heading up the path to the front door. "If these papers don't get to

Congressman Ford's office tomorrow morning so they can be sent to New Orleans, you may not get the passports." It was 20 December and the return flight to England was on the thirtieth. With Christmas falling in between, he had reason to be anxious.

Our visit was unannounced. One crooked slat of the blind covering the small door pane allow us to peek in. Spotting a small light on inside, Fred rang the bell.

Essie Mae's workday was always long and arduous. She had been on for three days and nights without a break, and to wake her was cruel. I whispered, "Let me come back tomorrow. I can find my way to the congressman's office."

Before Fred could answer Essie Mae had opened the door. I was embarrassed for him to see a portable cot set up in the front room where the residents sat throughout the day. It was single-bed size, narrow and low. Situated in the middle of the room, it looked odd surrounded by empty chairs and sofas. I knew that the caregivers had no permanent bed and used the living room for their sleeping space, but I noticed Fred's surprised eyes. Essie Mae was still dressed, and I was so busy apologizing for our visit that I hadn't noticed that someone was in the bed.

The house was quiet. Everyone was asleep and the TV was off. I looked down at my feet, trying to think of what to say. It was a relief to hear Fred whisper, "We've still got a paper for you to sign."

His smooth voice eased my tension, and my gaze slipped back to the bed. The body under the blankets was small and lay as still as a corpse. The head was concealed by the blanket, but a tuft of gray hair could be seen. There was no mistaking that the person huddled there was Ernestine. I gasped. A tide of possibilities rushed upon me.

Fred's eyes followed mine, but he wouldn't have known that my knees buckled. I was stunned to hear my own voice demanding, "Why is my grandmother in this bed?"

It was too small for two people to have slept in. Essie Mae looked sheepish and said, "Miss Hunt don't want to sleep nowhere but in here with me."

(*Right*) When I finally met her, Roberta Polk said, "Your grandfather told me, 'Daughter, you take my breath away. You look just like my poor, dear sick wife.'"

(*Below*) Frances Hooks, Benjamin Hooks, Ernestine, and me. His maternal grandmother and Ernestine's mother were sisters. It was a surprise that Ben and Frances came to the airport on December 30, 1994, to see Ernestine off for her flight with me to England. Despite my smile, I was deeply distressed because Essie Mae had not arrived to make the journey with us.

(*Above*) Ernestine on the Leas in Folkestone. Behind her is the Victorian crescent where I've had a maisonette since 1986. She stands looking at the sea.

(*Right*) Gentle and affectionate, only once have I known my grandmother to rebuff a hug.

Ernestine and me at the Arboretum in Boston, July 1995.

Ernestine in the kitchen in Folkestone.

Ernestine, age ninety-seven. When I showed her the Bible, she was able to read New Testament on the cover.

I had noticed a new female resident when I visited earlier and was surprised that she had been given the bed that had been Ernestine's. But as I stood there staring at my grandmother in that cot, I recalled a scene which had played itself out that afternoon when I came visiting. I was putting Ernestine down for a nap and the new resident, with ebony skin and eyes and a placid smile stood staring at us from the doorway. It took her awhile to say that Ernestine was in her bed. The one next to it had a bent square cut from a cardboard box which read MISS HUNT. But another old lady drifted in and out of the room to say that the bed with the sign above it was hers.

Fred and Essie Mae looked at me. I wanted to know why Ernestine was in that bed, but if I demanded an answer what would happen to her? It was after eight; I was spending the night at the Nelsons' and couldn't offer Ernestine a place to sleep, or even shift her from that heated room out into the night air. But knowing that Ernestine had no bed of her own made me want to drag Harry Mae outside and ask her how she could sleep at night knowing that Ernestine was not being properly provided for.

Fred took my elbow and guided me toward the kitchen. He could see that I was powerless to do more than get my grandmother to England. But I was determined to slip into what had been Ernestine's bedroom. I wanted to confirm what I suspected, and I tiptoed away from him and Essie Mae while he produced the paper she needed to sign.

All three beds in the small room that Ernestine had previously shared were occupied.

The following day I booked us into a double at the Econo Lodge. I couldn't even afford a single and my hand was shaking as I signed the register. But Ernestine had been abandoned long enough.

At Congressman Ford's

THREE YOUNG, IMPECCABLY DRESSED African Americans in the congressman's office had gathered around a desk where a clerk was selling beauty products. I sat with the secretary who was dealing with Ernestine's passport application. Jet lag made me impatient, but I tried to remain calm. "She's ninety-six years old and she doesn't have a birth certificate. They didn't issue them to blacks in Roanoke before the turn of the century."

The secretary adjusted her glasses and looked at me as though she had caught me in a lie. "You need something official stating that. Else this application may not go through."

"But it's December twenty-third," I whined. "Today's Friday, and if it doesn't go off today, we won't get the passport back in time. Our tickets have us flying out on the thirtieth and the date can't be changed. You don't understand. . . ." I put my head in my hands while I listened to her ringing the New Orleans passport office where the application had to be sent. Her tone implied that somebody on the other end wasn't being helpful.

Two sealed envelopes, one containing Essie Mae's application and the other Ernestine's, lay face down on the desk in front of me. Fred Hooks had spent ten days getting the various things required, but Ernestine had no birth certificate and my search for her history confirmed there wasn't one. Was this a sign that Ernestine wasn't meant to leave Memphis?

The pretty clerk with the beauty products made a sale and laughed, while the chestnut-brown secretary dealing with Ernestine's application nodded again and again to the voice on the other end of the phone.

I closed my eyes, hardly able to stay awake, and in that dreamy state of mind recalled that Ernestine was listed in the library on the

1910 U.S. census. I was out of my seat before the secretary hung
up her phone.

"My grandmother was listed on a census! Ask whoever you're
talking to if a census printout will do!"

The main library wasn't hard to find and the librarian on duty
was a member of O'Ferrell and Anne's church. Betty Blaelock had
the printout waiting for me when I arrived, and I got it back to
the congressman's office before it closed for Christmas.

 MIXING

A SOUL VERSION OF "I'M DREAMING OF A WHITE CHRISTMAS" floated
as gently as snowflakes from the café's speakers. Cutting above it was
the nasal voice of a white waitress shouting orders from the counter
to someone unseen in the kitchen: "Three scrambled . . . pancakes . . .
a side of bacon. . . ." She was wearing a strand of gold tinsel around
her neck; a few feet from her, a tall black waitress in a felt Santa hat
stacked clean plates. They didn't stare when I walked through the glass
doors guiding Ernestine, but several other people did.

It was Christmas morning and I had wanted to take her
somewhere special for breakfast, but every café we passed on the
highway was closed. She didn't balk when I said, "We'll have to
drive back to that waffle place," and maybe she was as glad as I
was to step from the icy morning air into the bright atmosphere
of a hamburger joint that doubled as a pancake house. But the
eyes that greeted us were unfriendly. I wanted to believe that
Ernestine's outfit drew their attention; draped in black from

head to toe, she could have been playing an old Sicilian widow.

Still, it was good to find somewhere warm where two handfuls of people were dotted about the booths or sitting with their elbows on the counter. Both blacks and whites were serving and being served but they weren't actually mingling, although the black waitress laughed at something the little white waitress said.

Ernestine sat opposite me in a booth near the cash register where a man in a red and white shirt hung about drying glasses. The agitated look he flashed me was meant to say something like, Sister, what are you doing playing nursemaid to that white woman? And in case I hadn't read his look, he glared harder when I showed my grandmother the menu, which had photographs of the breakfast offerings. I made a point of calling her Grandma, as though I needed to explain our relationship, but his angry eyes said that he wouldn't accept her as one of us.

Ernestine's mother had suffered because of how slavery made her and now it was Ernestine's turn. The pendulum of prejudice within our race is still hinged on skin color; that man drying the glasses must have assumed he was better than Ernestine, or better than me because I worked for her.

The couple who sat down in the booth next to ours also made a point of staring. But they were white.

THE GUARDIAN

HARRY MAE HEARD THE KNOCK on the bathroom window. I'd given up banging at the back door.

"Yes?" she called out.

"It's only me," I yelled. To arrive unannounced was meant to take her off guard, but I wasn't expecting her to have no stationery. So as soon as she sat me at her kitchen table, I had been on my feet again, grabbing my car keys and only half listening to her directions to the nearest store.

"Take the first left and turn right at the next corner. . . ."

On her Formica table lay a single sheet of white paper with the piece of cardboard that she'd used to write on a straight line. The uneven address which she'd managed to put in the top right-hand corner was her own. Farther down the page it said, "To Whom It May Concern: I, Harry Mae Simons, guardian of Mrs. Ernestine Jacobs Hunt . . . " Dissatisfied with her handwriting, Harry Mae insisted that she begin again but had no more paper. Had the letter been less important, it wouldn't have been possible to sit in her kitchen with her while she fussed over trivial details.

There was no love between us, although she said there was.

That Ernestine was living in such poor conditions was her guardian's fault, and every time I saw my grandmother in a shoddy dress or saw a roach on the wall at the nursing home or arrived to find her sleeping on a dirty sofa, my thoughts flipped to Grandfather's aged mistress.

She was still living in the house where he had lived as her boarder for nearly half a century. But the neighborhood had continued to slip since his death, and getting out of a car on side streets where the small wooden houses crumbled and teenage boys traveled in threes and fours wasn't advisable, so it was a relief after my quick trip to buy the writing pad to find myself back at Harry Mae's kitchen table.

She had become fragile during the eighteen months that I'd been away. Her answers came slower, she said her memory failed her, yet she retained control over Ernestine.

Would she try to stop me from leaving with my grandmother? It was possible, so I had avoided seeing her or discussing details about our departure. But a letter from Ernestine's guardian might be necessary at British Customs.

Harry Mae opened the fresh writing pad to the first page. "What do you want me to write?" she asked. But despite her smile, she was terse and gritty.

"One sentence will do. You only need say that you give Ernestine permission to travel with me."

Harry Mae reached for the piece of cardboard with its straight edge, which was still on the table, and asked, "How long will you be away with her?"

The refrigerator hummed but otherwise the house was quiet, and though we remained seated, we distanced ourselves behind the fences of mistrust that had been building between us since I arrived in Memphis in '91 and refused to stay in her house.

Harry Mae was still in her pink dressing gown, though it was late afternoon. As I watched her adjust her glasses and position her pen on the page, only her age saved me from socking her. Anger choked me, but I managed to say, "My grandmother hasn't got a bed in that place she's in. There's never toilet paper in the bathroom with all those people using one toilet. . . . No soap and no towels." What kept me from shouting, What has my grandmother got to come back to? was how badly I wanted Harry Mae's letter.

She felt her power with that blank sheet of paper in front of her and asked again sweetly, "But, sugar, how long will she be gone?"

I had avoided this confrontation during the eight days I'd been in Memphis, for to accuse Harry Mae of failing to ensure that Ernestine was properly taken care of might have meant risking Ernestine's right to leave. But perhaps the law was on my grandmother's side. Reaching for the phone I said, "Let's call my uncle. You've repeatedly said that you'll do whatever he asks you to where his mother is concerned."

In less than forty-eight hours, we were scheduled to fly to England, but we still needed passports for Essie Mae and my grandmother and we still needed Harry Mae's permission for Ernestine to travel.

Wilson wasn't at home. Dorothea answered the phone. Sitting there at Harry Mae's cluttered kitchen table, I saw myself at the Memphis airport boarding the plane home alone.

—⁂ UPS AND DOWNS

ESSIE MAE'S NEPHEW RICKY SWORE THAT he was honest, and while I listened to him list his qualifications, I kept my eyes on the road. He said, "I don't smoke, don't drink. And don't mess with drugs. Ask anybody. I don't do none of them things. So if you know anybody over there in England wanting somebody for work, let me know. . . . You can ask my aunt. She'll tell you that if it hadn't of been for me moving in with her, she'd be down, down, down."

He was talking about Essie Mae, and the reason he was sitting in my passenger seat was that he thought he might know where to find her. But when he directed me to the interstate, I got worried. "Ricky, the plane leaves in an hour and a half. There's no time for driving long distances."

The search for Essie Mae had begun almost seven hours earlier when I arrived at her door before 8 A.M. and was worried that she hadn't spent the previous night at home. Ricky had answered my knock. I wasn't surprised that he'd come to the front door as if I'd disturbed him, because as I drove there from the motel it felt like all of Memphis was sleeping in that Saturday morning.

Discovering that Essie Mae wasn't at home hadn't been the best way to begin my last day in town, and it took time for Ricky to convince me that I might find her at the nursing home.

"That's not possible," I snapped, "she promised faithfully that she wouldn't work after five last night and said that she was driving to Mississippi to see her brother." But she hadn't. Despite my reluctance to drop by the nursing home as Ricky suggested, I rushed there.

"You just missed her," Lula Mae said as she cleaned the kitchen. "She said she was going shopping with you and your grandmother."

O'Ferrell had assured me that she wouldn't make the trip, but there had been no reason to believe him, for although Essie Mae had admitted to being afraid of flights, she'd also cried about how shabbily she'd been treated at the nursing home and realized that the journey to England was a new hope and a brand-new start. Possibly I was more excited for her than I was for Ernestine.

"Essie Mae, people are going to love you in England. You'll probably get there and find a husband."

But as three in the afternoon approached and there had been no call from her, I became rattled by possibilities. Was she under a bus? Was she tied up at the nursing home? Had she run away? Was she stowed in a back room of her own house unable to admit that she'd changed her mind about going? Was she doing some last-minute shopping and planning to make her own way to the airport?

After my early morning visit to her place I returned again at noon, and although she wasn't there, a young man invited me in. Seeing a large suitcase resting on the back of the sofa was encouraging. The room was lit by the cartoons on the color TV. "Has there been any word from Essie Mae?" I asked.

"No. And everybody's looking for her," he informed me from the shadowy corner of her living room as I placed the clothes I'd brought over for her on a chair. Her home was barer than I expected it to be: one sofa, one chair, one coffee table, one TV— and the four walls.

I thought of the places I'd be taking her to: the flat in Folkestone where she could take walks on the cliff top or stroll alone safely by the sea. I envisioned her in the house in France sitting by the open fire or gathering daffodils by the armload from our small wood at the edge of our land. I had dreams of her meeting some well-heeled West Indian man who would whisk her off. But she had to get to England first and there it was, past noon and no sign of her.

O'Ferrell looked impatient with me when I turned up at his back door, so I made light of her disappearance and tried not to read "I told you so" in his expression. His son, Vincent, was in town and we were taking the same flight from Memphis to Nashville to make our connecting planes, so it was possible that O'Ferrell and Anne might come to the airport. It gave me an excuse not to say goodbye.

"My grandmother's at the motel with Archie Lachlan, my director friend from Glasgow who arrived yesterday." Employed by the BBC, Archie had come to Memphis to consider the possibility of making a documentary about Ernestine and agreed to sit with her while I searched for Essie Mae. "He'll be worried about what's taking me so long."

When I turned the key of the door to my motel room, Archie's expectant expression suggested that he thought that I had had word from Essie Mae because, sitting by the phone, he hadn't.

10

England

— ✂ IN FLIGHT

WHEN THE BREAKFAST CART GRAZED HER HEAD, I expected Ernestine to wake up. But she didn't stir, and for a split second I wondered if she was dead. More than one person had asked, "What if the flight kills her?" and to each I'd replied, "At least she'll die free." But that was bravado. I wanted her to be alive when we landed.

She had been sleeping with her head in the aisle for the third or fourth time, and I could tell from the cross look the flight attendant gave her that she didn't realize that Ernestine was non compos mentis.

Reaching over the empty seat between us to shift her head, I didn't dare adjust her body for fear of waking her. Covered by three airline blankets, she had been sleeping for most of the flight and I hoped that she hadn't wet herself, because I had no spare trousers for her.

It was the last day of December 1994 and we were approaching Britain. Would I have been as petrified if Essie Mae had been with us, or had I suddenly realized that I was traveling alone with someone who was totally unable to take care of herself? I had almost dared think about what I would do if she were refused entry, but that dilemma was a couple of hours away and it was dangerous to think beyond the next half hour.

Getting Ernestine ready to land was apt to take an hour, depending upon how long she spent in the toilet, but in case she woke perplexed by her surroundings, I was glad that she remained sleeping.

Of course, her passport was in my bag along with the letters from

Wilson and Harry Mae giving her permission to travel with me, and I kept checking that I had them. At least we weren't landing at Heathrow, I kept telling myself, but even Gatwick was likely to cause us difficulties. The corridors leading from the plane to Customs were as long as several city blocks, and while I expected to get a wheel-chair for Ernestine, I had a few heavy pieces of hand luggage.

I dared not think about what I had done by assuming responsi-bility for someone who didn't know my name, and yet I knew that it would have been unthinkable to have left her in a nursing home where I'd seen a woman washing herself in a basin of water brown with fecal matter.

Two breakfast trays were handed to me. They included yogurt, which she couldn't have, a sweet muffin, which might have given her the runs, and bananas—which I tried to view as a good omen.

Sniffing the air, I told myself Ernestine was still dry and tried not to think about what I would do if she wasn't. She looked com-fortable and safe and I took several deep breaths to quell my anx-ieties about getting her from the plane to the car in the long-term parking lot, because that was more than half an hour away.

Her head had fallen over into the aisle again.

⟶☙ FROM MEMPHIS TO MINEHEAD

AT THE MEMPHIS MOTEL, Ernestine had suddenly glanced at a print on the wall or eyed a lamp or stared long and hard in the mirror which covered the bathroom wall. But at Sid and Lizzie's home near Minehead, she touched things.

Sidney De Haan was the founder of SAGA, the Folkestone-based holiday company which had generously paid for our plane tickets. Lizzie was his Welsh sheepdog. They'd become inseparable after Sid's wife Margery died, and I was a little worried about his being alone over the New Year. He was in his seventies and we were unlikely friends.

In Sid's eighteenth-century house with its beams and open fire-places, Ernestine grew curious. She stroked the green marble lighter on the coffee table, which didn't work. She picked up the bowl of potpourri on the bedroom dressing table and emptied it, pushing the scented wooden shavings this way and that with her index finger.

It was 1 January 1995 and Sid and Margery would have been celebrating their golden wedding anniversary had she not died the previous summer. Whatever age Lizzie was, she was placid and patient and took little notice of Ernestine, who took no notice of her.

When Sid had invited us to stay, I'd imagined that we would have been arriving with Essie Mae. But only two of us turned up with champagne, flowers, and the box of jellied candies which Ben and Frances Hooks had given Ernestine in Memphis.

It was scary to be minding a ninety-six-year-old with unpre-dictable habits, nighttime incontinence, and no health plan who had spent fifty-two years in an asylum. There was no telling what kind of guest Ernestine would be and Sid needed to be a tolerant host. During the Second World War, he'd been a prisoner of war for five years and worked in a mental hospital in Northampton afterward, so I thought he'd understand my grandmother and for the most part he did.

His home was a large thatched cottage near Minehead in Somerset and Ernestine realized that she was somewhere different when we wrapped her in a hand-knitted blanket of brightly col-ored squares and sat her in a velvet chair by the fire. Had she ever seen the flicker of logs burning, or smelled their scent mixed with the aroma of roast lamb? And when had she last had a glass of sherry, if ever? She swigged it like a shot of scotch, as if playing a barmaid in a cowboy movie.

"Grandma! Drink it slowly!" I said as Sid poured her another.

She dozed before dinner beside the inglenook fireplace and didn't mind Lizzie sleeping near her feet.

Her dinner was roast lamb with homemade mint sauce and vegetables, and when she finished that and the ice cream, Sid offered her a chocolate from a box of the best and richest which Harrods had to offer.

"Sid, she mustn't."

She had been accustomed to the most basic diet and, tempting as the chocolates were, it was cruel to give her too much too soon. Furthermore, if she got diarrhea how much would she suffer and how would I cope?

She needed more protection than a newborn baby. To guess her fears took more forethought than guessing her needs. Did she know that she was safe with me, or had she lost the ability to trust anyone? Perhaps she was waiting for me to ask for more than she wanted to give.

Realizing that she had little experience with friendly white men, I cringed every time Sid bent over her to say something, but how could I explain that to an Englishman who hadn't experienced racial segregation? Being Jewish, he almost understood her circumstances, but could he ever appreciate how vulnerable Ernestine had been at Bolivar? Even as a woman I didn't pretend to comprehend it.

To let her open the refrigerator and cupboards, to show her how to switch on the light, to tell her that she could touch anything she wanted, to show her the bowl of fruit and watch her attempt to bite into an apple, fail, and put it back—these moments excited me, but I was also afraid.

We had a five-hour car journey to face and then a climb up four flights of stairs. Would she manage? Would I? Her nighttime incontinence had plagued me at the motel, and even at Sid's I didn't rest for fear that she would leak through her diaper and ruin his mattress. Old people's urine has a cloying stench and Ernestine's was no exception.

"You like this bedroom?" I asked when I tucked her under a mound of eiderdown and white candlewick spread.

"Yeah, hon," she chirped, staring at the white wall where framed bird prints were hanging.

Who did she think I was, and what did she think I planned to do with her? Or had she given up thinking at all? Or does she have flights of memory, even now recalling Sid's laughter between his inhaling gulps of Player's cigarettes?

FOLKESTONE

MYSTIFYING AND MYTHICAL, the great slabs of stone were there in the middle of nowhere with the grass around them as green as if it were a spring day. But there was no point in shouting Stonehenge! because neither the name nor the mysterious boulders would have meant anything to her. So we drove past silently although Ernestine had a perfect view of them from the passenger seat.

She'd said she liked the music that I was playing as we drove along, but we'd been in the car for over an hour since Sid had waved us goodbye. In case she was not aware that the din of soul music was affecting her, I turned it off and pointed to the rolling hills.

"This is England, Grandma, isn't it pretty?"

"Yeah, hon."

"And look at all the sheep!"

Her head was facing the right direction but could she see at a distance those few hundred sheep grazing? With my free hand, I tried to rearrange the long woolen scarf which I'd wrapped around her head. It was slipping down over her brow and she had no intention of adjusting either it or her coat, which was slightly bunched up under the seatbelt.

Wearing outdoor winter clothing was probably something she hadn't done in many years, decades even, and I'd forgotten that there was an art to keeping a coat on your shoulders and rearranging a scarf when it slipped. Did she care to learn how? I didn't know and was slow to understand that she knew nothing about herself. But did she want it this way? I wondered, as we headed for what was to be her new home. How could I prepare her for a life where she had choices?

Folkestone was now less than three hours away, and as much as I wanted to avoid thinking about how I would get her and our suitcases up the four flights of stairs leading to my maisonette—no, our maisonette—it was an obstacle which I would need to overcome. Had I not had major stomach surgery seven weeks earlier, carrying her would have been an easy solution, because she probably weighed less than ninety pounds. But instructions for my recovery had been, "Lift nothing, not even a teakettle."

We drove through every conceivable weather condition that England suffers in winter, except snow. That was waiting to greet us in Folkestone.

Assuming that Ernestine had seen snow, I hoped she wasn't unnerved by the sight of our seaside town colored white; recalling that she had lived in Boston and had written to her husband about the world covered in snow, I thought it was possible that she would even be excited.

We'd hardly spoken on the journey because I needed to focus upon the traffic and she seemed unable to hear me unless I aimed

my voice in her direction. But heading into town from the motor-
way, I turned to her to shout, "Look! Look down the hill. Can you
see the snow?"

No reply. Her wizened little face was hardly protruding from
the black scarf and she appeared to be sitting upright only because
the seatbelt supported her.

"Darling, are you falling over? Do you want me to stop?"

We had driven two hundred and fifty miles, and apart from one
break we'd made at a service station fifty miles east of
Stonehenge—where, after taking her to the toilet, I'd plied my
grandmother with a ham sandwich, a packet of chips, and some
orange juice—we'd been driving nonstop. Ernestine hadn't closed
her eyes once, which surprised me, but perhaps the speed I'd been
going kept her awake.

Why the rush? I was petrified, my jaws clenched, my heart
pounding; I made that journey in a state of sheer terror as questions forced their way into my attempt to remain oblivious to the
circumstances facing us. Will you be able to find someone to live
in to care for her? How will she adjust to seeing only white faces?
Will she be able to sleep in a bedroom on her own? And will she
miss Essie Mae and the nursing home? How will you get back and
forth to France with her?

Nothing that crossed my mind was as daunting as the fallen
snow, which clung to a thick layer of ice covering street and pave-
ments. Creeping along the wide boulevard which leads to the sea
and the crescent where I live, the car slid twice and I screamed,
realizing I had no control.

It was officially still the New Year holiday, but that wasn't the
reason the streets were deserted. Icy conditions made it suicidal to
be out. But I had to get Ernestine from the parked car into the
house. "Grandma, you're not going to be able to walk. I'll have to
carry you," I said, pulling into the curb.

An inch of snow covered the ice leading to my door and I put
my head on the steering wheel, reached inside my coat, and felt
my stomach. Was I up to the challenge? A seagull squawked repeat-

edly overhead and I peered through the tinted windshield in search of it; anything to forestall the inevitable move, which had to be made by limbs already aching with stiffness from the long drive.

Ernestine's profile was stoic; her head could have been chiseled in a Stonehenge pillar. Maybe the only place to be at that moment was in the void where I assumed she dwelled. Did she know I was staring at her? The black scarf had slipped again over her brow and she was a portrait of widowhood: wrinkled, silent, draped in black. Beyond her was a crescent of identical buildings as pale as her image was dark, but hardly much older than she was.

"This is where we live, Grandma." My voice was unconvincing. My eyes scanned the pavement leading from the car to the front door, desperate to spot a few feet at least where the ice had been worn away.

Getting the bags in the house was good practice, so by the time I came out for Ernestine, I felt more confident when I said, "I'll carry you, because of the ice and snow. But you'll have to help by being still."

I was wearing suede loafers with rubber soles and, despite the chilling air, I'd dumped my coat in the hallway to make lifting my grandmother less cumbersome. Opening her door, I found myself laughing at the sudden vision I had of us falling with legs flailing. The many windows that grace the tall Victorian houses could have been a thousand eyes. I was sure that neighbors were watching, because most of them were elderly and had little else to do.

Ernestine allowed herself to be carried to the front door with the ease of a ballerina trained in being lifted off her feet, and we reached the hallway without incident. But we were more Laurel and Hardy than Nureyev and Fonteyn when I tried lifting her upstairs.

"Grandma, don't grip the banister," I yelled in the middle of the first flight. But nonetheless her small fingers managed to seize the smooth walnut handrail and we nearly toppled before I could reach the landing. "You mustn't grab hold of anything," I begged, putting her down to catch my breath.

Her strength and determination amazed me as she fought to keep from being lifted to the second flight. So I let her sit on the top step and explained the position. "You'll die from a heart attack if I let you walk up these stairs, and I'll be back in the hospital if you make it so hard for me to carry you. You've got to trust me."

We'd been together for almost two weeks. She had a passport, a packed suitcase, and a return ticket to Memphis and maybe she knew she'd come too far to lose faith. So she merely held her arms around my neck on the fourth flight.

It was January second, and when I settled her in a chair by the fake coal fire, she looked happy and as if she belonged. But the ascent of the stairs had told me something which I couldn't yet face: I wasn't really able to carry her up and was certain that, even if she could manage to climb four flights, it would be stressful for her. But it was hard to admit that a nursing home was the only option.

 DESIRES

"SARDINES, GRANDMA? You're sure that's what you want?"

The lamp cast a flattering shadow across her face and she smoothed her hand over her dark-blue pleated skirt. Did she feel as elegant as she looked, sitting there in the lavender easy chair? By her feet lay the Bible I'd been reading to her and I placed it on the side table before arranging the wooden dinner tray on her lap.

It was rare for her to ask for anything and it was exciting to meet her request. "Sardines," I said, pulling up a chair so that I could feed her. She was as quiet as the fake coal fire which bathed the living room in a golden glow, and I wondered how long it would take her to feel comfortable and understand that this was her new home.

She gobbled the sardines, letting me spoon them into her mouth with the peas and mashed potatoes; the meal was over too quickly.

Unless I turned on the television, how would I occupy her? In case she had the answer, I asked, "What would you like to do now?"

Her stoic expression didn't change. She said, "Let's go pick some cotton!"

Folkestone in January with gale winds circling the roof was a light-year away from the visions she seemed to have of the world beyond our fireside, but she must have been feeling young and gay to have made the suggestion.

I laughed. "Pick cotton! Who do you think you're going cotton-picking with?"

"You, hon."

A NEW NURSING HOME

SHE DOESN'T CRAVE BANANAS ANY MORE and she often gets ice cream and cake, because, as the caregiver says at Romney Cottage, "Why deprive her of the things she enjoys at her age?"

Ernestine had been retrieved from a Memphis nursing home where the one thing worth taking with us was Essie Mae, who didn't come. Ernestine now lives some distance west of me. Had I dragged her from one ungodly place to bring her to another one? Certainly her new home is clean and bright and she has her own closet and drawers. And, yes, her sheets get changed every day and the room never smells, but I feel that she's been abandoned again when I spot her sitting in that room dotted with faded souls.

After she'd spent over two weeks with me between Memphis, Minehead, and Folkestone, she was responding regularly with very little prompting, but now I see her slide back into her silences. I arrive with a bunch of tulips and it takes her awhile to smile.

When we'd been together, I devoted all my energy to making events of daily occasions—asking her questions and offering options, dressing her to be seen, making a party of bath time—but it was easier entertaining a toddler. I couldn't give her all my attention, because I have a right to a life too.

But I can still see her in the passenger seat of my rental car in Memphis with her head held high. Attentive. Interested.

Yesterday I bought her some pretty secondhand clothes, and when she saw the pale blue nightie she fingered the fabric.

"You like it, Grandma?" I asked.

"Yeah, hon. They're yours."

"No they're not. I bought them for you."

The nursing home is fourteen miles away, and if it weren't for the car which a friend is lending me, I wouldn't be able to drive to see her, because my old wreck would never make it there and back. The Kent coast between Folkestone and Rye is in general one of the ugliest bits of the country's coastline, but there are some pretty stretches between Sandgate and Hythe. Sometimes the waves crash so high against the embankment that sand and pebbles are thick against the curbside after a storm.

I had Ernestine in the car driving that stretch and said, "Look, Grandma. Look at those waves. Isn't the water beautiful?"

"Yeah, hon," she said.

"You know what that is?"

"That's the Mississippi," she said.

The English Channel is much wider than the Mississippi River and not half as muddy, but one body of water must look like any other.

From her room at the home you can see across the golf course to the marsh. When I first looked out and saw the golfers in the distance, I realized that they were close enough to drive a ball through her bedroom window.

⟶ WITH CANON WOODS

ORANGE FLAMES LAPPED AT THE FAT, black coals in the small fireplace and Norman and Patsy's living room still felt like Christmas, perhaps because of the Christmas cake they served Ernestine with tea. It was rich with raisins and sugar and I had expected her to keel over with stomach cramps after swallowing the first bite. Instead, her little fingers gathered the leftover crumbs on her saucer and stuck them in her mouth. Norman laughed. "Oh, let her have another piece." He was sitting next to her with his back to the grand piano, while his daughter Juliette sat on Ernestine's left.

"She mustn't have any more, Norman, she's not used to rich food," I said, remembering how cautious they were at the nursing home about giving her anything sweet.

"Oh, just a little piece," begged Norman, who hardly seemed like a vicar when he was a vicar and now seemed even less like a canon. He turned to my grandmother. "You'd like another piece, wouldn't you?"

"Yes'm," said Ernestine. Her black southern accent sounded strange. She could have been an old English dowager sitting in that room in her red plaid jacket, but her deep voice was unlikely for someone so frail and European-looking. She accepted the second slice.

Norman had once been based at a church in a Philadelphia ghetto in the eighties and I had brought Ernestine to receive a blessing from him. He is open and tolerant and his church, St. Leonard's, stands on the hill opposite his vicarage, but when I rang him at five to ask if I could bring her around, it was already too cold and dark outside to have gone into the church. As it was, Ernestine had nearly lost a shoe walking from the car to his front door.

Patsy had served tea in china cups, and I wondered how Ernestine felt sitting in that room with three strangers who smiled at her and asked simple questions that she could answer.

"Do you like the cake?" Norman asked slowly and loudly.

"Yes'm," Ernestine said without dropping her head. She was sitting in a low, upholstered chair and I sat four feet away on the floor by the fire.

"Grandma, Norman is a minister. Would you like to say the Twenty-third Psalm for him?"

Surprisingly, she said yes. It suddenly seemed wrong. Was I making her perform? Her voice was not pretty, the words were distorted, muffled. But I wanted her to share herself and maybe she did too.

"The Lord is my shepherd, I shall not want. . . ."

The tension in the room was probably hope blended with pity and grace. I spoke the words too and Norman joined in. Patsy, sitting opposite me, had tears in her eyes She was a nurse at the local hospital but being off that day was in her jeans and running shoes sitting cross-legged on the floor. Her craggy face and sympathetic eyes made her appear more priestly than Norman, who had reached out to touch Ernestine's hand.

She repeated each word and when she had finished, Norman placed his right palm on her forehead and delivered a blessing which Ernestine repeated too. Everybody clapped, and Norman insisted that she sign the visitors' book.

"She writes best with a pencil," I said, because I had seen her hold a ballpoint pen and knew that she found it difficult.

Rummaging through drawers, Juliette produced a pencil and we watched as my grandmother's tiny fingers positioned it so that she could write *Ernestine*. It filled an entire page.

⟶⟳ VALENTINE'S DAY 1 9 9 5

TEA HAD BEEN SERVED. Ernestine's full cup was on the small table beside her, but the crumbs on her sweater and around her mouth were evidence that she had been more interested in the cookies, and she barely looked up when I greeted her. I wondered if she'd noticed that I hadn't visited for two days, but she gave me a hug when I knelt beside her.

The weather was good enough for an outing and I thought she might enjoy walking on New Romney High Street. I'm uncomfortable talking to her in the residents' sitting room, because it's necessary to shout, so we usually go to her bedroom when I visit, but I only stayed long enough that day to get her coat and brush her hair.

She never smells odd any more and a little glass egg on her dresser contains crème perfume which I dabbed on the back of her hands before we went out. Before leaving I asked if she knew where she was. "Ohio, hon," she said. But on an earlier visit she had said, "Roanoke. You always want to be in Roanoke."

Roanoke is her birthplace and I assumed that it had been decades since she'd heard anybody mention it.

On the high street we passed a florist and I asked her what color flowers she wanted. "Red, sweetie," she said. But being Valentine's Day, there was a long line and it didn't seem worth the wait, so we got back into the car and I drove her to a meadow where sheep grazed, so she could eat her lunch. It was scampi on wheat, potato chips, and a banana, and as I fed it to her on the backseat, I wondered if she missed Memphis and if she preferred sitting in the McDonald's car parking lot overlooking Elvis Presley Boulevard to sitting in that back lane where one could smell the sea. What I was forgetting was that she only went to McDonald's with me.

After she'd eaten, we said the Twenty-third Psalm and I tried to get her to sing "We Are Climbing Jacob's Ladder," which she didn't do, so I sang it as loudly as I could, because her hearing is bad. I noticed her lip was swollen on the right and although I didn't want to think that somebody had hit her, it crossed my mind.

A huge black cloud loomed in the west and there had been no sun for days. She sat there in the heavy woolen coat I bought her from a secondhand shop. The bad weather doesn't affect her and she has only had one cough since she's been in England.

Does she notice that her hands no longer shake?

THINGS SAID

MEMORIES REPLAY THE VOICES. "She's in the hospital, incurably insane." "All kinds of people used to end up here that didn't belong." "Maybe she never was crazy." "I don't think she talks."

"Maybe she never was crazy" were the words which drove me to find her, that and the presumption that my father's mother, the person who was behind his own torment, had been abandoned.

She. My father's mother. My grandfather's wife. Ernestine, my grandmother, who had become less than zero after half a century in asylums. Forgettable, because we convince ourselves that she has no feelings.

The owner of the Memphis nursing home had once said, "When she come to us they had her on about ten pills twice a day. So we took her off them and she calmed right down."

But how much chemical damage had already been done, and what would she give to wake up each day positive that her hands won't shake?

Her awakenings haven't been dramatic. But what has caused them? Does not being hungry any more have something to do with her improved state of mind? Or does sleeping between clean sheets and warm blankets allow her to get a deep enough sleep that her mind becomes more alert?

And how was she now able to accept realities which for so long she'd hidden from? So often I'd shown her my father's baby picture, asking, "Do you know where Bee Tee is?" and she'd answer with "I don't know, hon," or said, "He's out playing." Yet recently when asked, Ernestine looked at the picture and said, "He's in the cemetery, dead and gone."

We were standing in her bedroom that afternoon and rain had just begun to fall on the skylight in big drops. Ernestine's voice hadn't sounded sad and her statement seemed matter-of-fact, but did she need to talk about her loss?

"Grandma, do you miss him?"

She sighed. "Yeah."

⟋⟍ A Question of Color

"USUALLY WE CAN'T MAKE OUT WHAT SHE SAYS," began the woman, "but the other evening when one of us was waiting for her to use the toilet, Ernestine said, 'You're all the wrong color!'"

I chuckled because the aide did, but was it funny or sad? Did my grandmother feel uncomfortable surrounded by white faces? Was it strange for her to see white women cleaning rooms, serving meals, and attending to the residents? Did she miss dark faces? Was she confused about why she was being treated kindly by people from whom she may have expected abuse?

Pat, the caregiver who had spoken, had dark hair and broad features and looked Irish. She treated all the residents well and seemed to take an interest in them, whether she was passing out cups of tea or escorting them to the toilet, but I didn't suspect that she was interested enough in Ernestine for me to say that the statement about color was as disturbing as it was comical, coming from somebody who looked European.

Race.

What race is Ernestine and why?

She was perched on the edge of a chair in the sitting room, and I recalled how two weeks earlier we'd been in her bedroom when Clive Botting, the owner of the nursing home, popped in to say hello. I'd just asked her what song she wanted and he'd heard her clamor, "Three Cheers for the Red, White, and Blue." Normally she asked for "Gracious Lord," so her request for a patriotic song came as a shock. I laughed and tried to remember more than the chorus. Of course, the nursing home owner didn't know one line, being English, but he took professional pride in her looking so much more alert than she'd been when he'd accepted her as a resident on 4 January. Conscious of how afraid she might be with a white man standing in her bedroom, I reminded him that she was more accustomed to a segregated environment.

Eager to make her feel comfortable, Clive smiled and said in a loud voice, "You're completely welcome here."

So that she could see that he was friendly with me, I shook his hand and said, "It's okay to be 'colored' here." Having used the word which I thought she identified with, it was a shock to hear her correction.

"I'm a white girl."

Did she think that, because all the other residents were white, she had to be too?

"It's okay to be colored," I said. "You don't have to be white to live here. Nobody will put you out for being what you are. Clive here is the owner, and he's our friend."

At her commitment interview at Bolivar in 1929, Ernestine professed she was white. Was she confused about her racial classification or had her appearance caused her to have an identity problem?

That Ernestine had told a caregiver "You're all the wrong color" may have indicated that she felt free enough to raise the matter. But if she considered them the wrong color, what did she think about herself?

⌒ SHADES OF PALE

EVERY TIME I VISIT MY GRANDMOTHER I feel a need to explain why I'm so much darker than she or my father. But explaining that I'm a genetic throwback to her mother, Mattie, would make no sense to Ernestine, so I ask her questions, hoping that she can draw a conclusion.

I ask, "What color was Roberta, Grandma?"

"Brownskin," she answers without hesitating.

"And what color am I?" I ask.

"Brownskin," says Ernestine without looking at me.

Brownskin. Dark-skinned. Light-complexioned. Coffee-colored. Cinnamon. Toasty. Café au lait. Lemon-colored. Nutmeg. Walnut. Milk chocolate. Mahogany. Dusky. Dark chocolate. Ivory. Sepia. Chestnut. Straw. Ebony. Sienna. Oak. Copper. Tan. Reddish-brown. Dark chocolate. High yellow. Black. The shades of an American family, uniquely blended with a generation of this plus a generation of that. Where is the racial link between Ernestine and me? Does it matter and, if not, when did it cease to?

Ernestine and I. What race is she? What race am I? And why?

—⟶ ANSWERS

A FEW RESIDENTS AT THE NURSING HOME occupy the same places every day. Alf, for example, likes the green wingback chair by the door. Irene is usually beside him, while a few feet away two livelier residents play cards at the table. But that morning it was surprising to see Ernestine in Alf's chair.

Before I had a chance to greet her, she glared at me and shouted, "What do you want to kiss me for?" as I approached her.

Hiding embarrassment and fear behind my apology, I tried to make light of her anger. "Oh, dear." I smiled, reluctant to call her Grandma in case that annoyed her too. "Why didn't you tell me that you don't like being kissed?"

Ernestine's harsh stare made me look away, and I recalled that she'd given me no hello or welcoming hug on my previous visit. I didn't know her well enough to be able to recognize signs that would indicate her general behavior might change, and although Essie Mae had said that Ernestine had spells, I'd only known her to be gentle.

She sat primly; her hands were folded on her lap and she held her head up, but her air was that of a total stranger. Perhaps she'd had some sort of personality change. This thought made me wary. Was this the beginning of an extensive tirade, and how long could it last and how aggressive might she become?

One of the residents playing cards called to me, "Your little one's been naughty. Been very noisy yesterday."

Ernestine's eyes were icy. Had she cause to reject me? Did she feel that she needed to distance herself from me in the all-white nursing home? Was she reacting toward me in the way that I feared she might have done when I first visited her in Memphis in '91? Or was this a mentally disturbed woman venting her morning's anxieties?

Her silence is easier to deal with than her painful rejection. If this was the beginning of a new phase, I was overly sensitive.

The sun was staging an unexpected display for a March day and I dared ask if she wanted to come for a drive. "It's beautiful out and the air will do you good," I said cautiously, as I knelt beside her chair. The aides seemed to have stopped what they were doing in the kitchen. Perhaps they were listening. Ernestine and I were the odd couple, the foreigners, the mismatched pair.

When my grandmother looked into my eyes, her own were angrier than I'd seen them and I wondered if it was wise to take her out, but having offered, I coaxed her further. "I've got some cookies for you in the car."

Was she ill? Was she having an angry explosion before she was about to die? I had no one to ask but her. "How do you feel, darling?"

She said, "I'm fine, dear friend." It was the first time I'd heard her use that expression. Her manner was formal.

"Wouldn't you like to feel the sun in your hair? We could drive down by the sea."

Her blue eyes flashed and an indecipherable rush of words poured from her. I had never felt her detachment so strongly, and her intense gaze made it more chilling. As her eyes searched mine, I felt that she could read the doubts which plagued me: Why had I got involved, where would it lead me?

Something had prompted me to buy a blank notebook to keep a record of things that she said, and fingering it in my pocket, I waited for Ernestine to rise from the chair. Had I robbed this woman of the few things in life which gave her comfort, like southern accents and Essie Mae? For all I knew, my grandmother's anger was related to reality: I had plucked her from the world that she had known.

Unsmiling, she rose from her seat, and for the first time her mood frightened me. But I followed her along the passage, and in her usual way she allowed me to lead her once we were in the open air.

Suddenly she spoke. "No," she said, "we can't get out. We can't get out right away." Her expression was sober.

"Grandma?"

She looked away as I fastened her seatbelt, and I assumed that those fleeting words weren't meant for me.

Opening a packet of strawberry wafers, I broke one off and she gobbled it. Her fingers clutched the second one so tightly that it crumbled on her lap. Should I take it from her? I was thinking, but her voice interrupted. "Yes, girl, it ain't nothing but somebody stole our case. Mr. Brandon, I think."

Her voice was as clear as it was when she said the Twenty-third Psalm with me, but she spoke with such intensity that I could hardly believe it was Ernestine. It was almost like hearing the voice of a clairvoyant speaking for the dead. I headed for the coast, hoping that I could keep her talking.

"Can you tell me your name?"

"Ernestine," she said.

"And how old are you?"

"'Bout ninety . . . " On other occasions when I'd asked she had said sixteen or twelve. I glanced over at her. She was looking ahead but there was little to see but the modern brick houses, ugly and unimaginative, which line the road to Greatstone. I wanted to park so that I could concentrate on her.

She never remembered my name but soon after she had moved to the nursing home and I'd asked her who Marsha was, she had said, "An actress." It made me laugh, because I couldn't imagine that she understood the concept and assumed that she was repeating what she'd heard someone say at the nursing home. But that morning her lucidity made me ask, "Who's Marsha?" and Ernestine replied, "I thought you . . . Magnolia Davenport."

Had she said "Magnolia Davenport"? Her strangled speech was difficult to understand while I was driving, so I pulled into a space overlooking the beach. It couldn't have been more drab, a low concrete wall, and the sea bed so flat that it was impossible to judge where the pebbled beach ended and the muddy channel water began. Would she say so much I'd be unable to jot down all of it? Should I drive her back to Folkestone and get my tape recorder? I sensed that Ernestine had a lot to say.

"Who am I?" I asked.

"You said Marsha," replied Ernestine.

In case the seatbelt made her uncomfortable, I offered to undo it, but she said, "No. Don't take it off."

She didn't deserve a battery of questions, but when she fell silent, I was afraid for her sake. Not to encourage her to speak was unfair to her, so we said the Twenty-third Psalm with her repeating the lines after me. But when I said, "For thine is the kingdom," Ernestine added, "And the glory" without a prompt.

How much more was she capable of with regular stimulus? Thinking of questions that she might be able to answer, I asked, "Who is Emma Hunt?"

"She is a relative of Blair Hunt." My grandmother's answer was as stilted as a nervous contestant's on a quiz show, but she herself

sat calmly, staring ahead but seeming to focus on nothing in particular. Although the tone of voice was her own, there was something otherworldly about the way in which she phrased the
answer.

Emma Hunt was the name of my grandfather's mother. It had
also been his older sister's name, but since she had died at thirteen,
Ernestine never knew her.

"What did Blair Hunt give you?" I asked, unsure how she would
answer.

"A ring. He put it on the finger."

"What kind of ring?"

"It was a gold ring," she said.

A few other cars had parked either side of us. A couple sat in
one talking, a man and a woman who may have looked at my
grandmother and me. Who would have guessed how we were
related?

Ernestine remained silent as we watched a station wagon pull
up. A man was driving and a woman got out, draped in a raincoat
with its fur collar matching her fur hat. Two Alsatians leapt from
the back seat and she guided them toward the barren shore on a
lead just as my grandmother said, "I just want to say, go see Bessie
Clark."

"Why do you want to see her?" I asked.

"She sat in my chair almost."

The voice was accusing, and Ernestine seemed indignant as she
shifted in her seat, crossing her legs and arranging her clasped
hands in her lap. But her accusation didn't immediately lead me to
another question.

Lost for words, I asked, "Do you want me to sing?"

"I wouldn't sing," said Ernestine graciously. "I thought you were
a relative to your sister Susie Cloud."

Jotting the phrases down encumbered me. Had I had a tape
recorder, there would have been no need to interrupt Ernestine's
replies with silence.

When had she last spoken so clearly? Did she have regular bouts of speech, or was it the first time in years that she'd spoken more than a few simple words at a time and was it tiring to her?

"Grandma, want to go back home?"

"No, we can't go back right now," said Ernestine.

She suddenly squinted as if there were someone in the distance whom she wanted to focus upon but couldn't.

"Do you need glasses?" I asked.

"I don't know," she answered matter-of-factly.

"Would you like another cookie?" Having never been a secretary, dictation stumped me, and my grandmother stared at the small red notebook in which I copied her responses. While she watched me scribbling, I offered another wafer.

"No, darlin'." Her voice was kind. "Don't give me another cookie."

Mentioning names of places and people that she had known seemed an obvious way to make her talk. "Who was at ol' Kortrech High with you?"

"Lula Cloud."

"And how old is Lula?"

Hesitating as though she was calculating, Ernestine finally said, "About seventy."

Lost for questions, faced with nothing but a flat shore, a blue horizon, and a grandmother who was far more capable of stringing sentences together than I had imagined, we both fell silent, until Ernestine said, "It's a fire hospital."

I didn't reply, and after a few minutes she said, "Vivien Luston and Alberta Winston, lady."

"What about them?" I laughed.

"You had a pencil on your desk. . . ."

Whatever was responsible for this sudden willingness to talk wasn't clear, but I felt fortunate that I was there and that the blank tablet allowed me to record sentences that I might have otherwise forgotten.

Where did she think she was, as the gulls circled the shore with their haunting calls? Had she ever been to the seashore? It was hard to envisage how restricted her life had been. From high school to homemaking hadn't been unusual when she was a graduate, and America's entry into the First World War brought the opportunity to jump at offers of marriage from men who were to be stationed in Europe.

"Do you have anything special to tell me?" I asked.

"I'll tell you anything."

Was it cruel to continue questioning her, or did she like to hear herself making sounds? Did she enjoy conversing? In case it was the latter, I treated her to some easy questions.

"What's your husband's name?"

"Blair Hunt," she said immediately.

"And what does Blair Hunt do?"

"I don't know," she said.

"Is he a carpenter?"

"Schoolteacher," she replied in that heavy, dark southern accent, so reminiscent of the black rural South.

"And what did Ernestine Jacobs do?"

"Sew, difficult sewing."

Had she sewn, or was she confusing her mother's occupation with her own as a housewife?

A few pink flakes of strawberry wafer had settled in her lap. It was lunchtime and I didn't want her to miss it, but before starting the car, I asked if there was anything else we should discuss.

"Talk about snuff, I reckon," she said.

It wasn't the first time she'd mentioned snuff, but it was difficult to imagine the delicate Ernestine with a crust of snuff in her upper lip.

Back at the nursing home, I'd forgotten that our session that morning had begun with tension. Obviously she had too; before I left she said, "Don't worry. When you come, you and me will have to go on the train." And with that, she placed both hands on my shoulders as I knelt in front of her. The kiss she placed on my forehead was a whisper. That's why some days it hurt to leave her.

—⟲ ANGST

I GET INTO THE CAR AND TOSS THE BANANA and the bunch of daffodils onto the passenger seat . . . then I check that her half-eaten packet of wafers hasn't disappeared from the back and switch on the engine. As it idles, guilt has my stomach in knots and I resist openly accepting that I don't want to visit my grandmother. Isn't it my fault that she's in that nursing home where I now dread going?

Or is it Ernestine I dread? I can't admit that I don't want to see her or that I'm not in the mood to give the performance necessary to get her to communicate and make eye contact. It requires as much energy as giving a one-woman show to a packed theater. But there's no applause at the end.

Selfish thoughts, too strong to deny, increase my fears. God won't forgive me and I'll bring bad luck to my grandmother and me. I try to think of something pleasant as I head toward the coast, but I visualize a fat woman at the nursing home slumped in a chair and nodding like a junkie. Is that how I'll end up? Will that be my punishment for thinking about myself instead of Ernestine's needs?

The traffic creeps behind a beginning driver on the two-lane coastal road that leads to comatose New Romney and I wonder how Ernestine will receive me. Will she reject me after the tedious drive? Am I expending the sweetest juices of my middle age upon a woman who couldn't care less if I visit or not?

I imagine my arrival at the nursing home. In the hallway my eyes will avoid the depressing artificial flowers and the folded blue wheelchair, and I'll grin and grit my teeth before entering that sitting room where death keeps watch.

Where is my conviction? I wonder, as my sweaty palms grip the steering wheel and I try to free my mind of the negative thoughts that rush upon me. "She is going to outlive us all," I can hear her guardian saying, as I wonder if Ernestine is some demon who has come to destroy our family. Thinking about myself, my father, my grandfather, I cannot remember her suffering.

What happened to my sense of humor and why can't I see the funny side of my responsibility? I ask myself, as I drive past the dismal parade of one-room shops in Dymchurch. But nothing will relieve the sense of guilt. You could do more, my conscience keeps saying, until I release a long, loud scream before taking deep breaths. Perhaps it will get easier, I tell myself. But when, and how, and will the cost of keeping her at the nursing home finish me?

The car swerves so much on the last curve that the banana rolls off the passenger seat but I don't reach to get it. Keeping both hands on the steering wheel, I try to think good thoughts about my efforts on Ernestine's behalf. But more negativity erupts in me, and I remember the times when someone has asked, "How's your grandmother?" and I've nearly said, Don't get involved!

Ernestine has consumed my peace of mind. Seeing her reminds me that I am forty-nine and alone; she reminds me that I am all she's got and the weight of that sinks me farther down in the driver's seat.

The banana is still on the car floor. It stirs memories of Memphis that May of '93 when I kept bananas in the car for Ernestine after hearing Essie Mae say, "Miss Hunt loves bananas. If you don't watch her she'll come in this kitchen and steal 'em. . . . One time she ate seven!" But bananas don't excite Ernestine anymore, because she's no longer hungry.

Will she be pleased to see me?

Maybe. Maybe not.

⟋ SAFE

"Don't let's go outside," said Ernestine, rising from the chair in her bedroom. "That damn nigger James will be out there in the yard."

The owner of the nursing home was standing in the doorway. His grin slightly irritated me when he said, "Well, I understood 'damn nigger' but I have no idea what else she said!"

Ernestine wasn't talking to him. She had been addressing me, because I'd asked if she was ready to go downstairs, and the question was still in her mind when she said, "Let's stay right here. It's safe here."

"Grandma, it'll be safe downstairs. Honest." I wanted to reprimand her for calling someone a damn nigger, but her generation had used the insults which they had regularly heard used against them.

She had been talking since I'd arrived, making pertinent statements such as, "I don't think we better go in that store," when I parked outside a delicatessen and asked if she wanted anything from it. And when we returned to the nursing home and settled in her bedroom, she looked at me while I was combing her hair and said, "We got out the car too soon."

"Did you want to ride longer?" I asked. But she gave no answer. "Shall we go for another ride now?" I prodded.

"No, darlin'. I don't want to leave here."

She also didn't want her face or hands washed and didn't want to sing or say prayers, although her mood was positive. She liked the earrings and the red knitted cardigan which we had found for her that morning at the secondhand shop where she'd shouted "Keep your mouth shut" twice to no one in particular while I checked the shirt rack.

The elderly Englishwoman manning the till pretended not to have heard, but Ernestine's voice was bold and firm and unremitting. Grabbing her hand, I'd led her to the shirt rack, conscious that no one spoke above a whisper in that shop where they managed to contain that "worn before" smell which can make secondhand clothes depressing. Ernestine smelled the sleeve of a nylon blouse and forgot about whoever she wanted to silence.

She took no notice of the red cardigan while we were paying for it, but at the nursing home when she watched me hang it, she said, "That's so pretty." The mixture of surprise and enthusiasm in her tone was young and feminine, and for a fleeting five seconds, we could have been two women appreciating a purchase.

"You really like it?"

"Yes, darlin'."

It was moments after that the nursing home owner had arrived and I apologized for being two days late with Ernestine's room charges, which I paid each week, although I can't afford to. The first time she'd met the owner, she'd kissed him on the cheek, but while he stood in the doorway now she backed away from his handshake.

He was pleasant, a biology teacher at a Dover public school who ran the home as a part-time job. He asked very little about her history, which is just as well, because I'm still unconvinced that she needed to spend fifty-two years at Bolivar or that the condition which landed her there was hereditary insanity.

As she walked along the hallway ahead of us and opened the door leading to the stairs, I wondered if her fear of James plagued her or whether she realized that she was in a place where she no longer had to worry about her safety. She had slipped into her new life with such ease, it was hard to remember that although I didn't know her past, she had lived it, and many of the fears it had produced remained.

She was no longer living in the South, but she had lived through its crippling segregation. She was no longer a wife, but she had survived from a time when women had no rights.

MATTERS OF LIFE AND DEATH

WHAT'S WORRYING IS THAT SHE'S BEEN HOLDING ON for her sons' sake. Is she staying alive for them, or has she forgotten that the one choice left to her is death?

Would it disturb her to know that her eldest son killed himself and is it right to withhold that fact from her? If she understood that shock treatment, frontal lobotomies, and years in asylums were all that his future had promised, mightn't she be pleased that he had the foresight not to suffer?

Intelligence, the ability to learn, these had been my father's strengths. What ammunition did he have without his memory? A black male who had given his life to studying, what was his hope for the future when he found after shock treatment that he couldn't concentrate enough to read? Maybe he died for his family's sake. For his wife's sake, his brothers' sake, and mine.

Schizophrenia was his main interest. Why? Is that what he thought his mother had suffered from? That's the modern term for dementia praecox, which is what Ernestine's condition had been called.

More than a few times I've tried to explain to my grandmother that I'm Blair's child. The last time I tried, she looked at me with a blank expression when I said, "The reason I call you 'Grandma' is that I'm Bee Tee's daughter. You've been away from home for a long, long time and he grew up and got married. And he had me. But he's dead now, which is why he doesn't come to see you. He loved you, you know that?"

She was sitting in her room at the nursing home and I'd been brushing her hair while she sat with her head back resting on a pillow. Unsure whether there would be tears or denials from her, I stood back to let her take in what I'd said. But Ernestine didn't react; perhaps life and death have lost their meaning for her.

—☙ A SUDDEN CHANGE

HER ELFIN FINGERS CLAW AND SCRATCH AT THE AIR while her hands and arms jerk and jump, but her eyes are fixed on the last segment of the sandwich she's trying to eat. It's nerve-racking to watch her limbs flapping about while the rest of her is still. Any one of the five residents seated at the table could hand her that sandwich but nobody notices that she's incapable of picking it up. How does she keep from screaming when so many of her muscles twist and twitch her this way and that?

Right arm and left arm are at odds with each other until she grips her head with her left hand, so that for a moment, she is as still as the people around her who await the slice of cake which is about to be served. How long have her arms been out of control? Nobody can say when it started, but this involuntary motion is more exaggerated than I've ever seen and it hurts to watch her from across the room.

Her frantic fingers could be plucking an invisible harp, her restless arms could be taking aim with a bow and arrow. Suddenly her elbow snaps back with such force it lifts her off her chair, yet she continues to eye that excuse for a sandwich. The bread is almost as white as the saucer it lies upon. Spasms contort her wrinkled cheeks and, with her lips clamped, her mouth turns this way and that.

The aide serving Ernestine's table takes no notice and places a cup of tea in front of her. How many minutes before her flailing arms knock it over? Shifting her focus from sandwich to cup, in one unexpected sweep of her arm she has stolen up on the cup and draws it to her lips. Bravo! Despite her shaking hand, she snatches, a sip. Won't she spill it?

Unable to watch, I waited for the aide to pass my corner of the dining room. "My grandmother, when did she begin to shake? She wasn't doing it a few days ago."

The aide's smile was meant to placate and she threw a glance over her shoulder at Ernestine, who'd managed to place her cup back on the table. "Oh, the old ones do that from time to time. They're probably remembering things."

That made no sense, but her smile said it wasn't worth arguing with her. A deep sigh escaped me before I could say, "It's never been this pronounced before. Her fingers used to jerk about, but look at her. She's been trying to pick that sandwich up for ten minutes, but her arms are all over the place. Might this be a reaction to some pills she's been given?"

"We don't give them pills."

"She was noisy last time I was here. If she carried on into the night mightn't somebody have given her a sleeping pill?"

As we spoke Ernestine stared at that quarter of sandwich. Her fingers attacked the thin air, poking and pinching, jabbing and snatching.

Her body is a penitentiary and she is the chain gang.

⟿ SAFE AND SORRY

ERNESTINE WAS MORE AGILE THAN MOST of the others at the nursing home. To see her bend down and pick something up off the floor would surprise me, but I took it for granted that she could climb the stairs to her room whenever I visited. That had become our ritual; I'd arrive and we'd head for her room upstairs at the end of the passage. It was always spotless and to see her stuffed animals lined up on her dark pink bedspread was somehow a relief.

Pictures of Blair, Wilson, and Ernest stood on her dresser and I kept fresh flowers in a vase beside her small pot of perfume. Her maple drawers were full of laundered underwear and warm flannel nightgowns. The sweaters and jogging suits were always neatly folded and her blouses and skirts hung in her closet. Fresh sheets were on her bed every day and clean towels hung on her radiator.

While the cold weather held, her bedroom was a good place for us to pass time together. Having a sink near her bed let me indulge her, putting steamy towels on her face while she sat in her padded chair at the foot of her bed with her head resting on a pillow.

Ernestine would close her eyes and I'd recall places and names from her past. She could say my name, but she called me Lucy Cloud if I asked who I was without prompting her first.

While I brushed her hair we'd say the Lord's Prayer and the Twenty-third Psalm, which no longer seemed such a feat, because she repeated it so easily most of the time. The song she always requested was "Gracious Lord," but she usually got "Jacob's Ladder" because I know so few hymns.

The attendants on duty tolerated me, but I sensed that they thought my visits were too frequent. I tried to explain how important it was for her to see a black face and to hear English spoken with the accent that she was used to, and I believed it. When I spoke to her my voice was black southern.

My dream in taking her from Memphis had been to give her a family, so it felt like I'd failed her to have her in the nursing home. She was well fed, but I felt that she was missing the things that happen haphazardly at home—the impromptu hug, a shared glance.

The sitting room of a nursing home is such a dead space. Even at Romney Cottage, with the wall of glass leading to the patio and the golf course beyond, there was a feeling that the fourteen residents were only half alive. To walk into that room and find Ernestine sitting in a chair against the wall with her head bowed always made me sad, but it was the best that I could give her. With my flat on the fourth floor, I felt that getting her to climb those long, winding stairs on a visit was a punishment that she wouldn't have asked for.

When the weather was good we would take drives out by the sea and sit with the window open listening to the gulls. She always seemed eager to go for the drives, but I sometimes wondered if she could see through my phony good cheer.

Once we were sitting in the car with the windows open looking out at the sea. The landscape was flat and there was an uninterrupted view of pebbly beach, English Channel, and pale gray sky. Ernestine was getting better at answering questions, but I hadn't said anything to her for a few minutes. She was staring ahead and said, "You hurt for me."

The voice had been hers, but to whom did the thought belong?

We were parked in the same spot where we'd been when she'd talked a lot once before. So I sat still, hoping that she would say more. She was wearing her blue pleated skirt and a bright red hand-knitted sweater which I'd bought secondhand, although it looked new. Her hands were clasped in her lap. If she felt me staring at her, she didn't bother to look in my direction. She sat so still. It was spooky.

⟳ IN HER OWN WORDS

IT WAS TOO QUIET. THE RESIDENTS WERE AS SILENT as tombs. Age had crucified them. Even with the TV on, the atmosphere was heavy and I wanted to get away from the ones propped in chairs.

Ted and Sylvia were at the table. Thank God, they disregarded the NO SMOKING sign, and sucked on hand-rolled cigarettes. Skimpy strings of smoke settled on the flowers and the out-of-date magazines.

I said, "Mind if we join you?" and guided Ernestine in their direction.

Alf and Dora were sitting there too. So was Kathryn, who had a deck of cards in front of her and eyed Ted like a lover.

It felt as if what the residents needed was something to do, so after settling Ernestine, I said, "Let's sing something."

They did pretty well on "The White Cliffs of Dover" but "Danny Boy" was shaky. Still, it loosened them up, so rather than let them slip back into their silence, I said, "How about everybody telling two important things that happened to them?"

Ernestine was opposite me at the table. Her head was bowed and I didn't think she was listening. Sylvia had nothing to say and her nicotine-stained fingers rolled another cigarette. So Ted volunteered to go first. His story about parachuting into a duck pond in Belgium during the Second World War was supposed to be funny—but nobody laughed. In fact, Alf looked asleep until he got to talk about engineering.

Then came Ernestine's turn. She usually said, "I don't know, hon," to almost any question, and since she'd been staring at her hands while the others spoke, I thought it might be kinder to skip her. But she was still the new girl, and I was there to encourage her to mix, so I prodded, "What about you, Grandma? Wanna tell us something important that happened in your life?"

Ernestine's hands were clasped tightly together and her blue eyes flashed at me. In that southern black accent which doesn't match her looks she said, "I got killed."

I laughed, because I wasn't thinking. In fact it wasn't until I woke up in the middle of the night and thought about it that I understood the significance of what she had said. I wanted to cry, because of course she was right.

Ernestine got killed.

~ DESPERATE

APRIL DRIFTED IN AND HARRY MAE SIMONS was still witholding Ernestine's pension. I'd been paying the nursing home fees since January. The cost crippled me. Although Harry Mae had a legal duty to forward my grandmother's pension, I had thought her sense of moral duty would also motivate her to do the right thing.

In January, when I explained to Wilson and Dorothea that I was putting Ernestine in a nursing home, he had assured me that he was to become her guardian and would see that I received her income. Our phone conversation was pleasant and I thought he was relieved to know that his mother was near me. But Ernestine had entered England on a visitor's visa and I couldn't apply for her permanent stay until I could show that she had an income and wouldn't become a burden on the state.

Dorothea sent a contribution which showed good faith but did little to reduce my borrowing to cover Ernestine's costs. Wilson's promise to go to Memphis in mid-March to sort things out didn't materialize.

I had forgotten that Harry Mae would have wanted me to fail. It was Dorothea who said, "Ernestine ruined her life." I had never considered it in those terms, but my grandmother may have been the factor which kept my grandfather and Harry Mae from marrying.

Despite the fact that my aunt and uncle had contacted her repeatedly, requesting that she forward my grandmother's pension to cover costs at the nursing home in New Romney, I heard nothing from Harry Mae. I thought that Wilson was also negotiating the transfer of the guardianship to himself from Harry Mae, so I tried to be patient. But when I rang in early April to ask what delayed Harry Mae forwarding funds, Wilson said she needed a receipt. So I provided one, with a covering letter to show that in nursing home fees alone I had paid out $5500. I also listed all the clothing and items which I had bought for my grandmother and included pictures of Ernestine in Folkestone and a brochure about the nursing home. Copies were sent to Wilson and to Harry Mae, but she insisted she never received the parcel. Nevertheless, she wrote directly to the nursing sister at Romney Cottage. She included a check for $500 and said, "Kindly let me know if this is the fee per month or what." I saw this as a means of stalling full payment rather than as an act of good faith and was concerned that the check she sent was drawn on a joint personal account.

Whatever the reason for her sending me no money despite my sending the receipts she'd demanded, I had to think of a rational solution. I thought that my uncle wasn't being aggressive enough in taking over the guardianship, but phone calls about my desperate finances changed nothing. When Dorothea rang to say that Harry Mae had refunded Dorothea's contribution, I remembered that none of them knew Ernestine and they might have felt guilty about my involvement.

Money problems make me frantic. I saw myself facing bankruptcy and told my uncle that he had to do something. "By bringing Ernestine here," I said, "I let everybody off the hook. You can sleep at night knowing that she's cared for and has me visiting twice a week. Have you asked Harry Mae what she's been doing with your mother's pension money?"

I thought a threat to arrive on his doorstep would get him to act. But still he did nothing, saying that Harry Mae had assigned a lawyer to transfer the guardianship.

Nothing changed. Dorothea rang to say the last time they'd spoken to Harry Mae she admitted that she'd never seen Ernestine. I was sitting next to the kitchen window in Folkestone. It was dark and the blinds were closed. The gulls had stopped calling for the night. I was too depressed to be angry and said, "Ernestine is helpless. How have we let Harry Mae ruin what little life she has? She's ninety-seven. She's made an incredible adjustment settling in a new country—new climate, strange faces."

Dorothea said, "Harry Mae's lawyer never returned any of our calls."

"Does Wilson know that I can't keep Ernestine much longer?"

"He said he'd have to find a nursing home for her here because you couldn't take her back to Memphis."

Two weeks crawled by. My sense of failure wore down my confidence. I stopped laughing and forgot what it felt like to wake up raring to take on a new day. Seeing Ernestine made my guilt about disturbing her life soar and I hated myself for interfering, for thinking that I was capable of improving her circumstances. But what I hated more was the bill at the nursing home, which was rising.

At the beginning of May, I rang my uncle to give him a final ultimatum, because I knew that an uncontested change of guardianship couldn't be difficult to secure.

"You're leaving me no choice," I told him. "Can't you fly to Memphis and get this sorted out at the probate court?"

"Harry Mae is guardian. I can't make her give that up."

"But she's already agreed to. She's eighty-six—maybe she's not capable of organizing it. And Ernestine is the one who'll be losing out. I took her from Memphis because she wasn't being properly cared for. She didn't have a bed, there was no toilet paper or soap in the bathroom, and there were roaches crawling down the kitchen walls."

"What do you want me to do, take Harry Mae to court? I can't afford to do that."

"Harry Mae has agreed to hand the guardianship over to you, but you have to do more than you're doing! I've given Dorothea the phone number at the probate court and the name of someone who last dealt with Ernestine's case, as well as her case number. Call! Go down there! But you have to do something, because I can't hold on."

~❧ 15 MAY 1995

WHEN I TURNED INTO THE WINDING ROAD that led to Romney Cottage, it was after eight. I'd never been there at dusk. The golf course was deserted, and lights were on in the sprawling houses set back behind tended lawns. Flowers were blooming in front of brick walls and camellia bushes were heavy with buds.

Pulling up in front of the home, I felt like a criminal because I was coming to take Ernestine away. I opened the back door of the car and removed the two empty suitcases.

The night attendant who answered the door knew why I was there. I could hardly lift my head to say hello. Shame and defeat had played havoc with me while I'd been driving there. Asking the attendant not to tell Ernestine that I'd arrived, I headed straight up to her bedroom. I hadn't been there for five days, because I knew that I couldn't put on a happy face.

Ernestine's bed had been stripped but her roommate's had been turned down. With a faint evening light coming through the window, I packed in semi-darkness. I didn't want to see what was going into the suitcases; I just wanted to get them stuffed and get out of there. I'd left packing until the last moment, hoping throughout the weekend that something would happen to turn things around: an unexpected offer of a million-dollar job, a call from Wilson, a check to me from Harry Mae. But there had been no eleventh-hour rescue. The flight I'd threatened to take to Boston was leaving before noon the next day.

The middle-aged night nurse was a stranger. Her shoulder-length hair was dyed a reddish-brown. As she came and stood in the doorway it began to look blacker as darkness fell. The one thing she did right was to turn on the light. Bent over the open drawers, I kept my eyes down so she wouldn't talk to me, but she asked, "Why's she have to leave? She's like a little doll. I dress her in the morning and she's never any trouble." I didn't answer.

The only person I'd spoken to that day was a therapist I visited who I knew could throw some perspective on what I was about to do. I didn't trust my judgment.

Wilson and Dorothea had suggested that I postpone the trip for a month, but the air tickets were nonrefundable. I'd said, "We'll be flying in on the sixteenth, arriving at two P.M."

My uncle had said he couldn't pick us up because he'd be working that day. Despite his retirement, he continued to do psychological assessments. The night attendant blocked the doorway and claustrophobia crept over me as I folded Ernestine's flannel nightgowns and laid them in the suitcase. I grabbed my father's baby picture from the dresser and slung it on top without looking at it.

It was there in that room that I'd told her he was dead. I'd said, "The reason he can't come and see you is that he died, Grandma." Ernestine had been seated in her green chair by the door. I stroked her arm, stroked her cheek. She said nothing. But about ten days later when I asked if she was happy and she said she was sad, I'd asked why.

Ernestine looked at her hands and said, "Bee Tee's dead."

With a suitcase in each hand, my steps were heavy as I plodded downstairs to collect her from the sitting room. She was sitting at the table with her back to the door. Ted was opposite her, puffing a cigarette. He looked up and said, "Isn't she lucky. I wish somebody was taking *me* to the States."

11
Boston

THE PORTER

WHEN THE PLANE LANDED IN BOSTON, I braced myself for the cat-
astrophes I was expecting. I'd requested a wheelchair for Ernestine
but didn't think it would be waiting. We were last off.

Having slept through most of the flight, Ernestine staggered
down the aisle like somebody dazed, but even then she moved
faster than I wanted her to. I was in no hurry to face five days in
a city where I had no friends and felt I couldn't depend upon family. Lagging behind her with coats and hand luggage, I frantically
kept telling myself to take one hurdle at a time. Even to get her
from the plane to a taxi had become a crisis in my mind.

I emerged from the plane as Ernestine was being placed in a
wheelchair by a porter sent to help us. His brown skin was welcome in itself, but he didn't smile. He was a good-looking man in
his forties, with thin lips, a narrow nose, and freckles. To have him
push Ernestine in the chair unburdened me, so I resisted his offer
to carry the large holdall I'd smuggled onto the plane as hand luggage. He was slightly built and hardly taller than I am, but he
yanked the bag from my hand.

He looked mad at the world as he pushed Ernestine along. I
figured he thought I was her servant and wanted him to know
she was one of us. But he walked so fast, I almost had to run to
get ahead of the chair. Ernestine looked solemn, leaning on one
elbow. The crown of her hair was sticking up in a cowlick.
Smoothing it down as we moved along, I said, "This is Boston,

Grandma. Do you remember I told you we were coming to Boston?"

I hoped she didn't associate it with being committed to Foxboro there in 1925 and reminded her she'd once come with small sons to stay with her mother. But Ernestine's expression revealed nothing as the porter guided the wheelchair along the airless passage. I don't think she realized she'd been on a plane, so it seemed pointless to tell her that we were in an airport. The nondescript corridors may have reminded her of the halls of an asylum, but whatever was going through her mind she was calm and beyond taking an interest in the moment or in her fate.

That's what made my stomach churn. Despite knowing that she had a son, a daughter-in-law, and two middle-aged grandsons, I felt totally responsible for what was about to happen to her. I touched her hand to say I was there, but I felt useless and angry that Harry Mae Simons was still in control of Ernestine's life.

The porter looked like he was straining under the weight of my bulging holdall. I said, "At least let me push the chair."

But he resisted my help and asked, "She's your grandmother?"

I managed to say yes through clenched teeth. I was ten million exposed nerve endings and felt as raw as a boxer who'd been pummeled but refused to crumple to his knees. I thought I looked in control but maybe the porter sensed that I was ready to scream. His manner was suddenly caring when he asked, "How old is she?" There was a hint of sympathy in his voice. He no longer felt like a stranger, and I was desperate enough to want to confess to him that I'd ruined her life. Instead, I answered, "Ninety-seven." The stress of the previous days, my uncertainty about bringing Ernestine to Wilson, my sense of having failed to provide a decent life for my grandmother started overwhelming me as we moved through the corridor which led to Passport Control. I was sure that I was courting insanity and wondered if Ernestine had been feeling the same way when she arrived in Boston seventy years earlier.

"My grandmother lived until she was ninety-five," the porter offered. "She would have probably lived longer than that, but she had diabetes and refused to let them amputate her leg. Said she came with two legs and was leaving with two. . . . Anyway, I think it's great that you're looking after your grandmother."

"You don't know the whole story." What saved him from having to hear it was that I had to stop and look through my briefcase for the passports.

"Is somebody meeting you?" he asked, as though he thought somebody should have been.

I recalled my uncle ringing me in Folkestone three days earlier to say that if I brought Ernestine to Boston, he'd have to return her to Memphis. The news came as a shock, because in our two previous conversations he'd said that he would find a nursing home for her in Boston. I had tried to convince myself that he was proposing this as his way to stop me from delivering her to him, but I had to remind myself that he might be prepared to do anything to avoid getting involved.

I'd said, "You can't take her back to Memphis. It's cruel. She has no family there."

"Nursing homes in this area are a hundred dollars a day or more. I can't afford that."

"Nobody expects you to pay. Ernestine's got a pension, and when you become her guardian . . . "

The porter saw that I was miles away. I'd forgotten he'd asked me who was picking us up. The question threw me back to remembering my last conversation with Wilson, because he'd also said that he couldn't afford to lose a day's work to come to the airport.

I told the porter, "Nobody's meeting us. We have to take a taxi to Brookline." While I said it, I could see us both stranded outside my uncle's house, finding nobody at home when we got there. That's why I'd bagged a sandwich for her from the last snack we were served on the plane. For a moment it felt like I had stepped into somebody else's nightmare. It made no sense to me that I had taken Ernestine to England, nor that I had brought her to Boston.

I'd completely forgotten the horror I felt when my cousin Alan had rung me back in 1991 to say that Ernestine was possibly alive. It was 16 May 1995, and as the porter steered us toward baggage claim, I could only see my efforts on Ernestine's behalf as foolish. I told the porter, "I only met my grandmother four years ago. She's spent fifty-two years in a mental hospital. I tried to give her a home but I messed up."

The porter had put the brake on the wheelchair and Ernestine sat a few feet away from us. He looked me in the eye for the first time. His face had softened since he'd first collected us from the plane. His almond eyes were as dark as midnight. He would have let me lean on him had I dared ask. Stranger though he was, we were American descendants of slavery and therefore shared some deeply rooted complexities which bound us to each other despite our being strangers. I figured he could half read my family's history just by looking at Ernestine and me. Had I asked him to guess what might have been at the root of our family problems, I was positive that he could have told me that color played its part. Nobody talked about how looking white or not looking white affected us, but we were all familiar with it.

My jeans were torn at the knee and my hair was in a ponytail. I hadn't had any interest in my appearance or Ernestine's. To arrive at Wilson's looking like vagabonds wasn't going to help her case, but I didn't see a ladies' room and thought I'd find one in the main hall where we could change clothes and slap on a little makeup.

The baggage-claim area was almost deserted. The fluorescent lights must have made the bags under my eyes deeper. I was rushed by another sensation of not knowing what I was doing there, and the porter was the nearest thing to reality. I told him, "I don't know what I would have done had you not been here."

He lifted his cap to rub his forehead and looked at Ernestine. Her head was bowed, and she sat slightly slumped to her right, so I went to prop her up and kissed the top of her head. I felt guilty when the porter said, "She's got you. That's enough."

I knew that she didn't have me for much longer. I pushed her chair through Customs and the porter followed with our bags. In the main hall, the usual cluster of people gathered to collect passengers. My uncle's white hair and glasses hit me in the face.

"Wilson! I thought you weren't coming!"

Taken off guard by the sight of him, I forgot that he hadn't seen his mother in fifty-five years and was angry at myself for not having groomed her. She didn't look like the last flattering picture I'd sent him. I was flustered and smiled at my uncle while combing her hair with my fingers. Nothing she wore matched.

I stopped beside her chair. "Look up, Grandma." I lifted her chin, but her eyes shifted down. "Grandma, it's Wilson. It's your son. He's come to collect you."

For years I'd wondered what the moment would be like when Ernestine was reunited with him. But I'd never envisaged that she'd be sitting and he'd be standing or that the moment would happen as we were blocking the exit from an airport arrivals lounge. So there were no eyes staring into eyes, no sudden recognition. Wilson was standing behind a low barrier like most of the other people waiting to meet passengers. He was smiling but didn't rush forward or reach out to touch Ernestine.

"Grandma, come on," I said, "let's stand you up. This is your son. Can you say 'Hello, Wilson'?"

The wheelchair suddenly seemed cumbersome and its footrests awkward, but Ernestine managed to rise. On her thin legs she wore black tights and she had on black satin ballet slippers, which made her feet look less deformed. But the tights looked wrong with the navy-blue dress and her hair was sticking up again at the back. She didn't look like the grande dame who'd made an appearance at the Mississippi Boulevard Church, or the pretty gentlewoman who'd taken tea with Canon Woods or sat by the fire at Sid and Lizzie's. When she finally said, "Hello, Wilson," her voice was quiet, less forceful than usual. I couldn't see her eyes. But her presence was as subdued as his. She was most often the stillest pond. A hush reflected off her.

"Won't you give him a little kiss?" I asked, nudging her as he took her arm and I saw Dorothea approaching. She'd been outside to smoke a cigarette. It was warm for the raincoat she wore but she said that we'd brought the sun.

Weeks of fear and anxiety about Ernestine being rejected by her Boston family were almost forgotten as my aunt and uncle led us to their white Volvo wagon in the parking lot. The sun was blazing and the porter followed behind us with the two cases laden with all Ernestine's belongings. He'd detached himself a bit, but seeing him reminded me how close I was to screaming when I got off the plane.

Dorothea looked puzzled to see me kiss his cheek after I tipped him. But I knew the money didn't say thank-you enough.

—&> REUNION

ON THAT VALENTINE'S DAY BACK IN 1991 when I'd sat at my uncle's dinner table asking where Ernestine was buried, my cousin Alan was seated on my left. Four years later, Ernestine was sitting there. It seemed almost natural to have her dining with her family. With Ernestine present, we were four generations, because Will had come with his kids, Rachel and David, who had also been at the Valentine's Day dinner.

I remembered telling them about Ernestine in 1993 when they stood in Wilson's kitchen chomping huge triangles of pizza. I wondered if she was living up to their expectations as she sat opposite them at the table. She looked pretty in a pale apricot jogging suit and gray blouse. Her thick, healthy hair was swept back and showed off her silver earrings. I had told them that she was brave, but I didn't know what else they knew about her.

Ernestine took more notice of the bouillabaisse soup Dorothea had made than of the seven of us. My cousin Will was seated to her left and eyed me as I fed her; perhaps he was wondering why I didn't let her feed herself. But I'd weighed which would be better for her, to be seen dribbling food and maybe sticking her elbow in it or be seen being fed. It was a hard choice, like whether she needed a tea towel tied around her neck to protect her from spillage.

I felt that how she looked and acted would determine whether she was accepted, and therefore the smallest details mattered. When Dorothea noticed that Ernestine's nails were manicured, the implication was that she would have noticed had they not been.

A round vase of purple and white tulips picked from the garden sat in the middle of the long antique dining table, which glistened from years of polishing. Brightly patterned placemats protected it from the china and crystal. With Wilson sitting at the head of the table and Dorothea at the foot, it felt to me like Ernestine's celebration dinner, although nobody drank a toast or spoke about how wonderful it was that she was there.

I kept wanting to tell her, Grandma, that's your son, that's Wilson sitting there! because although we'd spent the day with him, I wasn't sure the fact had sunk in. He called her Ernestine, as did his sons and his wife. It made my calling her Grandma seem phony. But as I explained to Wilson the next day, how we addressed her would help her identify her relationship to us.

Alan hadn't come to dinner, and his son Valente was at a Scouts' meeting. He lived across town with his mother and being fifteen may have had other reasons for missing a family supper.

Something which had happened early next morning had made it less important that they see Ernestine that night.

Ernestine woke at 2.00 A.M. and after two hours of listening to her stir in the single bed next to mine in the guest room, I finally accepted that she wasn't going back to sleep and got her up, grate-

ful that her bed was dry. After that stressful day of travel I hated
missing another night's sleep. She noticed that I was impatient
when I hustled her from the bed to the bath. Glaring at me, she'd
said, "What's the matter with you!" and I hoped that her bath
would give me thinking time.

Wilson had gone to bed the night before, saying that he would
return her to Memphis and the nursing home. Hearing that drove
me to swear, which felt wrong in his sedate living room in the
lamplight. I was still in my torn jeans.

"You can't fucking take her back there!" I had yelled. "It's inhu-
man. Didn't I tell you that there was no soap in the toilet? No toilet paper? No towels? Didn't I say I arrived one morning to see
one poor old woman wringing out her washcloth in a basin of
water that had her fecal matter in it? And Ernestine had no bed!
Once I saw the state inspector observe a fire drill, and Ernestine
stood in the middle of the living room not knowing what was
happening."

My uncle spoke quietly. "What can I do? I can't afford a hundred dollars a day for a nursing home. That's the rate."

"She's got a pension."

"Even if I had the pension, and I don't, it wouldn't cover the
costs."

Dorothea sat on the sofa near his chair. I stood in the corner of
bookshelves where thick psychology books were pressed together
in their worn bindings.

I lost my temper. It was the first time since arriving eight hours
earlier, but I couldn't allow good manners to get in the way of good
sense. Having sat through a cordial supper while Ernestine slept on
the sofa, I'd finally put her to bed feeling as guilty as if I'd brought a
Martian into their settled midst. Gripping the bookcase to control
my anger, I reminded Wilson that his mother had a pension.

"You know Harry Mae's dragging her feet," he said.

"Harry Mae is eighty-six. It shouldn't be her job to look after
Ernestine. She says she wants you to be guardian. But we can't wait
for her to act. We have to."

Wilson let me rage, repeating myself. He was a practiced listener and must have heard clients shout and swear. It was easy for him to detach, and he didn't have anything to lose if he didn't care about Ernestine.

I still respected his right not to want to get involved. Knowing how it hurt me to see her, I sympathized that it might have been even harder for him. After all, she was his mother.

When I'd rung Wilson from Folkestone on 2 January to wish them a happy New Year, he had surprised me by saying that he had decided to become Ernestine's guardian and would thereby be able to make certain I received her pension. That he hadn't pressed for the guardianship was the reason Harry Mae remained in control of Ernestine's income.

But the guardianship still hadn't been transferred because Wilson had been lax about it.

When Wilson went to bed, Dorothea and I continued talking. She agreed that Ernestine shouldn't return to Memphis, but the decision wasn't hers. Earlier in the evening I'd rung Ben Hooks in Memphis. While she and I sat talking, he rang back. As he'd been a judge in Tennessee, I thought he would know how long it should take to change a guardianship in his state. He thought it could be instantaneous if both parties agreed.

Dorothea was encouraged by that news. By midnight, we'd shifted to the kitchen to go through a pamphlet listing all the nursing homes in Massachusetts. There was always the chance that Wilson would change his mind. Assuming that nursing homes in remote parts of the state would be cheaper than in Boston, I rang a few thinking that I might get some information from the night staff, but nobody I talked to was able to discuss charges.

I felt that I had failed Ernestine by removing her from New Romney. I didn't want to fail her again by allowing her to be returned to Memphis. I knew if she went back there I'd never see her again.

The overhead light in the kitchen cast shadows across the white table as I scanned the listing and Dorothea checked the telephone directory, because I wanted numbers for government agencies that dealt with the elderly. I squinted. Not only was the light dull but my brain was. I thought of what the therapist had told me when I'd gone the day before to talk about taking Ernestine to the States. He'd said I had no choice—"It's the only thing you can do." But I didn't believe he could see beyond my side of the story.

Dorothea, on the other hand, had a broader view. Married to Wilson for over fifty years, she knew things about him, the family, and his feelings about my getting involved with Ernestine which I didn't expect her to share with me. That she was sitting in the kitchen with her pen and pad jotting down the numbers of government agencies was a good sign.

Her list was still on the table the next morning when Ernestine and I came down after Ernestine's bath. Her apricot jogging suit was the same color as the mats on the round table. I was still giving her breakfast when Wilson appeared at six, smiling and fully dressed. I reminded myself that I was in his house, that Ernestine and I were uninvited guests, and that he alone had the power to save her. I imagined that the last thing he wanted to do was talk about her, so we made small talk and Ernestine was brighter than she'd been since our arrival sixteen hours earlier.

It was hard to believe that the day before we'd been sitting on a plane with me imagining that my uncle might have slipped out of town to avoid us.

I glanced at Ernestine. She eyed the crockery hanging on the wall as her son ate his breakfast. She touched the tip of a green plant which was growing in a little pot on the windowsill behind her. Then she fingered the fringe of the mat on the table. As Wilson swallowed a spoonful of cereal, we watched Ernestine suddenly rise to go to the sink. She stared into it before running her hand over the spotless work surface. Picking up a plastic sandwich bag, she laid it down again, pressing it into folds.

Wilson's expression brightened as it might have had he been watching a toddler make discoveries. On the side table behind him, I could see the listings guide of Massachusetts nursing homes.

I knew it wasn't the right time to discuss returning Ernestine to Memphis, but for her sake I couldn't let the subject rest.

Although we'd arrived the previous afternoon, Wilson still hadn't been alone with his mother. So with Ernestine still examining his kitchen I said, "I only got an hour's sleep last night. Will you watch her while I go into the living room for a minute?"

While they were alone together, I could hear him saying, "That's the stove. . . ."

Ernestine was silent. But I could imagine her tiny fingers touching things as they had when we'd visited Sid and Lizzie. There was a lot for her to look at in Wilson's kitchen, but in case she was beginning to feel dislocated surrounded by kitchen gadgets and mistook her son for a stranger, I rejoined them, asking my uncle if we could talk.

"After I pop out to get the paper," he said, leaving the table.

While he was out, I knew that I had to think up an economic reason for him to keep her. Money mattered to Wilson. So I calculated that two air tickets to Memphis plus the cost of renting a car and staying in a hotel could cost more than keeping Ernestine in a nursing home for a two-week experimental period, assuming I could find one for under a hundred dollars a day. I wrote out some figures on a piece of paper and practiced what I would say.

Ernestine was still sitting with me at the kitchen table when Wilson returned. I think it was his mother's presence more than my simple calculations and proposal which made him say, "If Dorothea agrees, I suppose we could try that." He was smiling. His hands were clasped together on the table and his calm air reminded me of Ernestine.

Dorothea's list of agencies for the elderly was on the small side table. I didn't know whether to laugh or cry. It felt wrong to shout. Both Ernestine and Wilson had that quietness about them, but I wanted her to know that her future had suddenly changed. My eyes were heavy and watering but I was smiling and so was Wilson when I said, "Did you hear that, Grandma? If I can find a place here for you, you can stay!"

Ernestine's head was bowed, and like Wilson her hands were clasped on the white table. Reaching to cover them with one of mine, I managed to suppress a loud hooray.

It was the same when we had sat at my uncle's dinner table enjoying the bouillabaisse soup. I wanted to make celebratory noises, but they were quiet people. I wondered if it was in their genes. Our genes.

Occasionally my cousin Will would stare at Ernestine as I fed her. I wondered what he was thinking. He had seen her the night before and didn't have to return with his children. I recalled having dinner with him in '93. Back then he'd been worried about how his father felt, about the family tragedies which Wilson had survived.

There was no question that Wilson was happy that night. In fact he'd been brighter since the morning when he'd agreed that Ernestine could stay in a Massachusetts nursing home for two weeks. When Dorothea had nodded her agreement he had even rushed downtown to buy a better guide to nursing homes than the one we had.

By the time he returned I'd already found Ernestine a place. It had taken less than an hour on the phone after one agency for the aged recommended various names. Ironically, there was room for her at the Norwegian Old People's Home, which I had joked about with Dorothea the night before. Considering how many hundreds of homes there were to choose from, it seemed uncanny that it had been the Norwegian Old People's Home which had caught my attention. It was another of the coincidences that made me wonder if my father's spirit was still guiding me. Not only was the price right, it was only a few miles from Wilson's house, opposite a beautiful park owned by Harvard called the Arnold Arboretum. Ernestine didn't need to be Norwegian, but for all we knew there might have been some in her blood.

FAMILY

THE NORWEGIAN OLD PEOPLE'S HOME was a fifteen-minute drive from Wilson in a suburb called Roslindale, which was also close to Will. From the outside, the building could have been mistaken for small offices, brick with no frills. Hidden by hedges, it was set back from the four-lane street. A sprawling Lutheran church was nearby, a Jewish Rehabilitation Center across the road was as large as a hospital, and diagonally opposite was the Arnold Arboretum.

Ernestine's room was a single next to the last bedroom at the end of the corridor. It had a sturdy bed. The beveled headboard matched the dresser to the left, and tucked in a corner was an easy chair in front of a window overlooking a patch of lawn.

After I'd registered her, Wilson and Dorothea helped me hang her clothes while she had lunch in the dining room with the thirteen other residents. We'd bought her flowers and a couple of small plants. With her stuffed animals arranged on her pillow and a shawl thrown over her chair, it looked welcoming. The framed baby picture of Blair was on her dresser next to a childhood shot of him with Wilson and Ernest.

The common rooms were at the other end of the single-story building. The lounge was large and attractively furnished to look like a family room. That's where we found Ernestine sitting when we finished organizing her room. She was wearing a soft pink sweater and a pleated skirt. She'd fallen asleep in a wingback chair near the small room that led to the office. Having made arrangements to spend the night in Connecticut, I kissed her goodbye while she was sleeping. I wanted to be alone with her, but Wilson and Dorothea stood nearby, with the redheaded registrar of the home. She saw my tears welling. In a broad Bostonian accent she said, "Hey, don't do that to yourself. You got her here."

Her name was Jean Ryan. Her deep tan was in sharp contrast to the whites she was wearing. She looked fit and energetic, like an assistant in a gym, and whenever she passed one of the residents, she made a point of speaking.

Ernestine looked elegant, sitting with her legs crossed and her hands clasped together in her lap. Her head was cocked to one side and her thick hair was still brushed into waves behind each ear. It seemed too cruel to wake her.

I had no way of knowing if she felt safe there. Although I saw no other blacks, I was hoping that her months in England had prepared her for seeing none. When I'd first brought her in, she had replied to anyone that spoke loudly enough to her and had answered most of Jean's questions. She'd even spoken to the attendant in charge of activities and a cleaner who was repolishing the shiny floors.

Trying to help her, I discovered that I'm weaker and more selfish than I thought I was. My self-respect was in tatters when I boarded that train for Connecticut. I needed a stiff drink but hid in a heavy sleep while the 2:15 out of Boston rolled to Bridgeport.

I had given Wilson and Dorothea the idea that I'd fly home from New York, and they'd said their goodbyes outside the station. He knew I couldn't leave the States without seeing that Ernestine was adjusting to her new home. But my confidence was blighted; the four days it took getting her from New Romney to Roslindale could have been decades, and I felt old. Depression gripped me; I couldn't remember laughing and needed to see my reflection in a friend's eyes, an old Berkeley friend.

Whenever I recall those two days in Connecticut, I'll always think of the flowering dogwood trees. Some were pink, some white, and they were everywhere. The prissy suburbs near Westport were too pretty to be real. At dawn I could stare out of my bedroom across a wild half acre of trees. So by the time I had made my way back to the Norwegian Old People's Home, I could almost concentrate and form sentences.

The sun was as brilliant in Boston that Sunday as it had been the day Ernestine and I arrived. I took the underground across town and wondered if she'd recognize me. Seeing her with Wilson made her feel less like she was part of me, and when we'd registered her, it had been Wilson who signed as next of kin. His and Dorothea's eyes had brightened when I'd shown them around the home and they had said more than once that if she settled they planned to keep her there.

Jean Ryan wasn't on duty that Sunday, so I introduced myself to the staff attendant and said, "It's such a lovely day. If I can borrow a wheelchair from you, I'd like to take my grandmother to the Arnold Arboretum." I'd never been there, but Wilson and Dorothea had pointed it out as a park worth seeing. I imagined flowers and bandstands and ice-cream vendors. But what Ernestine got was totally unexpected. While I was waiting by the storm door for the wheelchair, my cousin Will appeared with Rachel and David. That Ernestine had three other visitors excited me.

"What are you doing here?" I asked my cousin, who was as surprised to see me.

"No," he said, "what are *you* doing here?"

The children were less interested in seeing Ernestine's bedroom than in pushing her in the chair. Rachel is ten but has a sturdy build. She is a keen gymnast and David, who is lean, is state champion for his division. When we got to the park, they took turns with the chair.

Their father and I watched them steer Ernestine past cyclists and skaters, a grandmother pushing twins in a stroller, and some picnickers on the grass. The sun was in our eyes as I saw Rachel in her pink and white tie-dyed playsuit run ahead of the wheelchair to snatch up a twig of flowering dogwood. David steered the chair to the left as the path we were walking on declined slightly. My cousin Will watched with pride. They were handsome children and their mixed blood made their coloring unique. Rachel's blackish-brown hair made her gray-green eyes look unusual, whereas David's olive skin was unlikely with his chestnut-brown hair.

Rachel's thick little legs were fast. Her ponytail bounced as she ran to catch up with the wheelchair. She did a half spin, skipping on one leg as she passed the twig of white flowers to Ernestine, who held it between her thumb and forefinger.

Will said, "I think Ernestine likes Rachel."

"It's great that you came to see her today."

"Alan meant to come too. But he must have been held up at church."

David was wearing black running shoes and soccer shorts. I couldn't see Ernestine's face but I could see her small hand holding the dogwood flowers.

The day after we'd arrived in Boston, only a few hours after they'd agreed by phone to take her at the Norwegian Old People's Home, I'd asked my uncle to take us to Mount Hope Cemetery where my father was buried. I didn't know whether it was right or wrong to show her his grave, but something told me it was important. On the way there we passed some abandoned buildings and Wilson said, "That was Boston State Hospital. Blair worked there."

"Is that where he was also a patient?"

"No," said Wilson. Dorothea was sitting in front beside him. Ernestine and I were in the back. His windshield wipers squeaked against the glass, because there was so little rain.

I said, "I think that's the hospital Roberta said Blair had been admitted to, even though he'd worked there."

Dorothea said, "I never heard that."

It seemed as good a time as any to ask my uncle what he thought had caused my father's mental illness.

"What do you think happened to him?" I said.

"Well, he was skipped a grade. Maybe he was always a bit younger than the rest. And my grandmother wasn't an easy woman," he added, referring to Mattie.

Dorothea had once said that my father told her he should have been a plumber. He may have been implying that his ambition had been too great.

His headstone was in a plot at the far end of the cemetery. We had a hard time finding it. There were thousands of graves, some tombs, but no great sepulchers. Having seen the sketch that

Roberta had of his headstone, I expected it to be taller, broader. It was so inconsequential, a simple gray slab tucked in a long row of others just like it in a far corner easy to miss. As my uncle parked in front, I was still unsure why I wanted Ernestine to see where her eldest son was buried, but something pushed me to do it.

The falling rain was so fine that it settled like dew upon the grass as I helped my grandmother from the car and guided her to my father's grave. I thought about that moment at the nursing home in New Romney when she'd been sad and said, "Bee Tee's dead and buried in the cemetery." Pointing to his stone I asked, "Can you read that name, Grandma?"

"Hunt," she said as she stood in front of the space which was now reserved for her. Her expression didn't change as I explained that one day she could be buried beside Bee Tee. But Ernestine was very much alive and being pushed along by her great-grand-son in the arboretum; it seemed she was beginning an important new chapter.

Ernestine looked relaxed, leaning on one elbow in the wheel-chair as she rode past great tall trees that may not have been as old as she was. Will and I lagged several paces behind while Rachel, her curly ponytail bouncing, leapt ahead with so much enthusiasm that she seemed ready to fly through the air. A few people stared at the five of us. For such a small clan we all looked so different.

"Funny," said Will, turning to me, "I bet people think we're a family."

And we were. An American family. Made in the U.S.A.

—ᏽ Acknowledgments

MANY PEOPLE HAVE HELPED IN VARIOUS WAYS to complete this book, none more so than my daughter, Karis Jagger, who not only went to Memphis three times but helped with research and contributed a large portion of her time and savings. Financial help also came from Steve Lovi, Bassam Alghanim, and Sidney De Haan.

During each of my trips to Memphis, O'Ferrell and Anne Nelson did all they could to make me feel that I belonged there. Anne's continued interest in Ernestine was saintly. Harry Mae Simons allowed me to see my grandmother and her medical records and gave important information about my grandfather. Western State hospital employees, particularly in the medical records department, were very helpful.

In Boston, Wilson and Dorothea Hunt gave me photographs and information and made my visits comfortable and happy, as did their sons, Wilson and Alan.

Early encouragement to write Ernestine's story came from Michael Ratledge, Alexandra Pringle, Susan Sandon, Elaine Koster, and Audrey LaFehr. My agent, Virginia Barber, and Abner Stein gave continued support. In England Roger De Haan and Paul Bach proved to be monumental, while Clive Botting made her stay possible.

Friends who have continually given advice while I was writing include John Monahan, Patricia Van Der Leun, Caroline Coon, Diana Stainforth, Edna Tromans, Doris Troy, Tony Garnett, Ben

Churchill, Anne Forbes-Robertson, Colin Bell, and Fred Hooks. Roberta Polk was inspiring.

Editorial assistance came from my main editor, John Saddler, and more recently from Rebecca Lloyd. Her detailed advice about my final draft, along with Stuart Prebble's criticism, was crucial. Terry Karten has been a vital addition to my editorial team. She and Diane Reverand restored my confidence. Ashley Chase's comments were very helpful. John Saddler sustained a fighting interest in Ernestine's story, encouraging the support of publishers, agents, and subeditors. I can't thank him enough.

Ernestine's need for care is immense. At the various homes where she has resided staff members have been wonderful, and I wish I had the space to give them individual mention. She now lives at the Norwegian Old People's Home.

While concentrating on Ernestine I've neglected my mother, Inez, and my Aunt Thelma. My father has been a spiritual guide.

Finally, I thank Alan Gilsenan for his support, encouragement, and love.